MONUMENT BUILDERS

MONUMENT BUILDERS

Modern Architecture and Death

EDWIN HEATHCOTE

A.D. ACADEMY EDITIONS

Acknowledgements

I would like to thank the following people who have all assisted me in some way with the research for, and writing of this book: my wife Krisztina whose support and encouragement is always invaluable and who graciously listened to my musings about death; Christian Kerez for his superb photographs; the Swedish Institute for their valuable assistance; Stefan Buzas, Andrew Mead at the Architectural Press archive (EMAP) and Yoshi Oshima. Furthermore, I wish to thank Maggie Toy, Mariangela Palazzi-Williams and Iona Spens for their support, and Mario Bettella and Andrea Bettella of Artmedia for designing the book.

I would like to reserve special thanks for the assistance rendered by Mr A S MacDonald and Co-operative Funeral Service without which this book would not have been possible.

I wish to stress that the use of the words Man, Mankind and suchlike are not intended to be sexist, but are merely my own use of the language. The style and the opinions in this book are my own and do not necessarily represent those of John Wiley & Sons.

Photographic credits

All photographs are courtesy of the architects or from the Architectural Press archive, unless stated otherwise; every effort has been made to locate sources and credit material but in the very few cases where this has not been possible our apologies are extended: Hakan Ahlden pp108, 109, 112; Architectural Press archive pp36, 43 (below), 37, 46 (right), 51, 54, 58, 63, 65, 70, 72 (above), 77 (right); Stefan Buzas pp10, 204, 205, 206, 207, 208, 209, 210, 211, 212; British Film Institute p11 (above); Bengt Carlén pp2, 104, 106, 107, 110, 111; Barbara Burg and Oliver Schuh pp182, 184, 186, 190; Commonwealth War Graves Commission pp43 (above and centre), 44, 45, 46 (left); Edwin Heathcote pp13, 24, 28, 30, 34, 36 (right), 45(left), 67, 72 (below), 74, 76, 77 (left), 79, 81, 83, 158 (below), 159; Akelei Herzberger pp102 (below), 103 (below); Timothy Hursley p69; Toshiharu Kitajima pp146, 150-151, 152; Anders Rosenberg p113; Laszlo Saros p154, 158 (above); Shinkenchiku-Sha pp114, 115, 116, 117, 118, 121, 122, 123, 124, 125; Margherita Spiluttini pp41 (below), 60 (above); Hisao Suzuki pp166, 168, 169, 170; T Waki pp126, 127.

Cover: Mortuary Chapel, Bonaduz, Switzerland, Christian Kerez, 1993
Frontispiece: Lilla Aska Crematorium Chapel, Sweden, Ove Hidemark, 1990

First published in Great Britain in 1999 by
ACADEMY EDITIONS

A division of
JOHN WILEY & SONS
Baffins Lane
Chichester
West Sussex PO19 1UD

ISBN: 0 471 98368 3

Other Wiley Editorial Offices
New York • Weinheim • Brisbane • Singapore • Toronto

Printed and bound in Italy

CONTENTS

PREFACE

The desire for immortality and the inability to accept the finality of death are universal. The myths and stories weaved throughout history are attempts to explain man's place in the cosmos and to make sense of what lies beyond the knowable world. The perceived gulf between primitive and advanced societies disappears when faced with the prospect of death and the dealings with the corporeal remains of the dead. Attitudes to the body reveal superstitions and taboos which reflect man's deepest fears and existential *angst*, and the manner in which the dead are commemorated displays those fears; the conventions of the architecture of the dead derive from the most fundamental of roots.

The House of the Dead reveals as much, and usually more about society than does the House of the Living: the first substantial houses were the dwelling places of the dead. The body spends more time in its final resting place than in any dwelling inhabited when alive. Therefore it seems logical for the dead to be housed satisfactorily, discouraging them from returning to haunt the living. The tomb, or the city of the dead, becomes the home of the forefathers, a pivotal place which anchors the space of the living to a particular location and sacralises it, placing it in the world.

A society based on technological advance and the rational achievements of the past few centuries in understanding the basic building blocks of the universe at the sub-atomic scale, reveals the most primitive superstitions when faced with death. The gestures made towards the dead – the mourning, epitaphs, rituals, burials and monuments – have nothing to do with rational ideas and everything to do with taboos that reach back into pre-history and the cult of the dead: the worship of our ancestors. The Western world is becoming more reliant on a rational, technological base and an ultimate acceptance of Benthamite utilitarianism, and yet it has failed consummately to shed superstition, myth and religion. J B Priestley once said that when man ceases to believe in God, he will not believe in nothing, rather he will believe in anything.

The contemporary existential world view is based on anything from orthodox religion to cults which have no less absurd a basis yet are reviled for their bizarre beliefs and an increasing interest in all forms of occult philosophies from astrology to Eastern mysticism.

Attitudes towards the dead have changed little but the ability to address death has diminished. Death has no place in a society which is obsessed with youth and vigour; it has become taboo, and the art of expressing death has suffered deeply. Memorialisation has become a branch of catalogue shopping: funeral homes increasingly resemble shopping malls in their ambience and *muzak*-rich atmosphere. The disposal of the dead is treated similarly to garbage disposal; corpses are buried far away from the city in hygienic conditions with little thought for alternative options, for the tremendous waste of energy that is expended on cremation or the waste of materials (and money) which goes into coffins and other paraphernalia. However, a place for the contemplation of death is a fundamental adjunct to every town. The churchyards used to be at the heart of the settlement, but the cemetery is now usually on a ring-road or by-pass, accessible only by car. Death has been torn out of the heart of the city and a significant part of the city has died as a result.

In this book I attempt to examine the work of some of the architects and artists who have addressed these issues in recent years. It is only a brief cross-section of a moment in the tradition of the architecture of death, but it is a critical moment. Modern architecture has found it hard to address the notion of death, but the few architects who have engaged the subject successfully have created some of the most important buildings of the modern era. Gunnar Asplund's Woodland Cemetery, Stockholm, Carlo Scarpa's Brion Tomb, Aldo Rossi's cemetery in Modena and Enric Miralles' Igualada Cemetery are among the most striking and thought-provoking buildings of our century, and I have attempted to look briefly at these acknowledged masterpieces and to introduce some lesser known buildings.

The field is not well-covered. It is symptomatic of the contemporary taboos and an inability to confront death as a defining part of life that the subject of death in modern architecture has been largely avoided. This is curious, for in archaeology it is perhaps the most studied of all fields; the mausoleums of the eighteenth century have been studied intensely, along with the architecture of Etienne-Louis Boullée and his contemporaries, including Sir John Soane and others, who wallowed in morbid imagery and an architecture obsessed with both the expression of death and of the sublime.

I have confined myself here to a study of twentieth-century architecture, and specifically to recent buildings, although I have attempted to outline some of the major developments in funerary architecture which I believe exerted a formative influence on a modern architecture of death; for this I have reached back as far as the eighteenth century when death was a fundamental theme in many architects' work. I have briefly covered the emergence of the cemetery as a building type with a chapter on the cemetery of Père-Lachaise in Paris, but I have not followed up this history with a description of subsequent developments as other books do this admirably: J S Curl's *A Celebration of Death* gives an exemplary background to this theme, although it is sparse on modern architecture,[1] and Howard Colvin covers similar territory in *Architecture and the After-Life*.[2] The work of Richard A Etlin has been important in reaching a modern understanding of an architecture of death, and his writings on eighteenth-century French architecture in particular are to be recommended as the best source for an understanding of the period.[3]

I have generally addressed architecture and not sculpture or funerary art, although sometimes the line is so fine it disappears: many of the Holocaust memorials stand astride the boundaries of definition and some also embrace the museum as a building type (a tradition which reaches back to Soane and beyond). I have tried to cover a broad spectrum of work, from the monumental to the minuscule, and have included the work of artists and sculptors (Rachel Whiteread, Arnaldo Pomodoro and others) where I feel that it sits comfortably within a broad definition of architecture. However, I have omitted memorials to national heroes and to events, as these tend to be political gestures and connected with a language distinct from that of the art of death. The introduction and the subsequent essays are to be read not as a coherent history of modernism and death but as a series of brief, individual summaries of the state of the architecture of death at specific periods throughout the development of modernism.

I hope that this book will be able to promote discussion of a field of architecture which is all too often sadly neglected, and that the bringing together of these works for the first time will illustrate the diversity and potential of death as a theme and an inspiration; for it is as an inspiration that death should be seen. The proliferation of and thirst for ghost stories, haunted houses and the supernatural is a manifestation of the universal desire for the notion of the dead dwelling among us. This can be attributed partly to an absence of a physical place of death in our culture. This book attempts to explore the work of some architects who have sought to return to us the space of death as a fundamental part of the city.

Notes

1 James Stevens Curl, *A Celebration of Death*, B T Batsford Ltd (London), 1980 (revised 1993). In addition to Howard Colvin's book, this is the best study of funerary architecture. It is very comprehensive although curiously weak on twentieth-century examples.
2 Howard Colvin, *Architecture and the After-Life*, Yale University Press (New Haven), 1991; a fine study which gives the background of the subject up to the nineteenth century.
3 See especially Richard A Etlin, *Symbolic Space, French Enlightenment Architecture and Its Legacy,* University of Chicago Press (Chicago), 1994; and *The Architecture of Death: The Transformation of the Cemetery in Eighteenth Century Paris*, MIT Press (Cambridge, Mass), 1984.

MODERNISM, ARCHITECTURE AND DEATH

I. HOUSES OF THE DEAD – CITIES OF THE DEAD

The houses of the dead are of necessity more permanent than the houses of the living, and the landscape of death is an enduring ideal. The purpose of the tomb is to demonstrate the continuing existence of the dead in the minds of the living; funerary architecture represents the quest for immortality and is a concretisation of the notion of death as a rite of passage, where the tomb is both a transitory resting place in which the body undergoes the beginnings of the journey to the next, more real sacred world, and a monument to that world's existence.

A house has symbolic and ritual functions but its primary purpose is to give shelter. In the negative world of the architecture of death, the primary function of the tomb is not to give shelter – the earth itself can do that – but to memorialise and signify the existence of the sacred realm, the world beyond. This is a far more important function than shelter from the elements as it becomes the embodiment of the world-view, a model of the cosmos and an archetype which touches on the most profound sense of existential *angst*, but also of the visions of another realm of its builders. Thus, the great civilisations left us their houses of the dead and it is often from these that we create our picture of the mythologies which have shaped our world.

Houses of the dead became cities of the dead. The necropolis was a fundamental adjunct to the metropolis; indeed, Lewis Mumford has written that the city of the dead preceded the city itself precisely because of the importance attached to permanence in the architecture of the tomb.[1] The physical relationship between the two parts of the city is revealing. The necropolis occupied a boundary zone immediately outside the city; it became an impenetrable barrier, and the dead acted as a reinforcement of the city walls. The ghosts of the dead inhabited the necropolis as much as the living inhabited their cities: these were, after all, both cities of memory and *memento mori*, a place of contemplation upon life and death, of mortality.

In his novel *Invisible Cities* (1974),[2] Italo Calvino uses Marco Polo as a narrator who tells of the myriad cities he has seen on his travels, and only late in the book does it become clear that all the cities are metaphors for different visions of Venice. Among these cities are the 'cities of the dead'. Each is in some way an inversion of the city of the living; in one example an exact replica of the city of the living is built beneath its inhabitants' feet, and tended and maintained by the living, so the subterranean necropolis becomes indistinguishable from the city itself and there is no way of differentiating the living from the dead.

In another chapter a city is described in which the air has been replaced by earth, space becomes solid, houses and streets are filled with dirt and roots, and the city is invisible from the surface. A third section of the narrative describes a city where the growth of the necropolis is exactly parallel to its own, and the streets and blocks mirror its own. The city's inhabitants need to visit their dead counterparts in the necropolis in order to comprehend their own existence, and the speculative existence of those who will follow them.

As Calvino makes clear in his poetic way, the necropolis is the city in negative; it is a realm in which absence is celebrated. The dead are both physically present and yet missing, and the architecture in these cities of ghosts echoes this paradox, tending towards the archetypal dwelling and the opulence of the monument for which the occupants can have no use. Their world is now beneath the ground; they have been consumed by the earth. Just as the necropolis is a negative image of the city, so the reversal continues in the strata of the earth.

The cemetery is a world of darkness to its inhabitants and to those who come to visit. The figures in Canova's Maria Christina Monument (1799–1805) mournfully approach the darkness at the heart of the pyramid. The ghost story and the zombie horror film use the image of the graveyard at night because it is the natural location for a world of shadows, where our fears are exposed. To bury the dead in the darkness of the earth is to return them to the cosmic night, the chaos of the beginning, so that they can start their journey anew. But to the living, night is a frightening place – it is the void, the darkness in the soul of every individual into which he or she cannot bear to look, yet it is the shadows which give form to life.

Oswald Spengler made the connection between death and space and form. In *The Decline of the West* he explains that form is by definition finite and that grasp of its limitations engenders in us an appreciation of our own limited time on earth:

> A deep relation and one which is early felt, exists between space and death. Man is the only being that knows death; all others become old, but with a consciousness wholly limited to the moment which must seem to them eternal. We are Time, but we possess also an image of history and in this image death.[3]

Of the moment when a child sees himself or herself for the first time as a being in an 'alien extended world' Spengler writes:

> Here, in the decisive moments of existence, when man first becomes man and realises his immense loneliness in the universe, the world-fear reveals itself for the first time as the essentially human fear in the presence of death, the limit of the light-world, rigid space . . . Every great symbolism attaches its form language to the cult of the dead, the forms of disposal of the dead, the adornment of the graves of the dead. And thus every new Culture comes into existence with a new view of the world, that is, a sudden glimpse of death as the secret of the perceivable world . . . And thus the essence of every genuine – *unconscious and inwardly necessary* – symbolism proceeds from the knowledge of death in which the secret of space reveals itself.[4]

The most elemental of these symbolic gestures and languages is that of burial and interment: the return of the body to the earth. The great primitive tombs of mankind are exaggerated versions of a vision of the earth itself. According to Adolf Loos:

> When we find a mound in the woods, six feet long and three feet wide, raised to a pyramidal form by means of a spade, we become serious and something in us says: someone was buried here. *That is architecture.*[5]

Adolf Loos recognised the power of the gesture. The body is buried in a hole displacing a quantity of soil. The soil is placed above the hole so that a mound is formed. It is the tomb at its simplest and, as Loos recognised, architecture at its most archetypal. Most of the great monuments of the architecture of death contain echoes of that simple mound in the woods. The pyramids, the great barrows, cairns and chambers of northern Europe, the tombs of Mycenae and even the great mausoleum of Halicarnassus (the stepped roof of which influenced Loos' own design for a tomb for his friend Max Dvořak) blend the symbolism of the burial mound with the vision of the world as a mountain.

The mountain was the image at the centre of the cosmos, the place where height allows communion with the gods in the heavens. The tomb is a microcosmic version of that world order – just as the mountain top gives access to the heavens, an opening in the earth provides the path to the nether world, to the realms of darkness. Thus grottoes, clefts in the rock, caves and caverns become the focus for worship of the earth itself. To return to the earth through these sacred openings is to return to the womb of the earth mother so that the dead can be reborn into a new life.

In Christian lore, Jesus himself was resurrected this way, while his early worshippers found themselves praying in the catacombs beneath Rome; the place of burial became the place of worship. Exactly the same relationship can be seen in the expressionist vision of a nightmare urban future, Fritz Lang's *Metropolis*, where the cult around the dead heroine gathers in the bowels of the earth in a catacomb-type space pierced with grave-marker crosses.[6]

The proximity of the dead to the place of sacred ritual has survived: relics remain important elements of the Church's mythology and become places of pilgrimage, while the illustrious dead are buried and memorialised within the walls and floors of the building, their presence increasing the sacredness of the place and reinforcing the physical position of a church which may otherwise seem arbitrary, but also serving as *memento mori*.

With the rise of the notion of the individual in society during the Renaissance, the personal memorial became a new type, a vehicle for artistic expression and the expression of the wealth, standing and faith of the deceased. At the same time, inscriptions on the church wall appeared (as the space for burial beneath the nave diminished) to commemorate the burial of the deceased

Brion Cemetery, San Vito di Altivole, Italy, 1969–78, C Scarpa

in the grounds or in the church itself, but separate from the actual point of burial.

The idea of an empty memorial, or cenotaph, indicates a fundamental change in conception and a move towards the Enlightenment, based, like many other concepts of this era, on an idea taken from the ancients. In his novel *A Tomb for Boris Davidovich* (1980), Danilo Kiš eloquently describes the origin and meaning of the cenotaph:

> The Ancient Greeks had an admirable custom: for anyone who perished by fire, was swallowed by a volcano, buried by lava, torn to pieces by beasts, devoured by sharks, or whose corpse was scattered by vultures in the desert, they built so-called cenotaphs, or empty tombs, in their homelands; for the body is only fire, water, or earth, whereas the soul is the Alpha and Omega, to which a shrine should be erected.[7]

The idea of the cenotaph as a shrine is best expressed in Boullée's fantastic Cenotaph to Newton, who, as Hugh Honour has said, discovered 'order in infinity'. The building is no longer a representation of the earth but of the cosmos, and it is a monument to Newton's ideas, to his mind more than to his body which is absent. The great sphere, punctured to let in the light from the sky to represent the stars, becomes a model of the universe in which the visitor is placed at the centre of the void and left to contemplate and wonder at the enormity of his or her surroundings and the genius of the man who revealed its order to us.

Together with the awe at the scale of the universe, Boullée's architecture of death and that of his contemporaries reveals a profound existential terror and melancholy. This is a buried architecture, the immense weight of which has seemingly pushed its mass into the earth. Huge blank walls convey the finality of death and deep, dark shadows reveal a nether world of darkness and the negative image.

The visionary work of Boullée and his contemporaries represented a high point of funerary architecture, even though almost none of it was realised. These seminal works became models for all monumental architecture which would follow, especially that of the twentieth century. At the same time, the mausoleum had become a popular building type, a vehicle for architectural experimentation, and in the eighteenth century – an era in which the achievements of the ancients were almost equalled – the architecture of death reached its zenith.

ABOVE: Scene from Fritz Lang's Metropolis, 1927;
CENTRE: Cenotaph to Newton, 1784, E-L Boullée;
BELOW: Design for a mausoleum for Dvořak, 1921, A Loos

The development of the cemetery in the wake of the success of Père-Lachaise saw the re-emergence of the necropolis as a critical symbolic adjunct to the city and the secularisation of burial grounds provided a new creative impulse. But the notions of hygiene and an effort to move cemeteries away from city centres arguably led to a disassociation of death from the heart of the urban fabric and the destruction of a layer of history and consciousness. It is this trend which has largely triumphed, and the nineteenth and twentieth centuries have been subject to a real reduction in the relationship between the cities of the living and the cities of the dead, and an increasing reluctance to address death as the inevitable consequence of life.

The catastrophic holocausts of the twentieth century have drastically altered perceptions of death, of inhumanity, and have rendered the existing languages of memorialisation almost obsolete. New forms of expression were necessary as archaic symbols lost their power to express the tragedies of war and genocide. A new language was not found, although several noble attempts have been made and many of the most successful structures reinterpret the archetypes; Aldo Rossi, Jože Plečnik, and Gunnar Asplund and Sigurd Lewerentz all explored deeply engrained images trawled from Western civilisation's collective unconscious. Thus the modern architecture of death is an eclectic reflection of the pluralism of the late-twentieth century and of the uncertainty that death brings in its wake. Modernism has always had a deep and profound problem with the architecture of death.

Although hugely influential on the monumental aspirations of modernism, Boullée's 'Architecture of Shadows' and 'Buried Architecture' is in many ways the antithesis of the architecture of the twentieth-century modernists. Modern architects, and more specifically, functionalist architects sought to disassociate buildings from the earth. *Pilotis*, walls of seemingly frameless plate glass, were intended to lighten the building's contact with the ground, to do away with the need for a cellar, the repository of repressed Freudian evils and the darkness below and to create an international style which was not bound to the earth but could quite easily sit anywhere.

Functionalism is an architecture of light from all angles, of views and air and healthiness, and it has no place for lingering melancholic memories and death. There is a sudden, fundamental rupture with the conti-nuity of the architecture of death as the point at which the realms of the nether world, the earth and the heavens can commune. Cremation had become the modernist way of dealing with the dead – hygienic and efficient it is the functionalist approach – while cemeteries had become less like cities of the dead and more like gardens of remembrance. The notion arose that these cemeteries should be hopeful, pretty places full of birdsong and flowers. Consequently, the idea of the *memento mori* has gone completely out of fashion in an age where death is unmentionable.

Death seems to have no place in the modern city. The architecture associated with death is generally that of the neutral sympathy of the undertaker. Unobtrusive and bland like the piped music which plays on a loop in funeral homes, it is an architecture which does not attempt to address the gravity of its theme or the existential questioning and crises which death can prompt, but which attempts to disguise its purpose with the gentle forms of a neo-vernacular, or a simple but pleasing institutional modernism of the type used in hospitals and geriatric homes. Funerary art has suffered similarly and has degenerated into a catalogue trade with off-the-shelf models becoming the norm. Indeed, it is possible to buy entire mausolea from a catalogue and choose the colour of the marble; there is no hint of the irony of Marcel Duchamp's 'ready-mades'. But there are significant exceptions and it is upon these which this book aims to dwell.

I have attempted to briefly examine the history of modernism and the architecture of death. To do this I believe it is necessary to begin somewhere in the eighteenth century, when modern notions concerning death were largely formulated, and to travel briefly through the nineteenth century in order to offer a relevant perspective. Other books give a far more complete view of funerary architecture in the last couple of centuries but surprisingly few about modernism and death have been published.

The schemes which have been included were chosen because they were felt to represent significant attempts to address ideas of human mortality and the place of death in the modern city; they are predominantly in the Western tradition (although I have included a number of works from Japan where cremation has engendered a serious investigation of a new building type) and the buildings have been drawn from the work of both artists and architects. The list, however, is far short of complete, it can only be a brief, subjective cross-section of the state of the art of death at the end of the millennium.

II. ET IN ARCADIA EGO

Inscribed on the frontispiece of Sir John Soane's copy of Rousseau's *Confessions* (published 1782-89)[8] is a sketch by the architect of the great thinker's tomb on an island in the garden at Ermenonville. Encapsulated on this page are the preoccupations of an age of enlightenment which placed death firmly at the centre of the new Arcadia which it sought to create.

Rousseau's impact was in great part due to his notion of man as the noble savage in a garden of Eden, almost a reiteration of Defoe's Robinson Crusoe, the man stranded on an island who strives to create a new life, a life embodied in his creation of his house and his garden. These ideas placed man in a paradise, but the knowledge of that paradise was always tempered with an acute awareness of mortality. The title of this chapter takes a phrase which has been well used in the literature of art history and has had much writing devoted to its enigmatic message. Perhaps the best is that by Erwin Panofsky in his *Meaning in the Visual Arts* (1955). His chapter of the same title opens in 1769 with an anecdote about Joshua Reynolds showing his new painting to his friend Dr Johnson:

> It shows two lovely ladies seated before a tombstone and sentimentalising over its inscription: one points out the text to the other, who meditates thereon in the then fashionable pose of Tragic Muses and Melancholias. The text of the inscription reads 'Et in Arcadia Ego'.
> 'What can this mean?' exclaimed Dr. Johnson. It seems very nonsensical – I am in Arcadia.' 'The King could have told you,' replied Sir Joshua. 'He saw it yesterday and said at once: "Oh, there is a tombstone in the background: Ay, ay, death is even in Arcadia."'[9]

Panofsky's ensuing chapter discusses historical interpretations of the phrase *Et in Arcadia Ego*, outlined in too much detail for the purposes of this book, but his conclusion is that grammatically and philosophically, the king had got it right, whereas Johnson, the compiler of the dictionary, was unable to interpret the melancholia of its romantic message. Reynolds' painting was a part of a tradition of the *memento mori*, the insertion of an element into a work of art, the purpose of which is to remind the spectator of his or her own mortality.

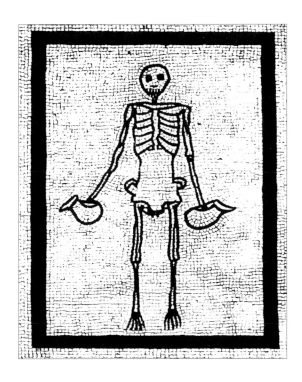

ABOVE: View of Rousseau's tomb, Ermenonville, 1778, J-M Moreau; CENTRE: Mosaic floor, Pompeii: a Roman memento mori; BELOW: Neo-classical tomb, Putney, London

This particular device (the inscription which is the title of this chapter) can be traced back to a pair of paintings by Nicolas Poussin, *The Arcadian Shepherds*, executed in the first half of the seventeenth century. One is housed in the Louvre, Paris, and the other in Chatsworth House in England. In Poussin's scene, the shepherds, who for our purposes can be seen to represent Rousseau's idealised primitives, have found an ancient tomb in their pastoral paradise. A rather detached female stands beside them and looks on as they trace the inscription on the tomb *Et in Arcadia Ego* with their fingers. The lady perhaps represents death as much as does the tomb and looks on approvingly as the shepherds become aware of her power.

The pictures encapsulate a set of themes which recur throughout this book and will provide us with a good (if perhaps surprisingly antiquated) starting point for our narrative of death and modern architecture. Poussin was illustrating the elegiac tradition and the idea of an Arcadia which, despite the idyllic state of the life which it supports, bears testimony to an earlier civilisation which has disappeared, here represented by the tomb. It is a version of the Atlantis myth, of a lost civilisation greater than anything we will know again, and a reference to the perfection of Adam and Eve's existence in the Garden of Eden, which Eve (perhaps here represented by the shepherds' female companion) destroyed so tragically. The neglected tomb is a memorial in the sense that it commemorates some long dead and forgotten figure but also in the sense that it embodies the memory of a half-remembered mythical past, a Jungian collective memory of a defunct paradise.

In the eighteenth century, many strands came together to form a new picture of death, antiquity and commemoration; it is this view, which rose paradoxically from Rationalism and Romanticism, that gives us images and landscapes which we today associate with death, the dead and memory. The new age of enlightenment brought with it new forms of investigation and expression. Among these, two in particular are of interest: the new science of archaeology and the idea of the romantic garden. Both these developments can be traced back to the Renaissance which was, after all, a 'rebirth' of classical culture based on a reconstructed and heavily idealised view of the world from which the artefacts of the classical age must have belonged conjecturally.

Poussin's shepherds, the amateur archaeologists in the pastoral landscape who come across the antique tomb's enigmatic message, are the embodiments of Rousseau's notion of the noble savage. And when Rousseau died in 1778 he became the first major figure to be buried in a garden (at Ermenonville) which represented the Arcadian settings to be found in the paintings of Claude Lorraine and Poussin. His final resting place was on an island on the estate of his friend René Louis, Vicomte de Girardin. The pervasive influence of the island burial can be seen in Princess Diana's tomb in Althorp Park.

The garden in which Rousseau was buried had originally been inspired by that in his own novel *La Nouvelle Héloïse*.[10] Sir John Soane, a great admirer of Rousseau's work, had been suitably impressed by this entombment, thus he sketched the island on the cover of his copy of *Confessions*. Soane however can also be seen to represent that other strand mentioned above – archaeology. He was a passionate collector of antique objects and his house stands, even today, as one of the most incredible of museums (we shall come back to his work in greater detail later in the book).

Theodor Adorno has pointed out that museums are displays of objects which no longer have a vital relationship to the viewer and are therefore in the process of dying (and he uses the German word *museal*, or museum-like, to illustrate this point). Archaeology is, in fact, the study of the dead: dead civilisations and artefacts which were made by and belonged to the dead. The museum is the memorialisation of those objects. But seen together as a collection the objects become a series of fetishes which tell us as much about the mind of the collector as about the collection. Freud's collection of primitive sculptures and phallic fetishes leaves us in no doubt about his preoccupations.

Soane's collection was in many ways about death itself. His house in London (1792–1824) culminates in the lower, rather than the upper levels, and particularly in the remarkable Egyptian sarcophagus at its heart, which is ultimately symbolic of the architect's presence. It is a house about death, a memorial to himself. However, its architecture is also an indication of his preoccupation with the idea of a route, as exemplified in the English landscape garden, a narrative journey through the building and through a series of experiences, moods and ages. This interpretation of architecture is characteristic of the Freemasonry of which Soane was a practitioner.

Masonic ritual places great emphasis on the route as a path of initiation. The ideas came in part from contemporary studies of Ancient Egyptian archaeology, temples and pyramids which were designed as a succession of spaces and halls leading ultimately to the most holy and sacred space. In masonry, this progression through space (often while blindfold) became a symbol of the journey through life and the rites of passage celebrated in all religions and cultures.

Other Enlightenment architects who occupied themselves with narratives and an *architecture parlante* (notably Ledoux) produced designs that were more manifestly expressions of masonic ritual. However, the principal impact of this idea of the journey was not in interior but in exterior space. The rise of the English landscape garden, also in the eighteenth century, can be linked closely with prevailing masonic ideas and iconography. The garden is not laid out like the formal gardens of the late Renaissance as an imposition of order on nature; rather, as an idealised landscape recalling the Arcadian setting of Poussin's paintings.

Man works with nature in creating the ultimate artifice and, within this Arcadian setting, deliberately places ruins, follies and *faux*, or real, memorials. These ideas can be seen at Castle Howard in Yorkshire (1699–1742), where Nicholas Hawksmoor placed a series of objects in the great gardens of the house designed by his master Sir John Vanbrugh. A huge mausoleum was built, a building devoted to death perhaps the consummate masterpiece of English classicism. Its crowded and curious classical composition makes a striking appearance on a skyline which is also punctuated by a temple, a pyramid and an obelisk. The Elysian Fields at Stowe in Buckinghamshire featured a monument to British genius, a temple set within lush gardens, and a walk at the garden of the Leasowes featured a classical urn inscribed *Et in Arcadia Ego*.

This brings us back conveniently to the idyllic setting of Rousseau's tomb. The Arcadian garden and the tomb as a classical fragment and *memento mori* set within that symbolic landscape has become an archetype of the burial ground in the Western tradition and it is hard for us to conceive of a time when the garden or the park was not the norm in cemetery design and for the setting of the architecture of the dead. Rousseau's tomb and the great romantic gardens of Georgian England represent the elegiac interpretation of the birth of a new type of architecture of commemoration.

However, there were practical issues which also necessitated the change from prevailing burial trends in the eighteenth century. In the following chapters we will briefly examine these circumstances in order to understand the genesis of the tumultuous changes which made death a fundamental theme of the architecture of the Enlightenment and a preoccupation which has reverberated through the ensuing centuries to reach our own age, where it remains a powerful artistic idea.

III. THE NECROPOLIS
A Resurrected Archetype

The necropolis, the city of the dead, was a classical archetype which had been forgotten. Roman cities had such burial places on their outskirts, so on approaching a Roman city, the traveller first encountered the dead. The Romans had been aware of the hygienic implications of burial in city centres and of the symbolic and iconographic significance of setting aside a planned area for the inhabitation of the dead. However, despite the Renaissance and the subsequent glorification of all things classical, this particular aspect of classical culture had not been revived.

The early Christians adopted the burial customs of the Romans and interred their dead in catacombs, which later became associated with illicit services and meetings and with the burial of saints and martyrs, taking on great iconographic and ritual significance. Christianity had its beginnings, quite literally, as an underground religion and the place of the dead became the place of celebration where the house of the living could not be used.

This connection of ritual and burial never completely faded away and has had great implications for both the history of the liturgy and church architecture and the architecture of death. Altar-tombs were often erected within the catacombs and when Christians were able to build churches above ground they tended to do so directly above or at least near to the remains of martyrs and saints which sanctified their construction and founded the location and the space as sacred. Subsequently, the connection with the catacombs and the burial of martyrs was maintained when relics or bones were brought from their resting-places to be placed inside the altars. The altar in Roman Catholic ritual still symbolises three concepts: the table of the Last Supper, the sacrificial altar and the Body of Christ.

Thus, by making it a reliquary it becomes a holy container in its own right while retaining the traditional iconography; the altar at the heart of the church retains a very close link with the tomb.

The presence of relics or sacred remains was seen to infer sanctity on their surroundings and it therefore became desirable to be buried close to these remains. The space beneath the church became a place of burial for those with the means or importance to request interment close to the altar, and the church itself became to some extent an expression of the architecture of the dead. Once the space beneath the church was exhausted, burials began to spread outside and a hierarchy developed: the best spaces inside the church were reserved for the wealthiest citizens, the spaces near the church for the emergent middle classes, and the spaces on the peripheries were communal graves for the poor.

The church became a repository of funereal sculpture, often crowded with memorials vying for the best position and the most dramatic architectural effect. The churchyard gradually also became sanctified and the property of the church, being reserved solely for burial. The oldest and the best burial places were on the south side of the church and the poorer graves were situated on the north side where the shadow of the church fell upon them (the devil was supposed to enter from the north side and to live in the shadow of the church). The poor were not memorialised and simply buried in pits, one on top of the other, wherever there was space.

The Church had become solely responsible for the burial of the dead and it was found to be a lucrative sideline. Fees were charged for burials and higher fees were charged for good plots in the churchyard and for interment and memorialisation within the church. The churches themselves became huge crypts crowded with plaques and sculptures, with constant digging up of the floors and disturbance of the services, and disposal of old, often foul-smelling, partially decomposed remains. The levels of the churchyards outside tended to rise with the constant cycle of burials, one on top of the other so that it often seemed that the church was drowning in a sea of bodies. As old bones were dug up to make room for new bodies, charnel-houses and ossuaries were filled to the brim with remains. In Paris, the Cemetery of the Holy Innocents was contained by arcaded walls which themselves contained the bones of the cemetery's previous occupants while the exhumed skulls looked down from open eaves. It was a sight that was at once *memento mori* and a reminder of the horrors of purgatory.

After the Middle Ages, cities began to grow at unprecedented levels and the cemeteries became full to capacity and began, sometimes literally, to overflow. The Romans had learned that there was a hygienic purpose in placing cemeteries outside of towns but, as the great Roman cities emptied leaving only a fraction of the population and Christianity began to take hold throughout the empire, so the lessons were forgotten. They were to be relearned of necessity during the Enlightenment.

The seventeenth century, for example, witnessed fundamental changes in outlook and attitudes towards cemetery design. In London, the growing numbers of dissenters were unwilling to pay the established Church the fees for being buried in churchyards (sometimes they were prevented from being buried in proximity to the church by the authorities) and they began to establish their own cemeteries. The appalling death-toll inflicted on urban populations by the Black Death intensified the demand for large, new burial grounds away from the centrally-located churches.

At the same time, Europeans were beginning to embark on monumental programmes of colonisation across the continents and there was a great cross-fertilisation of cultures. Europeans were deeply moved by the splendour and sophistication of Islamic memorials. The shrines erected to contain the bodies of prophets and sultans exerted a powerful impact on Western culture. In the lands occupied by the Ottomans, great figures were memorialised in mausolea, or *türbe*, which can be perceived as a continuation of the classical tradition even if the architectural language had altered beyond recognition. The Taj Mahal in Agra, India (1630–53), represented the zenith of Islamic funerary architecture and its setting in an exquisite garden surrounded by canals, pavilions and fountains seemed almost impossibly beautiful.

The life of the early European colonists was luxurious but short due to the intemperate hot climate and their susceptibility to tropical diseases. Within a brief period there was a demand for a great number of burial places and, influenced partly by local traditions, some of the first great garden cemeteries began to appear in the colonies.

South Park Street in Calcutta, a British colonial cemetery begun in 1767, was a resurrection of the necropolis. As its name suggests, it was organised along urban lines, anticipating the re-emergence of the classical form of the city of the dead: a street of individual mausolea, conceived as houses, each expressed in a neo-classical language; almost a museum of architectural styles and elements. In America, French settlers in New Orleans encountered similar death rates. The humidity and proclivity to flooding made burial grounds unhygienic. Therefore, rows of vaults were erected outside the city centre and remarkably modern 'oven tombs' (vaults arranged in a rational grid, the body being placed inside as bread is into an oven) were erected out of iron and stucco. These were forms which would reappear in Aldo Rossi's buildings two centuries later.

Back in Europe, churches were beginning to subside above foundations that had been gnawed away by centuries of burials and exhumations. The monopoly of the Church with respect to burials began to dwindle with the rise of vehement dissension. While the dykes built up around the churches swelled with piled-up coffins, and the charnel-houses overflowed with bones, the ideas of the Enlightenment were beginning to erode the Church's prominence in the field of learning, its philosophical position and its status as moral guardian. Rousseau's burial in a garden (Ermenonville) echoed the pantheistic classical overtones which ran through his work. Although the philosophers who followed in his wake did not question absolutely God's power, there was a subtle erosion of the Church's influence and of that of the crowned heads of Europe as God's official representatives.

One of the great vehicles for the spread of Enlightenment ideas was Freemasonry. This contributed to the decline in the Church's power, a de-Christianisation of society, and was also, as we have seen with the ideas of the narrative and the route in the garden, a fundamental influence of the revival of classical ideals in funerary architecture. The rational and the romantic seemed to conspire against the *status quo*. The revolutionary ideals which swept America and France at the end of the eighteenth century were to exert dramatic effects on the architectural interpretation of death and a return to the democratic ideals associated with the classical world in building radical new cities of the living, and a resurrection of the idea of cities for the dead.

IV. BURIED CITIES – DEAD CITIES

The discovery of Herculaneum in 1738 and of Pompeii ten years later exerted a profound effect on Western civilisation. The idea of the discovery of these lost cities can almost be compared to Sigmund Freud's discovery of the unconscious: a whole new world had opened up which, until then, had only surfaced in fragments, disjointed objects or concepts.

Yet the towns had continued to exist like ghost cities in the local myths and legends of people in the surrounding areas. These were vital towns which had been struck down by the unbridled volcanic power of Vesuvius. The inhabitants lay hardened into grotesque fossils – sculptures of themselves. The brothels, bars and shops and obscene graffiti on the walls were perfectly preserved. It was the perfect *memento mori* for an eighteenth century obsessed with itself, a decadent society based around a privileged few, on great inequality, and one which expressed itself in an art and architecture of ever and more fanciful Rococo flourishes.

The dead cities revealed surprises and disappointments. Roman society was seen to be as decadent as contemporary Europe, and not the idealised perfection into which it had been mythologised, and its wall paintings and buildings were often crude and vulgar. Yet the discovery of the cities was an undeniable impulse in the development of neo-classicism and a fascination with a new vision of the past in ruins, of fallen greatness. Pompeii was a museum before there were museums, a walk into a tangible past, back into a sacred time. It had always existed in the idea of a lost city, an Atlantis, but when it was exposed and excavated it became a true necropolis, a city of dead people on the outskirts of Naples.

As already mentioned, the Romans were aware of the need to position their burial grounds outside the cities, and Pompeii was no exception. The city of the dead at Pompeii was a crucial counterpoint to the city of the living but it was not set apart in an enclosed area, as was to become the custom with cemeteries. On the contrary, the Pompeiian necropolis, in common with the other Roman examples, was built around the roads which led into the city, around the city gates.

The Romans did not feel the need to place their dead in gardens of rest. Quite the opposite was true; the necropolis was positioned as a street of tombs and mausolea sited along the busiest and most bustling thoroughfares. The funerary buildings and mausolea became shelters for travellers who would rest under their arcades. Soon, the tombs became interspersed with traders who set up kiosks to service the resting travellers and it was seen as proper that the spirits of the dead (who were believed to hang around the area) should be able to participate in the everyday activity of city life.

In the same way as in the cities of the living, status was expressed in the scale, decoration and materials of the tombs in the necropolis. The simple benches which were part of the design of the tombs became transformed on the graves of the wealthiest citizens into arcades and small buildings, monuments to great men whose beneficence was such that even after their death they continued to provide shelter and beauty for the citizens. The familiar hierarchies of urban life continued on to the other side and the necropolis became a kind of forum, a place for public interaction, and for interaction and communion with the dead, who were left votive offerings and even fed through pipes (which culminated in amphora buried underground) into which wine or milk was poured, to assist their journey through the afterlife. Indeed, the relatives often joined the dead in their feasts; when Vesuvius erupted in AD 79 it caught one family banqueting inside one of the tombs near the Herculaneum Gate, creating a painfully ironic but very convenient blend of Last Supper, wake, cremation and interment, but illustrating the closeness which the living often retained with the dead.

In the *Satyricon*, written by Petronius around the time of the demise of Pompeii, Trimalchio, a major protagonist relates:

> It's a big mistake to have nice houses just for when you're alive and not worry about the one we have to live in for much longer . . . I'll put one of my freedmen in charge of my tomb to look after it and not let people run up and shit on my monument. I'd like you to put some ships there too, sailing under full canvas, and me sitting on a high platform in my robes of office, wearing five gold rings and pouring out a bagful of money for the people.[11]

The necropoleis were built in the surrounding area immediately outside the city gates, which was known as the *pomerium*. This zone acted as a metaphysical rather than a physical boundary. The power of the idea was such that early Roman cities often had no substantial walls and the presence of the *pomerium* was

enough to deter aliens. For a stranger to cross this sacred zone was perceived as a sacrilegious and disrespectful act which could incur the wrath of the dead, and this was adequate deterrence. This idea of the burial of the dead on the boundaries has proved powerful and enduring, while the notion that the dead continue to inhabit their resting places needs no further explanation.

While the discovery of these lost Roman cities of Herculaneum and Pompeii had a critical effect on Western civilisation, the rediscovery of Rome had similarly dramatic connotations. Rome, of course, had never disappeared, after all it was the great centre of the Baroque. However, it was rediscovered in a different sense: as a city of ruins. One figure more than any other is responsible for this reinvention of the eternal city – Giovanni Battista Piranesi.

Piranesi's drawings of the ruins of Rome give the impression of a gargantuan city, a city abandoned by giants. Awesome walls and arches and cavernous, infinite progressions of spaces indicate the artist's immense respect for Roman civilisation and the awe in which he held the achievements of Rome. The city is seen as half-submerged so that the buried elements conceal the true scale of their mass; like icebergs they appear enigmatically as indicators of the huge remains that still lay below, as if what we are seeing is only the merest hint of the whole, a fragment of the glory of Rome.

These and some of his other drawings inspired by the theme reveal a world of almost terrible mass, interior landscapes and architecture on a geological scale, all shrouded in impenetrable and frighteningly intense shadow. Piranesi brought together two fundamental preoccupations of the era, two ideas which are very relevant to an analysis of the beginnings of the modern architecture of death: the idea of fragmentation and the notion of colossal spaces being defined in shadow as much as by mass and form.

In Henry Fuseli's watercolour sketch *The Artist moved by the Grandeur of Ancient Ruins* (1778–91) we see a figure, head held in hand, overawed by the magnificence of huge fragments of a classical sculpture, a foot and a hand. The most influential of all art historians, Johann Winckelmann, who published a treatise on the imitation of the antique, stated that the aim of all artists must be to attempt to imitate the work of the ancients; yet he acknowledged that they were inimitable. The reverence for the works of classical civilisation (even in the light of Michelangelo and Poussin) was inestimable. It became a platonic idea of perfection to be imitated but one which could never be captured. The ant-like people clambering about the Herculean ruins of Piranesi's depictions of Rome and his imaginary *Prisons* are equally insignificant when confronted with the grandeur of the past.

The works of art which attempted to portray this sense of awe could only ever be realised on paper. The drawings depicted grandeur through ruin; the fragments of the ancients were more profound than the whole, they more fluently conveyed the sense of what it was that had been lost and the impossibility of recapturing that essence. The ruin, the fragment, the displaced piece became the ideal. The first chapter opens with an account of Rousseau's grave at Ermenonville: in the same gardens a shrine was subsequently built and dedicated as the 'Temple of Modern Philosophy'. Like the follies in contemporary English gardens, it took the form of a ruin, a building built as the fragmented essence of itself. Soane, whose sketch of Rousseau's tomb provided the inspiration for the opening lines of the first chapter, designed his house as both tomb and museum, a dwelling built around a vast collection of fragments.

The fragment, like the tomb, poignantly represents a lost whole. As the body stands for only the physical part of a human existence, the fragment indicates a similarly lost essence which leaves the departed whole to the imagination, just as a tomb or an epitaph gives only the most subtle of information and allows the viewer to form a picture of the commemorated deceased. The task of an epitaph or an inscription is to condense a life or a body of knowledge into a single sentence. The gravestone and the tomb then become disseminators of a sometimes arcane knowledge (see chapter II, 'Et in Arcadia Ego') and they take on significance as books in a library. But their inscriptions also take on the meaning of a milestone, a marker colonising a space and identifying the deceased's part in historical and territorial terms.

In Roman times, milestones were placed at the sides of the road, a transition zone of territory that was neither here nor there, neither road nor land but which organised and defined the abstraction of charted ground as a man-made grid placed on a natural landscape. The side of the road had similar characteristics

to the *pomerium*, a no-man's land which somehow remained slightly beyond the reach of order. When highwaymen were hung at crossroads and their ghosts returned (like the devil in blues music – Robert Johnson's 'Crossroad Blues' is a good example) we can detect a lingering trace of this fear of a transitional, hence uncontrolled space. To move a milestone was to destroy the imposed order and was an offence punishable by death. The idea of destroying or defacing a tomb retains for us these notions of sacrilege and an unforgivable offence against the order of things.

It is no coincidence that the period of the French Revolution also witnessed the opening of the first museums. Today the museum has become to our great cities what the church was to cities of the past – a place of gathering, education, awe and pilgrimage. In an age which saw the decline of the Church as the dominant force in society, something had to replace it.

The museum became a focus of national pride and a new *type* of building. It was, in effect, a collection of fragments which allowed a walk through historical time and a return to mythical time, and memorialised the past. It also provided a concrete memorial to the vision of an individual or a state: Sir John Soane's house and his Dulwich Art Gallery with its bizarre mausoleum are the purest illustrations of this idea, while in our own age the proliferation of the Holocaust museum as a specific type (see chapter XVII) represents a further blurring of the boundaries between the museum and the mausoleum.

One of the fundamental ideas behind many of the Holocaust memorials and museums is that of fragmentation. The destruction of lives is illustrated by a group of objects classified by type (the collections of suitcases and glasses or piles of hair at Auschwitz, for instance) while the architectonic language often also resorts to an expression of the fragmentation of a grid or a city.

While the notion of the fragment played a critical role in the understanding of the artistic period around the eighteenth century, the other idea which is crucial to us at this juncture was that of shadow. Piranesi, as well as giving us fantastically distorted images of an imperial Rome of impossibly gargantuan proportions, was also largely responsible for the effects of shadow as a decisive means of expression on contemporary architecture. Next we will take a brief look at the role of shadow in the evolution of what is almost undoubtedly the most dramatic period of the visionary architecture of death.

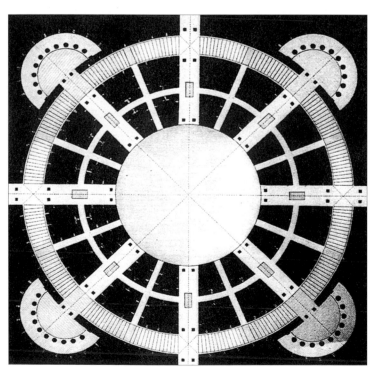

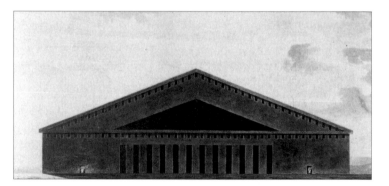

ABOVE: Design for a Cenotaph to Sir Isaac Newton, 1784, E-L Boullée; CENTRE RIGHT: Design for a funerary monument, c1785, E-L Boullée; BELOW LEFT AND RIGHT: Cemetery in Chaux, plan and section, 1804, C-N Ledoux

V. THE ARCHITECTURE OF SHADOWS

The ideas of darkness and chaos are inseparable. In the beginning, according to the Bible:

> the earth was without form and void; and darkness was upon the face of the deep. And the Spirit of God moved upon the face of the waters.
>
> And God said, Let there be light: and there was light. And God saw that it was good: and God divided the light from the darkness.

In darkness the earth was a void – light is the giver of form. The darkness represents the chaos and disorder of a primeval world. There is an automatic correlation between darkness and evil (Christ is the Light of the World, Satan the Prince of Darkness). Yin and Yang are represented as the fundamental division of darkness and light, each one giving form to the other and neither being able to survive without the other. Manicheism too sees the world principally in terms of darkness and light.

The more recent acceptance of the idea of black holes has given new expression to darkness, the space from which no light can emerge, as a focus for our deepest fears of oblivion and infinite nothingness. The shadow is traditionally seen as a negative side representing evil as the sun represents the force for good. As Heidegger has said, the world is founded by the creative light from above, so from below comes the destructive black light of chaos and of unmaking. Thus, in the shadows we can see another side to the world, the negative world of the unknown and of death. The shadow, like the fragment, denotes the absence of the object as much as it signifies its presence. De Chirico's powerful images of dream landscapes often feature shadows cast by unseen objects hidden behind columns or sculptures (as seen in the work of Aldo Rossi). These suggest evil, a threatening and doom-laden presence made more evil by its absence from that which can be seen.

Piranesi popularised visions of gargantuan ruins, semi-submerged in an overgrown landscape, casting ominous, all-consuming shadows. Colossal capitals jutted up above the ground hinting at the grandeur of the ruins which lay beneath and at the splendour of the civilisation which had created them, evoking a nostalgia and sentimentality for the unattainable glory of the past. It was as if these great monuments cast long black shadows over the hopeless inadequacies of modern civilisation. In his drawings of imaginary prisons, space becomes defined entirely by shadow; the artist created a nether world of the damned who were doomed to eternal existence, dwarfed in the darkness of these superhuman structures.

It was Etienne-Louis Boullée who developed these ideas a few decades later into a fantastic collection of visionary schemes which have continued to profoundly influence architecture in our own age and which have exerted an immeasurably deep influence on the modern architecture of death. Boullée combined these ideas of colossal scale, partial submergence and shadow into an extraordinary architectural language which was destined to remain almost exclusively on paper – perhaps in fact the designs' confinement to drawings has even added to their aura and mystique. The architect's description of the genesis of his development of an 'Architecture of Shadows' combines an Enlightenment existential crisis with a mood which seems to presage the darkness of the gothic imagination. In his manuscript, *Architecture, essai sur l'art*,[12] he explains:

> Finding myself in the countryside, I skirted the edge of a wood in the moonlight. My shadow caused by the light excited my attention (certainly, this was not a novelty for me). Because I was in a special mood, the effect of this image of myself prompted a feeling of extreme sadness. The shadows on the ground of the trees made the most profound impression on me. This scene intensified in my imagination. I became aware of all that is most sombre in nature. What did I see? the mass of objects detached as black silhouettes against a background of extremely pale light. Nature seemed to offer itself in mourning to my view. Moved by the feelings that I was experiencing, I applied myself, from that moment onward, to translate them in a precise manner into architecture.[13]

Boullée used shadows to denote the absent and the negative; his design for a 'Funerary Monument characterising the genre of an architecture of shadows' shows a huge, distended pediment, its roof out of scale with the structure it surmounts, which consequently appears to have sunk into the ground under the immense weight. The columns one would expect to see are replaced by vertical openings, so that the rhythm is of a pier, flush with the wall, followed by an opening which is narrower than the pier. It is a distorted classicism where the shadow becomes the structural element and the burden of grief is borne upon the blackness of empty space.

There is a distinctive duality present in all Boullée's designs; of above and below, light and shadow, the

ABOVE: Designs for mortuary depots, 1799, J Molinos; CENTRE: Designs for a Paris cemetery, c1785, E-L Boullée; BELOW: Engravings of Basilica of Maxentius, Rome and illustration from Carceri *series, G B Piranesi, 1760s*

massive quality of the architecture and the ant-like scale of the people depicted, the vast areas of smooth stone surface contrasted with equally colossal areas of impenetrable blackness, and of the changing mood of the scene from day to night. He often placed buildings below the level of the ground, partly to suggest an earth which was swallowing up the architecture, partly to connect the worlds of above and below and perhaps to emphasise the very idea of burial, while the columns he employed were frequently stumpy and ill-proportioned, suggesting partial submergence like those in Piranesi's drawings hinting at the wonders buried below.

The monumental scale and horizontality of these designs also helped bind them firmly to the ground; rows of columns, cypress trees and widely spaced chapels, pavilions and mortuary buildings gave the effect of an infinite horizontality – man's relationship to the earth while lying in a coffin rather than that while standing to survey the landscape.

Along with Boullée's enormous cemeteries set within Arcadian landscapes, the most powerful use of his 'Architecture of Shadows' and the employment of his peculiarly bleak and endlessly vast, smooth surfaces was achieved with his designs for a cenotaph for Newton. Isaac Newton was the icon of the new-found order in the cosmos. His name had come to embody the principles upon which a new age of rational thought was built, so what more appropriate motif could there be for his monument than the cosmos itself? The dome has traditionally been seen as the symbolic representation of the vaults of the heavens, but had been used in an ecclesiastical context. Here Boullée used the dome as a representation of the universe, the all-encompassing sky for its own sake; the wonder of the heavens was wonder enough without looking to a purpose beyond, other than the order in the stars found by Newton.

Obviously inspired by the great memorials of ancient Rome, Boullée conceived the monument as a gigantic sphere, pierced through with a plethora of tiny holes which admit light during the day to represent the stars in the heavens. At night, a powerful light burning inside would turn the memorial into a beacon to the exterior world. Man stands at the base of the sphere looking up in awe at the endless volume above; a tiny temple structure represents the pitiful scale of mankind against the awesome expanse of space. This poetic vision proved to be one of the most influential images in the history of a modern architecture whose devotees rediscovered Boullée as a precedent for their own visionary versions of a geometric autonomous architecture.

Boullée's other funerary schemes included buildings in the shape of grossly exaggerated sarcophagi, pyramids which doubled as triumphal arches celebrating the victory of death over life and colossal cone-shaped towers reminiscent of Claude Ledoux's charcoal burners at his visionary settlement of Chaux – huge smokestacks to celebrate the corporeal return to ashes. Many of these images would be resurrected by the Italian neo-Rationalists from the 1960s onwards, and the conical tower formed the centrepiece of Aldo Rossi's design for the Modena Cemetery. These were images which would come back to haunt a twentieth-century society permeated by the same revolutionary desires and rational beliefs which fuelled this remarkable creative era in France.

Boullée's vast cemetery designs bore similarities to notions inherited from the English garden design of the narrative journey through a constructed landscape to deliberately evoke moods and sentiments at particular points. The aspect of follies and grottoes within the garden would then change according to the light, the position of the sun, the season and the darkness of night. However, it was not Boullée but one of his contemporaries, the French architect Jacques Molinos, who created a design that demonstrated the closest affinity with the ideas embodied in the English garden.

His design for the *Champ de repos* of 1799 (the year of Boullée's death) was for a landscape garden in Montmartre which would have encompassed grand mausolea, paupers' graves, a giant central pyramid (like that later proposed for Père-Lachaise and subsequently for London by Thomas Willson) and a series of catacombs. But despite the ambition of the scheme (proposed as a private profit-making enterprise with the blessing of the state) it was perhaps the inclusion of a series of buildings within the city of Paris to serve as mortuary depots which was the most interesting facet of the design.

Molinos proposed a set of individual pavilions as mortuary stations (Richard Etlin suggests that these were inspired by Ledoux's *barrières*, or tax gates for Paris, a series of experimental constructions which proved to be one of the finest achievements of the *architecture parlante*).[14] What was so interesting about these constructions was that they were conceived as

Views of tombs in Père-Lachaise cemetery, Paris, which opened in 1804, including the tomb of Oscar Wilde by Epstein (above centre); a Holocaust memorial (centre); and fin-de-siècle *sculpture by P Bartholomé (below left) situated opposite entrance to cemetery*

outposts of the cemetery within the city. Their function was as the final destination for the funeral cortège from whence the bodies would be picked up by carriage to be taken on the last leg of the journey to the cemetery.

If Ledoux's *barrières* are the modern equivalent of the city wall, then these buildings represent the Roman relationship with the city of the dead, a distinct urban presence imposing itself on the edge of the city. The mortuary depots did indeed echo a number of classical themes; one with a stepped pyramidal roof clearly takes its cue from the mausoleum of Halicarnassus, while another, a sphere set within a circular temple, recalls Boullée's Cenotaph for Newton and Lequeu's fantastic Temples of the Earth and of Sacred Equality. These are urban *memento mori*, deliberate reminders of the presence of death in an urban setting so that the fact that the cemetery has been banished to the city's edge should be no excuse for forgetting mortality.

VI. THE PARISIAN ELYSIUM

On entering the cemetery at Père-Lachaise through the portals of the main gate, the visitor is confronted with a long vista which terminates in a remarkable sculptural monument, the centre of which is defined by a dark brooding opening. Completed exactly a century after the death of Boullée by the sculptor Paul Bartholomé, this monument superimposes a group of neo-classical mourning figures on a starkly simple structure with battered Egyptian-style walls. A bleak, black door seems to draw in the mourners like a magnet, or a black hole, the gravitational pull of which is too great to resist. The romantic figures against the stark, walls create a juxtaposition of the unadorned stone surfaces of Boullée's visionary structures and the exquisitely detailed neo-classical sculpture (particularly Canova's Maria Christina monument of 1799–1805) which bridges the romantic age and the emergent Art Nouveau.

The trees which surround the structure cast constantly moving shadows on the stone in a manner which evokes Boullée's revelation in the forest, which led to his formulation of an 'Architecture of Shadows'. These are suitable images as an introduction to the cemetery which has shaped the modern vision of the city of the dead more than any other.

Although the cemetery of Père-Lachaise opened at the dawn of the romantic age in 1804, it is just as much the fruit of the age of the Enlightenment and the increasing secularisation of society that had accompanied it. The great expanse of green at the edge of Paris was a response to the overcrowding of urban cemeteries and the developing notions of hygiene, but it was also inspired to a great extent by discoveries in the relatively new field of archaeology; the finding of necropoleis at Pompeii and Herculaneum and the new-found fashionable qualities of the Roman Via Appia.

The final influence which provided a framework upon which to weave these ideas together was the admiration for the English garden, a narrative landscape inspired by Claude and Poussin, an artificial Arcadia, a journey through the landscape which could relate a story – a walk through real and mythical time and a return to a lost age.

The cemetery was brought into being by Napoleon, then acting as First Consul, whose wide-ranging reforms across continental Europe ultimately led to the foundation of many other cemeteries. As well as being a tremendously successful architectural paradigm for other cemeteries to follow around the world, it was a highly fruitful speculative financial exercise: the official who bought the land for the city, Nicolas Frochot, later managed to sell a plot to the landowner from whom he purchased the site for a higher figure than he had paid for the entire piece of land.

Frochot was also responsible for bringing the remains of a handful of great figures from Parisian history to his new cemetery. The presence there of the bodies of Abèlard and Héloïse, Molière and La Fontaine was in part responsible for the huge popularity of Père-Lachaise as a fashionable burial place for Parisians and it was also instrumental in demonstrating to the world that there were huge profits to be made from this kind of enterprise. (The Church had learned this lesson during the Middle Ages and it was still smarting from the effects of losing this lucrative source of revenue.)

As such, it also constituted a significant move away from the French revolutionary idea of the cemetery as a 'Garden of Equality', in which there was an attempt to introduce greater elements of equality, democracy and fraternity into the final resting place than has so far been achieved by the revolutionaries. Père-Lachaise was a place to show off the illustrious dead and for wealth to be made manifest in the remarkable monumental mausolea which make up its landscape. It remains the place for a corpse (and its relatives) to be seen.

Alexandre-Thèodore Brongniart was commissioned to design the cemetery, which would have culminated in a spectacular pyramid atop the crest of the site had the planned chapel been built. The pyramid is absent but the site is no less dramatic, crowded with thousands of tombs and sepulchres and arranged in a part romantic and part formal manner with the most expensive and fashionable plots at the centre. The effect is of a deserted city, a landscape of curious sentry-boxes punctuated by larger imposing memorials. The cemetery is arranged in a series of streets in which the plots are numbered like urban blocks. The densely packed quality of the mausolea gives real definition to the winding paths, while signposts and cast-iron street furniture reinforce the feel of a city of the dead.

Père-Lachaise continued (and continues) to attract the fashionable and wealthy dead: Oscar Wilde's tomb by Sir Jacob Epstein, with its weird bulky angel, is a fine example of twentieth-century funerary art, while Jim Morrison's tomb attracts more attention than most of the others including those of Proust, Chopin, Hugo, and Modigliani, and is now permanently guarded. The burial of eminent figures helped to weave the necropolis into the consciousness of the metropolis, becoming, like the Roman necropoleis, an inseparable part of the city and a chief site on the itinerary of the traveller. One wall exhibits a plaque to the last surviving fighters of the Paris Commune who were lined up against it and shot, while nearby, bleak memorials of very fine quality, commemorate the deportation of Jews and others to the camps under the Vichy regime. Thus the cemetery becomes like a text; a book in stone narrating the turbulent and revolutionary history of the city.

The Romanian anthropologist and writer Mircea Eliade has suggested that in reading a book we transport ourselves into another realm, a mythical time which takes us momentarily out of our own existence. He states that in doing this we are simply indulging our ancient desire or impulse to recreate the sacred time of our ancestors, just as shamanistic cultures escape through trance and the shaman's dreams and the sacred time is relived in each Christian service, the Last Supper and the Transubstantiation.[15] These ideas infer a return to a lost age, where time becomes suspended and we put ourselves in the hands of the author or the priest.

In the cemetery we can guide ourselves through the history of the city and its inhabitants, losing ourselves on the borders of the city of the living and the city of the dead. The memorials to the dead co-exist with the wandering figures of the relatives and the curious; it is at once cathartic and the deepest of engagements with the history of the city and the layers of the past upon which it stands. William Godwin's *Essay on Sepulchres* similarly suggested that the place of memorials in a society was comparable in function and importance to the position of the library as a repository for knowledge and history.[16] Père-Lachaise is the supreme example of this interdependence of city and cemetery, and its effect on the architecture and planning for the dead has been inestimable.

VII. JOHN SOANE
Display, dwelling and death

In the buildings of Sir John Soane (1753–1837) the distinction between the architecture of death and the architecture of the living became blurred. Soane even conceived his own house as a memorial, an inhabited mausoleum. He was not unusual in his preoccupation with funerary architecture; many of his contemporaries saw the sepulchre as a practical vehicle to investigate the sculptural possibilities of architecture. Hawksmoor's mausoleum at Castle Howard set an important precedent as the first major freestanding classical mausoleum since antiquity, and the type became a stock item in the design repertoire of students, dilettantes and professional architects, even if only as a fantasy, remaining on paper.

However, Soane's interest ran deeper than that of his contemporaries, who often saw the sepulchral monument as a chance to experiment with the Orders and with a heavily mannered style which would have been unfeasible in a building needed to execute a function for living beings. For Soane, the architecture of death provided the architectural framework with which he created an artistic *oeuvre*, which is of particular interest to this book because it presages in many ways the development of modernism and, more specifically, of modernism and death.

During his studies in Italy, Soane had been profoundly impressed by the ruins of antiquity (his collection of drawings by Piranesi attests to this impact) and, in particular to Piranesi's view of these dead cities as the creations of a colossal race, an unparalleled civilisation. It is a sentimental and melancholic view of an idealised and impossible past. That Soane himself was a melancholic character was in no small part responsible for this view and for his fascination with ruins, with fragments

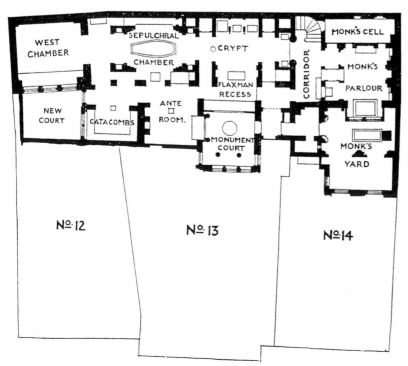

ABOVE: Fantasy vision of the basement of Soane's house in Lincoln's Inn Fields, London, 1815, J M Gandy; CENTRE: Section through house; facade (1792–1824); BELOW: Plan of house; RIGHT: Engraving of the Sarcophagus of Seti in basement of house, J Le Keux after F Arundale

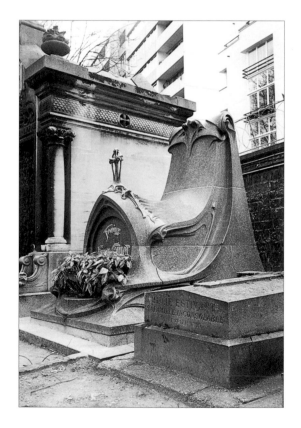

ABOVE: Soane family tomb, St Pancras, London, 1816; BELOW: Caillot tomb, c1905, Père-Lachaise cemetery, Paris

as the essence of an unattainable past and with architecture as *memento mori*.

Soane lived in an age which witnessed the dawn of archaeology. At this stage it remained essentially a form of pillage, but there is no doubting contemporary fascination with (and subsequent value attached to) antiques and the vestiges of antiquity. The great museums were founded at this time and Soane very much reflected the passion for collecting. The stone sarcophagus which lies at the heart of his house was rejected by the British Museum as too expensive, which explains how Soane came to purchase it from its importer. That the centrepiece of his house should be a sarcophagus is justification of our attention to him in this book, but it may be beneficial to briefly look at some of his other funerary designs before we return to his house.

Soane's other highly significant architectural tomb also resides in an early museum, at the Dulwich Picture Gallery in London (1811–14). He had already designed a private mausoleum in the London house of the original owner of the art collection and when the collection was moved to a purpose-built gallery in Dulwich, a new mausoleum was incorporated to house the bodies. It has often been noted that a museum is part of the expression of a desire for immortality. To have a great collection immortalises its owner while the pieces stay together. After death, the name lives on in the name or location of the collection – it becomes a monument to the collector.

At Dulwich, Soane was faced with making this connection, this desire for memorialisation, even more explicit. The focal point of the building is the founder's mausoleum, which is both separate from and central to the art gallery; seen from outside it appears to be an independent pavilion, from within it leads off the central axis. It is lit from above with an entirely different quality of light from that which persists elsewhere in the gallery, immediately denoting it as a special space. Steps lead down into a shallow circular well in which the tombs are situated – thus Soane introduces the idea of descent into another plane. The separateness of this area is further emphasised by the columned circular space which precedes the tombs as a kind of ante-chamber.

The monuments themselves are illuminated from a lantern above which gives the building its primary elevational interest: a curious cube surrounded by three sarcophagi representing those buried within and surmounted by five cinerary urns. The architectonic language of this whole composition is enigmatically bare, a stripped classicism, elegant and exquisitely proportioned but hauntingly elemental, as if only the essence of a language remained: the orders abandoned, a simple lintel instead of a cornice casting a heavy shadow on the wall below, and doors recessed into deep aedicules while simple brick piers replace columns and are doubled up to bear the heavy burden of death in the form of the sarcophagi they support.

Soane's own house in Lincoln's Inn Fields, London, can be read in a similar way as a dwelling built around the presence of death. At its heart is an enclosed atrium, the light filtering down from a lantern above and becoming ever fainter as it finally reaches the huge stone sarcophagus at its nadir. A bust of Soane himself sits high-up and is surrounded by other classical heads and fragments of cornices and capitals. Descending through the hole at the heart of the house the nature of the fragments changes; through cinerary urns to fragments of sculpted feet to darker collections of gothic carvings and funerary art. Soane's original drawings for the remodelling of the house show segments of the basement labelled as 'catacombs' and 'mausoleum' and, although it is probably not the case that he wished to see himself physically interred in the house, the great sarcophagus at its centre certainly seems to be a symbol of the architect's obsession with what John Summerson called the 'furniture of death' and a very profound *memento mori* indeed.[17]

Soane's house is, in effect, the first museum of architecture and, like most museums, it is a collection of fragments. But while we would expect a semblance of didacticism in a museum designed to educate and enlighten, there is none here. There is no order imposed on the objects other than Soane's own whimsy and some vague 'theming', perhaps more reminiscent of the idea of a 'cabinet of delight'. Fossils mingle easily with carvings as found fragments – things that were lost and have been brought into the light, resurrected. However, it is only a museum in the sense that a human mind is a museum.

Soane's celebrated lectures at the Royal Academy illustrate the breadth of his learning, the importance he attached to the study of the past and the subsequent use of this knowledge to create a continuity with the past. A walk around the architect's house is almost a posthumous lecture; the fragments of a ruined

greatness are visible all around, while the exquisitely thoughtful architecture of the building itself seems an abject lesson in what to do with this knowledge, how to bring it into a modern context – this is, after all, a common London terrace. Thus to walk around Soane's house is to wander among the architect's thoughts, fears, mourning after the demise of his wife, and his loneliness. In short, the house is a model of his mind.

In a small light-well Soane created a 'Monk's Garden', an absurd collection of gothic ruins piled up to create a sham monument to Padre Giovanni, a monk in Soane's own image; the architect buried his *alter ego* and then his dog in the same place. There is sentimentality, humour and pathos in the designs, but also more than a trace of the architect's genuine melancholia; grief over a lost wife and a son who had bitterly disappointed him (the house was at least in part a didactic tool to inspire his son into architecture; however, he became a journalist).

Other references to death abound inside and outside the house. The facade is decorated with four column capitals acting as brackets but supporting nothing except their own weight; they are both fragment and absence. The breakfast room is surmounted by a shallow dome inspired by a device on a Roman tomb. A similar architectural device crowns the tomb in which Soane buried his wife and in which he lies himself, and it can also be seen elsewhere in his works in a dome that represents the vault of the sky, though it is a low, brooding sky which hangs ominously like a threat (this device was also apparently the inspiration for the original red London telephone box).

The reason I have dwelt on a house designed at the beginning of the nineteenth century in a book about modern architecture is that its architecture expresses a complex web of ideas about death, memory and memorialisation which have subsequently fed architecture but have never again been addressed in such a comprehensive manner. Rossi and Scarpa share much with Soane, albeit expressed in fundamentally different architectures: concerns about the place of the fragment in architecture; about the subtle subversion of an existing architectonic language (particularly of classicism) to express abstract concepts connected with death: longing, grieving, missing, absence and so on.

Soane also presaged the idea of architecture as a Freudian analysis of dreams and desires, of ego and self-image, the notion of a house as a place of memories,

of dark basements and walls covered with successive layers of pictures and ornaments, each burdened with association and meaning. Just as Soane stripped the classical detail from his austere facades and these gave way to rich interiors loaded with meaning and symbolism, his house is a journey to the depths. The fragments largely belong to a classical world, and the symbolism too is drawn from myth and legend; what there is of the gothic is the atmosphere, the gargoyles and the ruined fragments of churches.

Soane's Freemasonry was well known and indicative of a man of the Enlightenment moving away from traditional notions of God towards an almost deist outlook. Looking inward to the workings of the mind, to repressed memory and a mysterious and unknowable subconscious seems a contemporary phenomenon but in Soane these traits are instantly recognisable. The architectures of memory, death, fragmentation and narrative blend to create the dwelling, the architecture of life. The house of the architect becomes the arena in which death and life cross-fertilise, a cathartic engagement with the house as a tomb from which we emerge paradoxically enriched by an enhanced consciousness of the inevitability of death.

ABOVE: Gries family tomb, Budapest, 1907, B Lajta;
BELOW: Design for a tomb, 1904, E Hoppe

VIII. DEATH AND THE BIRTH OF MODERNISM
The *Fin de Siècle* and the Sepulchre

> The grave, which knows my endless reverie
>
> (Graves understand the poet's vision)
>
> In those vast nights which know no lullaby.[18]

Baudelaire's elegy to the grave, like that of Gray earlier, imbued death and death's place on earth with an intense melancholy, a Gothic sentiment split evenly between a place of regret and an artistic muse. The romantic interpretation of the grave has its roots in the *memento mori* in classical art, but with the sentimentality and fashion for melancholia which defined artistic feeling in the nineteenth century, images of art and death became as closely intertwined as ivy covering an ancient tombstone.

This vision of death has never really left us but in the nineteenth century it met with utilitarianism and developing notions of hygiene and new methods of disposal of the dead in a curious collision which sometimes proved fruitful and, perhaps more often, did not. The association of the classical fragment, the Gothic ruin, with death became inseparable, and the mausoleum as a form remains dominated, even today, by a heavy classical architectonic language.

Modern ideas and architectural developments rarely penetrated through to memorial architecture. But the incredible explosion of artistic activity which engulfed the final years of the nineteenth century and the early years of the twentieth century inevitably exerted some effect on the architecture of death. It is to these few exceptions that I would like to turn, not because I believe them to have more value than other classical monuments but because they play a larger part in explaining the narrative leading to a modern architecture of death, if ever such a thing can be said to have developed at all.

Architecture in continental Europe and the USA was dominated in the nineteenth century by the academy system, in which students displayed their skill in design and drawing through the detailed exploration of building types using an accepted set of architectural forms and elements. The monument was often to be found among these prescribed building types, occupying the same importance as that of a century earlier for Soane's contemporaries; a device which allowed considerable creativity and experimentation (within the set parameters) due to its lack of function and the necessity for monumentalism inherent in the function of memorialisation.

The national monument and the monument to an important local historical figure became a critical *type* within architecture and gained further importance during the successive waves of nationalism which spread throughout Europe after the 1848 revolutions and before the outbreak of the First World War. The plethora of tombs and monuments to the illustrious dead of Europe from this period amply demonstrates the importance of the type to urban design. But the family tomb, the mausoleum and the gravestone remained largely untouched by new developments; the traditional conservativeness of the accoutrements of death prevailed.

In the USA, Louis Sullivan had begun to bring the blocky simplicity and exquisite decoration of his buildings to his mausoleum designs. While still firmly traditional buildings in a vaguely Byzantine mode, these beautiful structures presaged the developments in European Art Nouveau. The Getty Tomb of 1890 in Graceland Cemetery, Chicago, features the broad arches familiar from Sullivan's urban buildings and decorative schemes which evoke Islamic designs.

The Mausoleum of Charlotte Dickson Wainwright in Bellefontaine Cemetery, St Louis, built about a year later, is a piece of proto-modernism which bears a great resemblance to the designs of Josef Hoffmann a decade or so later. These tombs are one of the few rare examples of funerary architecture exerting a significant effect on secular design; Sullivan's intense and fine decorative motifs deeply impressed many designers who were later responsible for the emergence of European forms of Art Nouveau.

Walking around the necropolis of Père-Lachaise one can see little evidence of the Art Nouveau that was sweeping Paris at a time when many monuments were being constructed, but the quintessential Parisian architect of the *belle époque*, Hector Guimard, did manage to sneak in at least one curvaceous work among the sombre sepulchres: the Caillat Family tomb is a remarkable piece of work which stands out dramatically from the heavy classicism of its neighbours. The sweeping organic curves of the sepulchre seem to suggest a trail following in the wake of an ascent to heaven, yet the heavy black marble of the monument sits heavily on the ground, inferring the grief-stricken burden of death and the weight of the earth which pushes in at the bodies of the interred. The treacly cross

ABOVE: *Design for a war memorial, 1908, E J Margold;*
BELOW: *Design for a tomb, 1907, E Hoppe*

which sits at the front seems to melt into the flowing, lava-like stone of the monument.

The sepulchre is a fascinating blend of the organic and inorganic, the dynamic curves and the awful weight of the marble. Its very separateness immediately suggests the reasons why the style never affected sepulchral design too dramatically. Relatives may want to compete with their neighbours in the scale, size and elaborateness of the family tomb, but they do not want to compete with its style, to introduce a new language, as if there were something sacrilegious about changing the vocabulary of an immutable architecture of death.

Headstones and sepulchral sculpture were more readily embraced than monumental buildings by the flowing tendrils of Art Nouveau. Contemporary art and architecture journals show a plethora of extravagant, flowing Art Nouveau and Secessionist designs for tombs and memorials, particularly in France, Belgium and Germany (Britain remained largely immune despite the early emergence of the Arts and Crafts Movement as a precursor to continental trends). However, these memorials still represent the exceptions in an age of conservatism; the real impact of the turn-of-the-century avant-garde on funerary architecture can only be seen where the strands of classicism, an emergent functionalism and the architecture of the Secession merged, and the confluence of these design characteristics occurred most completely in the Wagnerschule.

The sepulchral designs of Otto Wagner's students represent one of the most fruitful bodies of work in the creation of a modern architecture of death. The huge Austro–Hungarian empire embraced myriad different cultures and all to some extent played a part in influencing the extraordinarily rich designs which emerged during this period. The simplicity of Mediterranean vernacular had struck Loos, Hoffmann and others, while Byzantine grandeur played a significant role in the formation of a Viennese art; the Secession building itself appears like some great mausoleum of antiquity. In the designs for the new building type of the crematorium, the Byzantine aspirations can be seen clearly, while in the sepulchral designs the primitive, blocky simplicity of Mediterranean vernacular was often used as a base to create monuments of great power defined by the use of elemental forms to create an 'autonomous architecture'.

The move away from flowing Secessionist designs of organic Art Nouveau type is evident in the work of a number of architects from Wagner's office. Jože Plečnik's early sepulchral designs are characterised by elemental forms tapering into blocks of stone in a Michelangelesque evocation of the spirit of the sculpture pre-existing within the rock; the role of the architect, like that of the sculptor, being to free the image trapped within. In each of his works there is a remnant of the idea of the shrine or the grotto, the monument as place of pilgrimage within the rocks.

This same notion of the tomb as an access to the sacred spring (which is the meaning of *Ver Sacrum*, the title of the Secession's journal), or grotto defines Bohumil Hubschmann's design for a sepulchral memorial in Semmering, Austria (1903). The powerful elevation is composed of a single slab of concrete let into the rock, its geometric smoothness contrasting with the rough geological forms of the stone background. Four square windows are shown, cut into the elevation so that the space between them forms a cross, and the attenuated niche for the door bears a lengthy inscription above the opening. Square openings in a random pattern beneath the windows allow the craggy rock to show through, partly achieving a kind of referential rustication and showing the strength of the rock which is able to break through the flimsy creation of man.

In Karl Maria Kerndle's design for a sepulchral chapel of the same year a similar strain of powerful primitivism manifests itself. There is something disconcertingly ominous about Kerndle's drawing; there can be no doubt that this is a building of death, an entry into a realm of no return. A pair of monumental pylons rise from the earth and the crevice between them becomes the entrance to which access is gained via a long stair sandwiched between two high walls. These walls exclude the view; manifestly this is an entrance to a hermetic world, apart from our own and defined by the darkness and shadow of the entrance. The door is like that to an ancient tomb, a huge slit of a window looms above it and this is capped by a triangle which terminates the interior space, like a spirit eye, or the all-seeing eye of the God of Masonic symbolism, an aperture at its centre implying that this is a world guarded by unknown spirits and forces.

The image of this design continued to exert a profound influence on architecture throughout the century and strikingly similar motifs can be seen in Aldo Rossi's City Hall Square monument in Segrate (1965) and his Via Croce Rossa Monument in Milan (1988).

A similar emphasis on solid geometric forms, but with less of the dark intensity of the above two designs, informed the work of several other architects who followed in the wake of Wagner. Emil Hoppe's study for a tomb of 1904, with its deliberate asymmetry and Greek-influenced head, reveals his debt to the ethereal work of Gustav Klimt, while his design for a tomb from 1907 shows his progress towards the more rigid symmetries of Hoffmann and the *Wiener Werkstätte*.

Rudolf Tropsch's sepulchral designs indicate this tendency towards a monumental, cubic classicism far earlier. His funeral chapel of 1902 displays a solidity that is characteristic of designs which would emerge a decade later. The later designs were heavily influenced by the work of Hoffmann, who designed a significant group of mausolea and tombs which are simple, elegant and defined by an elementality which effectively denotes their function. His sources were the Mediterranean sketches he made on his travels, the unmistakable qualities of Roman mausolea and the sparsely decorated geometric classicism which he developed in his architecture. These modest designs for memorials inspired far more ambitious schemes in the work of his contemporaries and students, including the dramatic fantasies of Emmanuel Josef Margold, whose funerary works seem, bizarrely, to presage the great Art Deco movie sets of the 1930s (perhaps not so unusual as both Art Deco and the Secessionists were influenced to a degree by early Central American motifs).

Margold's design for a war memorial (1908) amasses a huge pile of blocky forms into a pyramidic bulk, while his designs for a columbarium are characterised by a ghostly minimalism and the haunting presence of the simplicity of the central domed cylinder appearing like a vast cinerary urn. Wilhelm Foltin's designs for a war memorial display an even greater adherence to simplicity, and the pointed arches and grand scale of the scheme foreshadow later developments in Expressionism.

The designs of the years before the First World War tend more towards the monumental; colossal schemes conceived as great piles of masonry to equal the great Roman mausolea. These buildings were to influence the young Italian architects Sant'Elia and Mario Chiattone, whose designs are the natural extension of the impeccably drawn perspectives of the visionary monumental schemes emerging from the Wagnerschule.

Outside the Wagnerschule, in the Empire's twin hub, Budapest, a number of architects were experimenting

ABOVE: Schmidl tomb, Budapest, 1903, B Lajta;
BELOW: Design for a sepulchral chapel, 1903, K M Kerndle

with similar forms but tailoring them towards their cultural backgrounds. Just as Plečnik was to attempt to create a Slovenian necropolis with his cemetery in Žale later in the century, young Hungarian architects were working towards the creation of a national architecture which would embody archetypes embedded in a collective unconscious and also assert cultural and aesthetic independence from Vienna. The Wagner role of mentor to the new generation was played in Hungary by Ödön Lechner who had created an architecture that was as independently and eccentrically Hungarian as Antoni Gaudí's was Catalan. His protégé came in the form of Béla Lajta, one of the most underrated of the architects of the period.

Lajta's sepulchral monuments fill the cemeteries of Budapest with their eerily heavy classical forms. His Schmidl family tomb of 1902–3 (designed in conjunction with Lechner) is a florid vault covered in glazed tiles that reveals a richly decorated interior of gold mosaic, a powerful realisation of the *fin-de-siècle Gesamtkunstwerk*.

Later mausolea begin to realise a true internally consistent language. His Gries family tomb with its parabolic dome is based on the shape of the Hungarian peasant oven built-up of mud, a metaphor for the ashes to which the body reverts. Its features are articulated in a heavy, almost Norman architectonic vocabulary which occurs in many of the architect's buildings. Inside, however, it reveals the Byzantine richness of a world beyond – sumptuous gold mosaics depict trees of life, lions and folk motifs. Many depict Jewish mythological symbolism as these tombs were often commissioned by rich and progressive Jewish families who were more willing to hire an architect who worked outside the traditional conventions of funerary art.

The Schwarz tomb is a masterpiece of primitive classicism; tightly bunched up columns enclose a space of terrible shadows beneath a massive pediment. The sarcophagus protrudes as if it were being slowly swallowed by the darkness within. The Guttmann and Greiner tombs reveal the same dreadful darkness of the space within and beyond, contained within the massive elements of an oversized architectural language stripped to the fundamental essence of the parts.

Lajta's collaborator, Lajos Kozma, worked in a less emotive manner that is more reminiscent of his Viennese contemporaries. However, as his crematorium designs of 1909 indicate, he, too, was concerned with the development of a separate and recognisably

Hungarian language of architectural form, while moving to a functional approach which he would later embrace fully. The design (which is reminiscent of later German crematorium plans organised around a central circular chamber) contains no plans to use architectural euphemisms to disguise the nature of the structure; the smokestack is in full view, introducing a harsh asymmetry to the central hall.

In Slovakia, similar moves towards the formation of a national architectonic language were in the hands of Dušan Jurkovič. His designs for the chapel in the military cemetery at Pustki and Luzna (1916) powerfully evoke the silhouette of the timber bell-towers of Slovak churches. Pavel Janák would realise a similar result in his Pardubiče crematorium, which recognised the traditional timber architecture of Czech houses to create a house of the dead which sits awkwardly but fascinatingly in the midst of the explosion of Cubist architecture.

The designs of another Hungarian, Móric Pogány, see the return of the dome to the Central European architecture of death. The golden sphere which crowns the Secession building proved an enduring symbol. Otto Schönthal's designs for a funerary church in Vienna's Central Cemetery (1901) featured an enigmatic globe, symbolising the earth and the vaults of the heavens above in much the same way as Boullée's efforts a century earlier in his cenotaph for Newton. His earlier sketches reveal an expressionist vision of an elongated sphere flanked by two apparition-like columns, the design reminiscent of Fischer von Erlach's Karlskirche (begun 1716) and Wagner's Church of St Leopold but in a haunting, sketchily organic manner.

The idea of the central building of the cemetery and the crematorium as a single circular space was one which spread to become a hugely influential starting point for a number of designs, and one which would have continuing repercussions after the First World War. Fritz Schumacher's Dresden Crematorium of 1907 had dispensed with the decorative niceties of the Secession, leaving only the brutal masses of classicism to express the monumental finality of death. The main hall culminates in a curved apse which appears from the outside as a circular hall set within a massive block of stone. The powerful axiality of the scheme is given emphasis by a long reflecting pool which mirrors the terrible mass of the chamber, while a columbarium is set within cloisters on the other side of the block, sheltered by the mass of the building.

Schumacher's sketches for a crematorium project from 1889 already show the massive approach which was to become his characteristic style; the circular main hall is extruded skyward to become monument and landmark as well as functional building element. The idea of the oval or sphere at the heart of the crematorium as a quintessential Central European motif was reaffirmed in Bedřich Feuerstein's crematorium in Nymburk (1921–23). Characterised by an almost unbearably heavy stripped classical vocabulary, this massive building bears a great weight of grief on its stumpy columns.

In the end, the dramatic developments of the *fin-de-siècle* art movements had a surprisingly limited effect on funerary architecture. The emerging nations which made up the sprawling Austro–Hungarian empire perhaps experienced the greatest advances, partly due to the dynamic impetus of central European culture during the years around the turn of the century, and partly due to the desire for new forms of national artistic expression. Elsewhere, as has been the case through most of our century, conservatism dominated the architecture of death and designers were content to work within existing architectonic languages, principally classicism.

IX. CONSUMED BY FLAMES

Cremation is the most final method of disposal of the body, the most literal adaptation of the words of the funeral service 'ashes to ashes, dust to dust'. Its very finality meant that it was not accepted in the West until the end of the nineteenth century or later, despite a rich, pre-Christian heritage of cremation which stretched back to the Bronze Age.

The radical and secularising impulses which were responsible for the shift away from the use of the churchyard as a burial ground in the nineteenth century and resulted in the model cemetery of Père-Lachaise in Paris, and the cemeteries across Europe and North America which followed in its wake, were also partly responsible for the adoption of cremation as an efficient and hygienic method of body disposal. The development of new, more modern notions of hygiene and the revulsion at the insanitary conditions of overcrowded and foul-smelling burial grounds played an important part in establishing large municipal burial grounds, and these same concerns were instrumental in the rise of

Woodland Crematorium, Stockholm, 1935–40, G Asplund

Père-Lachaise Crematorium, Paris, 1809, Formige

cremation as cemeteries began to grow into alarmingly huge land masses to cater for rapidly expanding urban populations.

The development of utilitarianism as a philosophy in Britain and elsewhere also contributed to an eschewing of burial and entombment as a wasteful technique which occupied excessive amounts of valuable land and resources. The same impulses led to a decline in romantic and elegiac ideas, and the idea of the narrative landscape which had emerged from the English garden gave way to a simpler, gentler notion of the cemetery as a wistful park.

Meanwhile, European colonial expansion had opened up minds to other traditions of the treatment of human remains. Just as the high death rate in the colonies had inspired secular graveyards before they had gained popularity in the countries of the colonial powers, the native techniques would often have a profound impact on colonial officials and soldiers. The Indian tradition of cremation on a funeral pyre inspired many British colonialists, and when Shelley's body was burnt, the idea of cremation gained a powerful image of the romantic poet whose heart was plucked from the flames. Another poet, the symbolist Maurice Maeterlinck, also proved influential in the encouragement of cremation. He glorified the notion of cremation as a noble, spiritual end to life:

> Purified by fire, the memory lives in the heights as a
> beautiful idea; and death is naught but an immortal
> birth cradled in flames.[19]

So the move towards cremation gained ground in the second half of the nineteenth century. In France and Italy, cremation carried with it particular anti-clerical connotations which dated back to the French Revolution for their potency, and this gave cremation

an impetus among free-thinkers and radicals. The huge, imposing crematorium which was built at Père-Lachaise by the Paris city architect Formigé, testifies to the importance the method of disposal was gaining. The impressive building is executed in a blocky, powerful Byzantine style. It seems to presage Wagner's functional Church of St Leopold am Steinhof in Vienna and the synagogues of Theophil Hansen. The twin columns, Jachin and Boaz of Solomonic symbolism become two undisguised chimney stacks framing the dome, and a place is defined in front of the crematorium by arcaded columbaria. The whole is simple, elegant and functional.

Germany was very much in the vanguard of the movement towards cremation. A series of impressive, if often stolid buildings were created to accommodate the increasing demand for cremation; although, until the rise of Expressionism after the First World War, these were largely academic and conservative structures using an ecclesiastical tectonic language.

Other impressive crematoria were built in Milan and Genoa and combined a sombre monumentality with the ritual and functional requirements of this new building type. The rich, overtly pagan iconography of cremation – urns, flames, inverted torches and ashboxes – was used in abundance to inform the early architecture of cremation but, perhaps curiously, a real architecture specific to crematoria never arose and the only area where a consistent development of thoughtful and meaningful crematorium architecture developed was in Scandinavia. In most other places a reticence and an apparent unwillingness to confront the reality of death and of cremation led to anodyne, neutral designs. This sub-section of the architecture of death is therefore examined in a lesser way than intended in this book.

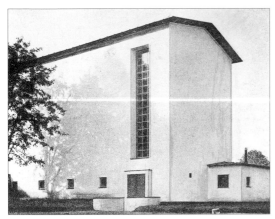

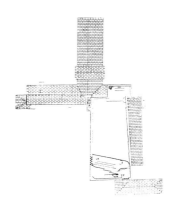

Abo Crematorium, Turku, Finland, 1941, E Bryggman

Abo Crematorium interior and roof plan

There are, however, notable exceptions. Gunnar Asplund's Woodland Crematorium, Stockholm, is one of the most recognisable and iconic buildings of the Modern Movement. Its themes of death and eternity, of man's place in the landscape are the same themes that have fascinated architects since Vitruvius and before. But the building has much more in common with classicism than merely a familiar set of themes. One of the reasons that Asplund's work has proved so enduring is that he is one of the architects who has emerged from modernism relatively unscathed. He is upheld by architects from all sides who wish to illustrate that modern architecture can be successful, on a human scale, and can take part in the meaning, symbolism and archetypes which have become familiar to us without reverting to an overtly classical language.

The Scandinavians, with their strong traditions of Lutheranism, took to cremation more avidly than other Europeans and the architecture which they created for their crematoria displayed a more honest approach to the process, a form of modernism which has somehow failed to penetrate the consciousness of many other Western countries. Ragnar Östberg's crematorium in Helsinborg, Erik Bryggman's famous and exquisitely simple crematorium in Abo, near Turku (1938–41), Fritz Schlegel's crematoria in Sondermark and Mariebjerg both in Copenhagen, Sigurd Lewerentz's Malmö Crematorium and the consummate simplicity of Otar Hökerberg's crematorium in Eskilstuna are buildings that do not attempt to hide their function, and they are among the relatively few buildings of this type which have gone some way to creating an architecture of death in the twentieth century.

The idea of the crematorium as a new building type was examined seriously in the years immediately before and directly after the First World War. In the work of Lewerentz and Asplund we can see the beginnings of serious investigations into the development of an architecture to accommodate and encourage the new rituals and processes necessitated by cremation as opposed to the traditional burial service. Many of the innovations they pioneered in their buildings were dropped and the services reverted to an approximation of their original forms as a result of either conservatism, lack of willingness to change, or of some mundane problem encountered with an unfamiliar new building type which led to it being used incorrectly, draining the intended drama away.

A number of outstanding crematoria were designed and built in the newly formed Czechoslovakia in the early 1920s. The abstracted folky style of Pavel Janák's design for the Pardubiče Crematorium (1921) is in total contrast to the hauntingly sparse meetings of classicism and modernism which defined Alois Mezera's crematorium in Prague, while Arnost Wiesner's crematorium in Brno and Bedřich Feuerstein's crematorium in Nymburk both attempt to create a new language of architecture which uses geometric, archetypal, symbolic and expressionistic forms.

The Russian Revolution was also followed by a wake of crematorium building in a kind of socialist efficiency drive, while the Germans and to some extent the Austrians took to cremation in great numbers in the years directly preceding and following the First World War; the product was a remarkable collection of crematoria which went a long way to formulating a new language of architecture combining monumental classical archetypes and new Expressionist-influenced forms. However, the development of this new architecture was stunted (or at least taken in another direction, maintaining the monumentalism but dropping the innovative expressionist elements) by the rise of conservatism and the subsequent coming to power of the Nazis.

Erich Mendelsohn produced a sketch as a series of studies for archetypal buildings, essentially character studies in a new *architecture parlante*, in which one of the featured buildings is a crematorium. The sketch conveys a new direction which may have arisen in giving expression to an architecture of death, a direction related closely to the visionary works of Sant'Elia and Chiattone and in many ways connected spiritually to the revolutionary architecture of Boullée and his contemporaries. But the international conservatism of the 1930s hindered most real developments in the architecture of death (with the exception of Scandinavia) and buildings of this period which contributed to a real development were the exception rather than the rule.

Crematoria became another form of municipal institution and only rarely have they shaken off this image when architects have attempted a true expression of the nature of a building type which embodies man's deepest fears and existential *angst*. The process seems too traumatic to be tackled and architects and authorities too timid to attempt this. Yet the smoke rising from the stacks of a crematorium and the smell of burning wafting through the air is one of the starkest experiences one can undergo – one which brings to the fore our deepest existential fears.

No amount of architectural sanitisation can hope to succeed in glossing over the elementality of the function of the crematorium. It is only surprising that so many try, and that the architecture of the crematorium is a theme barely talked about in a world that is quite naturally both obsessed with and terrified of the prospect of death. The architecture of crematoria has evolved largely as a language of avoiding the subject. A few exceptions can be seen in this book, and there are others, but it is largely a field of tragically wasted opportunities.

X. THE PRISM, THE PYRAMID, THE GLASS MOUNTAIN
Expressionism, Cubism and the Architecture of Death

Although I have grouped Expressionism and Cubism together and there are some stylistic similarities between these two essentially Central European artistic impulses, they are connected only vaguely. Nevertheless, both artistic strands were critical to the development of modern architecture and produced plentiful supplies of funereal architecture which is of interest to us in this context.

Cubist architecture (which is almost exclusively a Czech phenomenon) and Expressionist architecture (confined mainly to the German-speaking lands) used the form of the crystal as a primary inspiration. To the Cubists, the crystalline structure was seen as a device to imbue a facade with the extra dimension of time. The crystal, formed over millions of years, provided Cubism with the metaphor of dynamism, a seemingly eternal yet changing and responsive mass. Thus the symbol of the crystal proved ideal as a metaphor for eternity, for burial within the earth and for continual regeneration.

Albert Einstein's new ideas about time and space led to a dramatic reassessment of man's place in the universe and the stability and validity of our perception of the world. Oswald Spengler actually related the concept of space to the concept of death, stating that the two were inextricably linked in perception ('symbolism proceeds from the knowledge of death in which the secret of space reveals itself',[20] see chapter I).

The Expressionists, however, viewed the crystal as the embodiment of their dream of a new world. Leaning heavily on the poet Paul Scheerbart's visionary writings, the aim was to create a new glass architecture. The idea of the crystal mountain as the symbol of the new cosmos – clean, clear and sparkling with the divine light of revelation and spiritual enlightenment – was omnipresent in Expressionist imagery. The quick sketch, the capture of the fleeting moment of divine inspiration was the medium of these architects. Buildings were cumbersome, weighed down with details and functions and structures. The sketched images, the essence of an idea transferred to paper in the twinkling of a glass mountain, sometimes depicted buildings, sometimes merely an archetype. The one building type which gave itself perfectly to these flashes of inspiration was that which had no function other than to convey an idea: the monument.

The architects who created the language of the Expressionist monument were the same artists who would soon become the builders of the canonic structures of early modern architecture. Walter Gropius' design for a monument to the March Dead at Weimar (1921) displays many of the characteristic qualities of Expressionism: dynamism, a crystalline angularity and a vertical aspiration redolent of a soaring northern European Gothic. The drawing is rendered in heavy blackness, lit against a doom-laden black sky, probably in the hand of Farkas Molnár, a young Hungarian colleague of Gropius at the Bauhaus who later concentrated on a severe functionalism, the pure opposite of these early expressive experiments.

Bruno Taut, whose drawings represent the most complete vision of the Expressionist world-mountain as a glittering crystalline summit, designed the remarkable Wissinger family tomb near Berlin (1920), a crown of thorns in spiky metal which stands like a canopy over the grave. Taut was, like Molnár, later revered for his functionalism and mass-housing experiments. Dominikus Böhm's design for a Memorial Church in Gottingen was a realisation of the vision of the temple as the sacred mountain, the blackened pyramid of the spire still manages to exude rays of light which illuminate the darkness of the sky.

In Hendrik Petrus Berlage's design for the Lenin Mausoleum (1926), this same sacred light bursts through the roof to illuminate the body of the great revolutionary. A great central octagonal oculus above the sarcophagus affords a view from within the pyramid, while outside a series of blocky forms rises into a pair of slender towers supporting great glass prisms, the crystal held aloft as a symbol of the hope and vision that was Lenin's legacy. (The crystal in fact re-emerged in Konstantin Melnikov's initial, unexecuted design for the glass top to Lenin's sarcophagus.)

Of those mentioned above, only Taut's tomb design was realised, yet these paper buildings exerted a powerful effect on those who saw them and, in many ways their legacy remains. In the roof of the chapel of Scarpa's Brion tomb we can see echoes of Berlage's Lenin Mausoleum, and in Daniel Libeskind's fragmented, spiky monuments can be found traces of Gropius' memorial. These are images of death which returned to haunt the functionalism their creators gave birth to.

Cubism had a similarly indirect influence on modern architecture. Essentially a Czech curiosity, Cubist architecture arose through a complex confluence of circumstances. Although its name suggests a desire to emulate the innovative approach of the Cubist artists' depiction of space, this was only a part of the development of this short-lived but influential movement. Likewise, central to its growth was a dramatic juxtaposition of the spatial acrobatics of Czech Baroque

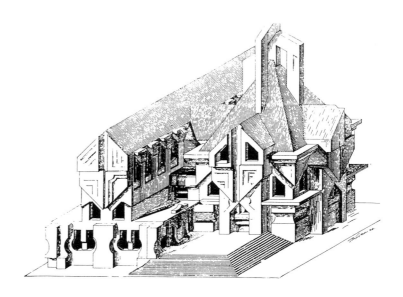

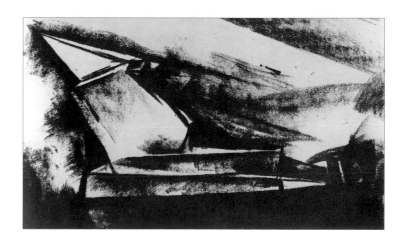

ABOVE: Design for a crematorium, 1921, J Kroha;
CENTRE: Design for Dabliče cemetery, Prague, 1912, V Hofman;
BELOW: Design for a memorial to the March Dead, 1921, W Gropius (probably drawn by F Molnár)

architecture and the spiky, ascending forms of northern European Gothic. To this was added the impulse to create a Czech national style, motifs suggested by some sketches by Jože Plečnik and the same crystalline obsessions which had occupied the Expressionists.

Curiously, the Cubists had perhaps more success in realising their architectural vision as a coherent body of work than did the Expressionists in the German lands. That vision was applied with particular vigour to funerary works, particularly designs for monuments and crematoria. The critic Karel Teige wrote of the Cubist architects' obsession with the trappings of death:

> While A Loos in the entire sphere of architecture would grant only to tombstones and monuments the character of art, since they were objects without any practical purpose, it became significant for cubist architecture that it selected these very themes and showed more interest in the homes of the dead than those of the living.[21]

Czech Cubism spanned both sides of the First World War. It emerged as part of a growing impulse to develop a national architecture, to assert independence from Vienna and the prevailing style. After the war the architects were in a position to express the ideals of the newly formed Czechoslovakia in built form. Architecture based on the expression of national ideals tend to give great prominence to the dead. National heroes are memorialised, legends are created and the cemeteries are full of martyrs to the cause of independence and war. Cubism was no exception. Indeed a plethora of buildings related to the architecture of death emerged from a fascinating chapter in Central European architecture. Perhaps the figure most associated with this period in Czech history is the novelist Franz Kafka, and it is his tombstone, designed by Leopold Ehrmann (1924), which best encapsulates the attraction of the crystal as a symbol in the architecture of the time. In this small structure, a simple stake of stone, octagonal in plan and capped by a prismatic peak, is the essence of the Cubist idea.

Pavel Janák, one of the principal figures of the Cubist movement, proposed that there were two fundamental forces in nature expressed in the horizontal plane (the horizon, the plain, and the natural level of water) and the vertical pressure of the effects of gravity on mass. The crystal displayed a third direction, the jagged angles caused by the juxtaposition of these two forces plus time. This third force is perceived as the soul of matter, an indefinable essence. But it can also

be perceived as the human element in structure, the dramatic force caused by man's intervention and the effects of time. Thus the single crystal of Kafka's tombstone becomes a mark of man, of Kafka's characters' search for humanity and reason in an unforgiving and absurd world. This little memorial comes at the end of the movement.

Not far from Kafka's tomb in Prague is the Dabliče Cemetery designed by Vlastislav Hofman. In Hofman's original drawings (from 1912) a central chapel is portrayed as a prismatic mountain, flanked by a pair of columns in a reference to both Solomon's Temple (with the columns of Jachin and Boaz) and Fischer von Erlach's Karlskirche in Vienna, a powerful symbol of the Austrian dominance which the Czechs were to shake off. In the event, a complex which was to have consisted of a crematorium, ceremonial hall, mortuary and offices only amounted to a pair of entrance pavilions and a perimeter wall, but these begin to give a good idea of the Cubist vision of an entry to a new world: a necropolis built with the intention of expressing a new perception of the forces in the cosmos; buildings which, like crystals, grew out of the earth and spoke the language of creation which had hitherto been buried deep in the mountains.

Hofman's crematorium in Ostrava dates from 1920 (destroyed in the 1970s) and displays an even more explicit homage to the Baroque. The building's squat cupola, compressed by the weight of an overbearing lantern, is a new experiment in the bizarre Baroque architectural language formulated by Giovanni Santini-Aichel in the Cemetery Chapel of St John Nepomuk, Zdár nad Sázavou, of exactly two centuries earlier.

Jiři Kroha's design for a crematorium (1921) is executed in in a spiky Cubist style which disposes of angles other than those of 45 degrees. The result is an odd axonometric building, where consecutive layers of frames develop into a complex series of planes giving depth, movement and drama to the elevations in a highly theatrical manner. In fact, the design almost resembles a stage-set: elements of anthropomorphy entering the great face of the facade with its droopy, mourning eyes. Its plinth begins to introduce elements from the Rondo-Cubist style which succeeded the angular Cubism of the immediate pre- and post-war period.

One of the finest buildings of this last manifestation of Cubism was Pavel Janák's weird Pardubiče Crematorium of 1923. Another stage-set building, this

ABOVE: Nymburk Crematorium, Czechoslovakia, 1923, B Feuerstein and B Slama; BELOW: Vienna Crematorium, 1922, C Holzmeister

remarkable structure incorporates elements of national romanticism and folk architecture into the avant-garde language of Rondo-Cubism. The effect is of a gingerbread house, the forester's-hut as the final resting place. A long ascent up a broad flight of steps leads into the dark shadows of the verandah above, with the banded gable representing both the form of the pyramid and an infinite ladder into the sky. The pediment is broken by a rose window, like a clock at the heart of the facade.

At exactly the same time as Janák was working in this curious manner, Bedřich Feuerstein and Bohumil Slama were building the Nymburk Crematorium, a small but nevertheless monumental construction which bridges and links elements of late Rondo-Cubism, monumental classicism and the emergent functionalism of which Czechoslovakia was at the forefront. The bulky, oppressive columns of the portico are a gross caricature of the elegance of Greek columns, and the squat rotunda which emerges above is compressed from the sides into an oval and from the top by a heavy square roof acting as cornice and entablature terminating the structure. The plan is asymmetrical and formed from a series of apsidal spaces. The focus of the central hall is a semicircular apse containing the bier on axis with the entrance. To one side the columns continue around the wall to create an arcaded columbarium.

The Nymburk Crematorium is one of the most haunting buildings to emerge from the twentieth century architecture of death. It is both oppressive and expressive, and speaks eloquently in a way that few modern buildings do of the burden of grief and the weight which descends upon the mourners at this moment. Yet the building remains pure and abstract, a cathartic monument along the path of grief. It was also one of the buildings which would link Expressionist and Cubist ideas in architecture into the mainstream of modernism, and it foreshadowed the remarkable series of monumental crematoria which were to emerge from this small country in the ensuing decade.

XI. WAR MEMORIALS
The Expression of Wasted Life

The twentieth century will be remembered for one thing at least: the century of war and holocaust. The inconceivable carnage of the First World War was followed shortly by another war which brought civilians even closer into its cold embrace and during which the Nazis began executing a plan to destroy whole peoples. In a recent survey to find the single word that would best encapsulate the century, it was found overwhelmingly to be 'holocaust'.

The American Civil War (1861–65) had demonstrated to the world the horror of an all-encompassing modern war. It was introduced to Europe via the Franco–Prussian War (1870–71) but it was not until the First World War that the full carnage of modern warfare was revealed. It was no longer the sole domain of small armies of professional soldiers, and virtually all European families suffered losses among the more than eight million dead of 1914–18. The casualties who had been dispensable in life became important in death.

All sides saw the necessity of making permanent gestures towards the dead for the sake of their families and the survivors. Permanent cemeteries for the war-dead were a relatively new invention. Gettysburg was the site of one of the first such cemeteries, where a chaotic landscape of monuments lies scattered around the battlefield, eloquently expressing the randomness of war.

The scale of the First World War and the pointlessness of the endeavour induced feelings of guilt in the governments of the respective participants. The least a government could do after the senseless waste of so many of its citizens' lives was to erect memorials and to build dignified monuments to the dead. Apart from the myriad memorials which would be erected in town and village squares, municipal and public buildings throughout Europe, the battlefields would inevitably become places of quasi-pilgrimage; there had to be something for the pilgrims to see when they arrived.

The approach of each country towards these memorials varied. The Germans created a plethora of fine, stiff sculptures and a large collection of enigmatic buildings, many deliberately evoking the primitive – dolmens and sarsens – as if there seemed no other way to address the catastrophe than this massive archetypal forms. Other architects employed a brutal, vast classicism which had originated before the war and spawned Bruno Schmitz's gargantuan Leipzig Memorial, while strands of Expressionism could be detected in some interesting monuments.

The Italian response was remarkable and perhaps the most truly monumental of all the participating countries. Harsh memorials were carved into hillsides, part of the hilly scenery which Robert Musil had described as *Totenlandschaft* (landscape of the dead), unromantic but striking. Only the Italians began to address memorial architecture with anything other than classicism; the work of Giovanni Greppi created a new architectural language of forms which reeked of ruins, of a lost age, and which cast great shadows like the haunting buildings in De Chirico's paintings (see chapter XIII for a more detailed look at these memorials).

The French response was perhaps more sentimental, peopled by grand sculptures and reliefs often characterised by monumental figures metamorphosing into rock, in a manner the diametric opposite of Michelangelo's Neo-Platonic idea of freeing a figure, the essence of which was contained within the stone. These were ossified human figures, soldiers portrayed as impregnable barriers of stone, the inscription on the walls of Verdun reading *Ils ne passeront pas* ('they shall not pass').

However, the ossuary in Douaumont was one of the finest of all architectural memorials. It contains the bones of hundreds of thousands of French soldiers who perished during the senseless waste of the defence of Verdun. The building was designed in 1923 and completed in 1932 by architects Azéma, Hardy and Edrei in the form of a single monumental barrel vault. From its centre an expressionistic tower tapers towards the top displaying an attenuated cross on each face. The simplicity and plainness of the vaulted interior is relieved only by the inscribed names of the dead along the stone surfaces. The barrel vault gives the effect of a subterranean crypt even though the structure is lit brightly and wholly above ground.

There is a special connection between the soldiers of the First World War and the earth which goes deeper than the condition of the dead now lying within it. The war on the Western Front was fought almost solely in the mud, in trenches dug into the soil, and the dead lay in huge craters formed by heavy artillery shells. The wounded drowned in mud, the dead were consumed by it, the battles themselves were over a few feet of the barren earth which had been turned into a nightmare landscape of sludge and human remains. Before the great offensives, soldiers marched past huge mass burial pits that had been dug in expectancy of the great casualties to follow; they would look down into the earth and see their own graves. In the German war novel *All Quiet on the Western Front* (1929), one of Erich Remarque's most powerful passages dwells on this special relationship:

ABOVE: Blighty Valley Cemetery, Aveluy, France, 1918; CENTRE: Jerusalem War Cemetery, inaugurated 1927, J Burnet; BELOW: Douaumont Memorial, 1932, Azéma, Hardy and Edrei

Menin Gate, Ypres, 1927, R Blomfield

Corbie cemetery, France, 1920s, C Holden

To no man does the earth mean as much as to the soldier. When he presses himself down upon her long and powerfully, when he buries his face and his limbs deep in her from the fear of death by shell-fire, then she is his only friend, his brother, his mother; he stifles his terror and his cries in her silence and her security; she shelters him and releases him for ten seconds to live, to run, ten seconds of life; receives him again and often for ever.

Earth! – Earth! – Earth!

Earth with thy folds, and hollows, and holes, into which a man may fling himself and crouch down. In the spasm of terror, under the hailing of annihilation, in the bellowing death of explosions, O earth, thou grantest us the great resisting surge of new-won life. Our being, almost utterly carried away by the fury of the storm, streams back through our hands from thee, and we, thy redeemed ones, bury ourselves in thee, and through the long minutes in a mute agony of hope bite into thee with our lips.[22]

The most evocative memorial to the all-consuming earth is at the Trench of Bayonets, Verdun. The memorial commemorates an apocryphal event, a myth which purports that in 1916 a French regiment stood its ground and refused to vacate its trench: the bombardments and explosions led to a collapse of the walls of the trench and all were buried alive. All that remained of the soldiers were their bayonets which protruded from the earth as they stood to attention, dead, below. Although it seems more likely that the bayonets were inserted into the ground to mark the burial place of the dead, the myth was so powerful and occupied such a place in the national consciousness that a memorial was built around the protruding bayonets.

The memorial was funded by an American, George F Rand. He had been moved by the story but died soon after and thus it became partly a memorial to its benefactor. Its architect, André Ventre, promised a design that would survive for five hundred years and indeed the building has an eternal, brutal solidity. A massive expressionist bunker of reinforced concrete, the memorial powerfully evokes the weight of the earth which consumed the soldiers, its stocky language speaks eloquently of the burden of grief.

Unlike most other war memorials, the Trench of the Bayonets commemorates the place of burial rather than simply functioning as a cenotaph. The power of the myth is that the unfortunate soldiers are buried beneath the land they stood to defend, and the protruding bayonets became a target for souvenir hunters. This was a mausoleum to protect the remains that substantiated a myth, and it was necessary to validate that myth for the purposes of morale in the darkness of the immediate post-war years, in a nation which had lost over 1.3 million men.

The architecture of Douaumont, the Trench of the Bayonets and the war cemeteries which dominate the Western Front is an architecture of the earth, the same earth which sheltered Remarque's soldiers, consumed their bodies and is now covered in a landscape of individual concrete crosses for the French and white stone slabs for the British dead. The soldiers were dispensable when alive but when dead were deemed to each deserve a stone rather than a single collective memorial. The British war cemeteries with their vast expanses of hauntingly white headstones present almost absurd landscapes, the form of the grave-marker, like some Duchamp 'ready-made', becoming art by the simple act of endless repetition. Among the

The Cenotaph, London, 1919–20   Memorial to the Missing of the Somme, Thiepval, 1932, E Lutyens

memorials it is the simplicity and eloquence of endless fields of white stones, slabs rather than crosses for cheapness of production, each the same in complete democracy for officers and Other Ranks, which constitute the most moving memorials. However, British architects also made a great impact at the time with their sombre classical designs. Reginald Blomfield's Menin Gate, Ypres, is a triumphal arch with the triumphalism removed; rather than the fleeting spatial impression of a gate, Blomfield's structure becomes a terrible tunnel, from which one re-emerges in a town which was comprehensively levelled. More moving than the architecture are the tens of thousands of inscribed names which overwhelm the interior and which poignantly underline the scale of the losses.

Charles Holden's Communal Cemetery in Corbie is built in a blocky, stripped classical style; unsentimental and unforgiving it remains one of the starkest yet most dignified of memorials. And Sir John Burnet's Chapel in Jerusalem Military Cemetery is in an almost Expressionist idiom more reminiscent of some of the German memorials, yet is also a fine and hauntingly bare building. However, without doubt the most influential and profound of all the British war memorials were built by Edwin Lutyens.

Lutyens' masterpiece is an understated stone pylon in London's Whitehall, home of the British government. The Cenotaph (1919–20) – literally 'empty tomb' – is a monument to all the soldiers of the British Empire who died in the war. Its finesse and utter lack of triumphalism or self-importance made it the most fitting and sympathetic of war memorials, but its simplicity is deceptive. Initially constructed of timber, the design was so popular that a replacement was commissioned in stone. It later also came to serve as the memorial for

the dead of the Second World War since another memorial would have seemed superfluous next to the poetry of Lutyens' eloquently simple monument.

Although his memorial has become the definitive British symbol of remembrance, Lutyens' first reaction when he visited the cemeteries on the Western Front before the end of the war was that no memorial was needed other than the 'ribbons of little crosses' which lay scattered across the land. His cenotaph is one of the few memorials to truly achieve simplicity and, to a degree, timelessness.

Essentially, the work is in the form of a coffin extruded into the air to form an attenuated catafalque beneath it, and it was designed in a such a way that not a straight line can be found within it. A subtle entasis (based on the proportions of the one in the Parthenon) ensures that the monument's vertical lines meet at a point 1,000 feet (about 300 metres) above the ground and again 900 feet (270 metres) below it. The implication of an ethereal point in the sky and a position deep in the heart of the earth presents a poignant symbol of the heavens above and the hell of a war fought in the mud and from trenches within the earth.

Lutyens wanted the flags on the memorial also to be of stone – somehow petrified like the trees in the no-man's land between the trenches – but he realised this ambition only later with the haunting design for the cemetery at Étaples.

His other great achievement in the field came with the Memorial to the Missing of the Somme at Thiepval. This is a sombre and tragic monument as it commemorates a prolonged, bloody and futile campaign (20,000 British soldiers were killed on the first day of fighting, with allied forces eventually losing 600,000, two-thirds of which were British) culminating in an allied advance

Canadian Memorial, Vimy Ridge, 1936, W Allward

Leipzig War Memorial, 1913, B Schmitz

of only ten miles. Essentially a triumphal arch, the classicism and the glory have been stripped away to reveal an altogether hollow structure which merely appears massive. The building is composed of openings piled one on top of the other; the structure exists for the holes. The absurdity of this can be seen best from the memorial's weird plan: a tartan grid vaguely displaying a cross at its centre.

This subtle symbolism is the only gesture Lutyens made towards Christian iconography here and in the Cenotaph. He was otherwise scrupulously thorough in avoiding clichéd, mawkish motifs and the plan is largely determined by the need for as much vaulting as possible upon which to inscribe the names of the dead. Seen in elevation, the memorial appears to be a slender brick arch with a pair of smaller openings at its sides. Yet from an angle its bulk becomes apparent (this view is best represented by Lutyens' original sketch). Arch upon arch stacked up in a mountain of brickwork, its stark massiveness is reminiscent of the hulks of the ancient mausolea and monuments where only the structure remains, the ornament having been stripped away by thieves and the elements over the centuries. Only the bones are left. The monument is exemplified by the gaping hole, which Vincent Scully has described as a screaming 'open mouth of death'.[23]

The last of the Commonwealth monuments to be completed, the Canadian Memorial by sculptor Walter Allward, unveiled in 1936 in nearby Vimy Ridge, is another powerful work. A great stone pylon seems to have been cleaved down the middle, sculpted figures populate levels of a kind of Dantesque world, mourning angels and triumphant glory figures, while powerful, heroic figures populate the massive plinth from which it rises. The memorial exerts its mighty presence on the flat landscape, its verticality a stark reminder of the complete levelling of the area during the war.

Although largely popular, these memorials were by no means universally acclaimed. There was a significant socialist strain whose motifs were somewhat puritanical and which saw the erection of such memorials as a waste. William Lethaby articulated this view in his essay 'Service or Sacrifice?':

> Is it necessary, is it what the fallen themselves would have wished, that four and a half years of war and destruction shall be followed by a great outpouring of unproductive, and indeed futile, labour? Must a sort of murder be followed by a sort of suicide?[24]

The suggestion was that the money should be spent on housing, schools and towns, not on 'useless' memorials. Lethaby and his colleagues were also dismayed by the standard of memorial building, which was often mawkish and dull. Despite Lethaby's own preoccupation with the symbolism of ancient architectures, he believed that these 'mere memory memorials' could not hope to become imbued with the symbolism which grew out of an architecture springing from a Jungian collective unconscious. With new, forward-looking regimes of both left and right, this view gradually began to take hold in the years between the wars throughout Europe. Thus it was that the outpouring of monumental architecture which followed in the wake of the Great War was essentially the last wave of specifically memorial architecture of this scale in the Western world.

Although the totalitarian regimes which came to prominence across Europe during these years produced much monumental architecture, the obsession was with monumentalising the nation, embodying a new vision, not of memorialising the dead, and consequently few buildings of interest to this book were built.

Liebknecht and Luxemburg Memorial, Berlin, 1926, M van der Rohe

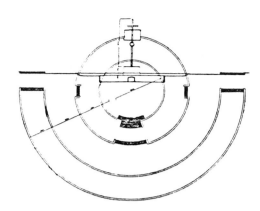

Schlageter Monument, Düsseldorf, 1931, C Holzmeister

(There are a few exceptions to this which we will take a brief look at in the next chapter.) However, a curious paradox emerges in the memorial expressions which followed the First and Second World Wars.

The First World War was a pointless slaughter on an inconceivable scale, but it was a war of soldiers and its memorialisation was a clear-cut affair; the 'glorious dead' were remembered in stone despite the protests of many left-wingers. The Second World War carried within it the spectre of the Holocaust. The war was memorialised most vigorously in the Communist countries where it was perceived as a victory for Socialism over Fascism. In the Capitalist West, Lethaby's ideas had come closer to fruition over the war dead, but it was the Holocaust which was to provide the source for the memorial builders.

XII. BETWEEN THE WARS: THE MONUMENTAL ERA

There would seem to be a convincing argument that a monumental neo-classicism was the architecture of the twentieth-century dictatorships. The era between the wars saw the rise of Hitler, Mussolini and Stalin, and in the wake of each arrived a vogue for a colossal, self-aggrandising monumentalism like that beloved of their illustrious and admired forebear, Napoleon, who had celebrated his victories with monuments the like of which had not been seen since Imperial Rome (on which he had modelled his empire).

But the argument is not watertight or consistent; in fact, a grand neo-classicism was almost universal during this period and its ultimate achievement was not to be seen in Berlin, Rome or Moscow but in Washington DC, the only major capital city which is conceived as a huge monument to a man and an ideal.

Neo-classicism and monumentalism have simply become more associated with the inter-war dictatorships and that association persists today. In fact, the grander of the memorials erected after the First World War were executed almost exclusively in a sombre and often expressionistically stylised classicism. This style did not spring from nowhere: it was merely a logical continuation of an architecture which had been developing steadily in the years before the war throughout Europe and North America.

There had been a considerable reaction to the decadent decorative excesses of the Secession and Art Nouveau and this generally took the form of a sombre, bulky classicism, the genesis of which can be seen in the pre-war works of the Viennese avant-garde and their German counterparts, and which later divided into a number of strains, one of which (personified by Adolf Loos' later work and by Peter Behrens and his followers, including Walter Gropius) can be said to have been the beginnings of modernism in architecture. The curious interconnections binding the classical and the modern inextricably together can be fruitfully explored through the architecture of death in this turbulent period.

The Weimar Republic which followed the First World War in Germany saw a remarkable flourishing of early modernism in all the arts, and the various architectural strands co-existed for a brief moment, embracing Expressionism, proto-functionalism and an austere stripped but monumental classicism. The staggering breadth of innovative architectural expression is evident in a handful of memorials from these years.

Clemens Holzmeister's exquisite Schlageter Monument in Düsseldorf is a masterpiece of understated minimalism, one of the finest of modernist memorials and a remarkable contrast to his brooding, expressionistic

*ABOVE: Temple of Honour, Munich, 1934, P Troost;
CENTRE: Design for the Lenin Mausoleum, 1924, I Fomin;
'Red Wedge' Monument, N Kolli; BELOW: Design for a
crematorium, Petrograd, 1919, I Fomin; Piranesian design for a
columbarium, Moscow, 1919, I Golosov; BOTTOM: Sketch
for a crematorium, 1914, E Mendelsohn*

Vienna Crematorium (1922–23). The simplicity of the round hole cut into the earth and the spectral, spindly cross which rises above it distils an archetypal language of the simple cross grave-marker and the pit that gives physical and symbolic access to the underground realm of the crypt.

However, perhaps the best known of the memorials of this period is Mies van der Rohe's monument to Karl Liebknecht and Rosa Luxemburg in Berlin, of 1926. This blocky composition of recessed and protruding brick panels blends Mies' minimal house plans with an aesthetic reminiscent of the De Stijl play of planes to create a brutally severe monument appropriate to two heroes of the proletariat. Its genesis was soaked in controversy; Krupps, for instance, the firm which was to supply the hammer and sickle insignia, agreed only to deliver them separately as two individual elements, such was the animosity to the Left. Its power as a monument and effectiveness as a symbol was attested to by the Nazis who wasted no time in destroying it.

The potential sculptural power of sheer cliff-faces of brick was realised early by the Expressionist architects, as well as by the classical modernists (who sprang from the tradition of Karl Friedrich Schinkel and Friedrich Gilly) like Mies himself. Walter Johannes Kruger's Tannenburg Memorial containing Hindenburg's sarcophagus is a powerful blend of images which encompasses the great megalithic stone circles, the classical auditorium (which was to influence Speer and Hitler so profoundly) and a great medieval castle. Munzer's monument to the German sailors at Kiel (1929–36) is a dynamic tower, a leftover from Expressionism very much in the same vein as Luigi Brunatti's memorial in Brindisi to the Italian seamen.

Ideally suited to the symbolism and emotion of an architecture of death, the Expressionism which flourished briefly in Germany and the German-speaking countries did not survive long enough to take a real hold. In Erich Mendelsohn's sketch for a crematorium a powerful Expressionist Constructivism emerges, but these fascinating experiments were cut short by the new conservatism. The grand classicism which had emerged as the almost universal language of commemoration after the First World War was to become the language of memory between the wars.

Franco Borsi has defined the kind of monumental classicism which triumphed in European architecture between the wars as the embodiment of a desire to challenge both space and time through grandeur and durability respectively.[25] The enemy was seen as the chaos, political and economic, which ensued after the war. Architecture was seen as the tool to impose a new order, and for inspiration the regimes looked to the ancient empires which still defined contemporary ideas of the successful state.

The ideas and plans of the French Revolutionary architects and their reinterpretation of classical and Platonic forms as an *architecture parlante* became a prime source of inspiration, and when the new architecture talked, it would talk of power. The Germans looked back to a golden period of Goethe and Schinkel, when Prussia was a nation in the forefront of European art, and this was the period of neo-classicism. The British looked back to an era of colonial and cultural supremacy, to their most powerful era as the victors over Napoleon and the age of the British museum. The Italians looked back to Imperial Rome, the French to Napoleon and the neo-classical and Revolutionary masters. The Scandinavians, too, reflected upon their northern rational roots. In the USA, neo-classicism was seen as the architectural embodiment of democracy and the republic, in the wake of Jefferson. The results were often remarkably similar.

Around 1799, Prussian architect Friedrich Gilly produced a design for a mausoleum. The theme of death has often prompted an architectural return to the elemental, to the archetypal forms, stripped bare of ornament; Gilly's design is the exemplary paradigm. The construction is absolutely elemental, only that which is necessary remains – post, lintel, and roof. The design is both strikingly modern yet redolent of the antique. In the Woodland Crematorium near Stockholm (1935–40), by Gunnar Asplund and Sigurd Lewerentz, the same themes are explored with virtually the same architectural language. Richard Etlin has pointed out that Paul Philippe Cret's Pennsylvania War Memorial in Varennes, France (1924) shares its roots with Gilly's design.[26]

In Paul Troost's Ehrentempel (Temple of Honour) in Munich (1933-34), the archetype of the Greek temple is explored again, and the results are strikingly similar to Cret's designs. The temple, in fact, consists of a pair of identical buildings positioned opposite the Propylaean gate in Munich's Königsplatz, each housing eight sarcophagi of the sixteen Nazis who died in the unsuccessful 'Beer Hall' *putsch* of 1923. Each building is defined by twenty squared, fluted columns at the edges of a perfectly square plan. The Nazi sentries who stood at the entrances lent scale to the buildings and were as much a part of the threatening, militaristic appearance of the memorial as the buildings and the sarcophagi themselves. Bronze torches inside were lit with an eternal flame of remembrance. The centres of the roofs were left open to the sky. Troost's widow, Gerdy, explained: 'No damp vault encloses the coffins of the fallen. Surrounded by pillars they rest under the open sky of their homeland, flooded with sunlight (or) covered with snow.'[27]

Among the most sinister of monuments to the dead, this pair of buildings displayed a politicised, militarised classicism which had been robbed of its soul. In his will of 1938, Hitler provided the ultimate testimony to the status of the Ehrentempel when he specified it as his preferred burial place. The chilling significance of the structures was confirmed when they were destroyed by the Americans in 1947; they were too powerful as symbols and, potentially, as rallying points, to be left to stand.

Yet despite the Americans' role as victors, liberators of Europe and destroyers of such potent architectural symbols of Nazi power, there are undeniable parallels between the formal neo-classicism of the European Fascists and the more or less contemporary monumental constructions of Washington DC. The USA's capital is in the curious position of itself being a memorial, from its name to its key monuments. The dazzling white stone monuments that punctuate its skyline are seen as the embodiment of the republican ideals of democracy – shining beacons of hope. The Lincoln Memorial, designed by Henry Bacon in 1911 and completed in 1922, was based on the Parthenon. Its thirty-six columns represented the number of states in the Union which Lincoln had defended so vehemently; thus it revives to some extent the idea of an *architecture parlante*, embodying the noble ideals of ancient Greek democracy and thought, as well as being a physical manifestation of the union it seeks to represent in monumentalised form.

Across the reflecting pool is Robert Mills' Washington Monument. Its eloquent subtlety is the result of the misguided temple at its base being omitted from the final design, leaving only the elegance of the slender obelisk. Jefferson's Memorial was designed by John Russell Pope (who had narrowly missed out on the design of the Lincoln Memorial) and completed in

1943. Its smooth, blank surfaces are reminiscent of Boullée's 'Architecture of Shadows' but its gleaming whiteness in its artificially pastoral setting is perhaps more likely to evoke the follies of an English picturesque garden. The city is a wonderful monument, a true necropolis, but its monuments are dead architecture as well as being an architecture of the dead.

The colossal designs which characterised Soviet architecture under Stalin were derived from the same neo-classical sources as the architecture of Washington DC, but to this was added a hint of the more dynamic architecture and the vertical aspiration of the New York skyscraper. To some extent, all major Soviet architecture was monumental, in that it was a conscious attempt to memorialise the regime which built it, to assert the parity of the Communist regime with the great civilisations of the past. But the memorials themselves tended towards sculpture and landscape rather than architecture. In the true tradition of Socialist Realism these were literal, not necessarily allegorical monuments which were to be easily read and interpreted by the masses.

Thus the earth itself was memorialised in many schemes, a direct tribute to the land which was fought over, to Mother Russia (Lev Illin's Fields of Mars in Leningrad is the finest example of landscape as memorial to emerge from Communism). This tradition continued and gathered real pace after the Second World War, while huge sculptures of Mother Russia, or of soldiers and leaders, were self-explanatory, stemming from the tradition of the colossus rather than from received notions of funerary design.

The huge figures of Stalin and Lenin which dominated towns throughout the Soviet Union and the Eastern Bloc were made focal points for ceremony and subsequently for dissent. These symbols of oppression were inevitably destroyed at the first opportunity. If anything, the architecture was confined to the (admittedly often spectacular) bases of these new colossi and to bunkers, pyramids and domes which formed part of these memorial landscapes, referring to Russia's great neo-classical past, their inspiration drawn straight from Revolutionary rationalism.

A true modern architecture of death was never allowed to develop in the Soviet Union. Yet this was despite relatively auspicious beginnings. For the Bolshevik revolutionaries, the iconoclastic value of cremation, the deliberate offence given to the Russian Orthodox, Jewish and Muslim communities, held the same attraction as it had to the architects of Revolutionary France.

Cremation was seen as the urban solution to the disposal of bodies, and as the Revolution was based largely around the urban proletariat, the introduction of cremation with its egalitarian overtones, functional and hygienic processes became a key aim early on in the new Russia. Indeed, one of the first major architectural competitions of the Communist era was held in 1919 to design a new crematorium and columbarium for Moscow. A prerequisite for the building was that it should, categorically, not resemble a religious building (it was to be sited in the midst of a monastery) although it was to use the existing foundations of a chapel on the site. Submissions were fantastic and many were truly revolutionary but of all the competition entries perhaps Konstantin Melnikov's was the most exciting. His proposal combined an industrial aesthetic with elements of Expressionism and Constructivism. A glass frontage (its transparency was an important feature as this was not to be a place of hidden ritual) opened on to a blocky, factory-like structure, the centre of which was dominated by an open-work tower resembling the lift tower of a mine, which was connected back down to earth by a series of powerful, stepped flying buttresses. Although theatrical and in many ways confusing, the ideals of the Revolution were embodied in this design, yet it did not receive the winning vote and the successful entry proved to be a disappointingly bland building.

The exploration of ideas of death, or more precisely, immortality, proved to be a fundamental cornerstone of Revolutionary art and literature; the Revolution and its leaders had to be seen to be immortal and cults were built up around them. Of no one was this more true than of Lenin, whose figure dominated the public squares of every Russian city, yet who is now strangely absent from their townscapes. His mausoleum, however, remains firmly at the centre of a city which has otherwise fervently attempted to destroy all traces of its Communist past. It contains the embalmed body of Russia's greatest revolutionary leader, and remains too potent and powerful an icon to be tampered with. For generations, Russia's leaders have stood on the mausoleum's podium and watched tanks and parades rolling by. Millions of Russians have queued to pay their respects to its contents. The mausoleum is curiously absent from the many histories of modern architecture though it is one of the most powerful buildings of the century and one of the most important works in defining a modern architecture of death.

The death of Lenin at the beginning of 1924 proved to be the end of the dynamic phase of the Russian Revolution. Soviet art and architecture was already shying away from its boldest achievements and state patronage was becoming increasingly suspicious of the avant-garde. However, this was merely a strengthening of existing suspicions; the tension between the state and the radical arms of Soviet art and architecture had always been pronounced. Lenin himself, who had lived in exile next to the Dadaist Cabaret Voltaire in Zurich, developed a profound distrust of modern art, and it was therefore appropriate that his final resting place in Red Square should be less a piece of agitprop and more a work of seemingly archetypal simplicity and power.

The Soviet regime was constantly attempting to set itself up as the new natural order, through a process of Darwinian evolution. The Communist state had become an inevitability – it was here to stay. The flux and impermanence of agitprop had served well in the early years of motion, revolution and civil war but the priority had become the portrayal of a new permanence. Lenin's tomb had to demonstrate the stability of the new state and the monumental importance to the world of its founder. What then could be more appropriate than a pyramid? The form denoted power, glory and the permanence and durability of a civilisation, and it was also the most fundamental expression of the death of a great leader. The symbolism and meaning were already in place.

Alexei Schusev, the architect of Lenin's mausoleum, had spent a number of years on archaeological sites in central Asia. S Frederick Starr (Melnikov's biographer) has suggested that the form of the Persian pyramid may have been the genesis of the mausoleum design. He also asserts that the pyramid and the triangle carried with them the Revolutionary associations of Suprematism, Constructivism and the idea of the 'Red Wedge' (particularly as adopted by El Lissitzky).[28] In this way, the monument hints subtly at both the avant-garde and the traditional iconography of death in Russian architecture which saw the pyramid being used as a memorial to great battles and figures in a manner much influenced by Boullée and the French Revolutionary architects in Russia's earlier Francophile historical incarnation, another fitting precedent for the new order.

ABOVE: Stages in design for the Lenin Mausoleum, 1926–30), A Schusev; BELOW: Design for the Lenin Mausoleum, Moscow, 1926, H P Berlage

Schusev had been one of Russia's most successful church architects before the Revolution but he managed to convert his workload to the secular, proletarian buildings called for by the new regime. However, in the Lenin mausoleum he was called upon to design a new place of pilgrimage. Lenin's body, like those of the saints, was to be preserved in what was, to all intents and purposes, a reliquary. It was initially built of timber and finally of red granite to match the Kremlin Wall which was to form its backdrop, so that the whole would be seen as an ensemble, one inseparable from the other, the iconography of power, state and revolution reinforcing each other.

The commission for the reliquary itself, a glass sarcophagus, was given to Konstantin Melnikov after a competition and he submitted his designs under intense pressure, armed guards at his side urging him on, apparently on pain of death, to complete the designs in time. He worked on a series of designs for the sarcophagus, each a variant on a crystalline theme which had much in common with the contemporary experiments of the Czech Cubists and the German Expressionists, in particular the visionary work of Scheerbart and Taut in which the crystal is seen as a semi-mystical source of enlightenment and knowledge. The most dramatic of the variants would have consisted of a complex system of glass planes with peaks over Lenin's head and feet, while the final, simplest version was a prism extruded above the body like a laterally stretched glass pyramid.

As well as the image of the reliquary, the designs conjured up curious visions from mythology and folklore, including the notion of the sleeping beauty or of a body preserved in ice, ready to be thawed out and resurrected. All these designs would have been awkward and expensive to build, but the sarcophagus that was ultimately fabricated was a simpler affair, easy to construct and nominally more in keeping with the new austerity of the New Economic Policy. The final version of the mausoleum was realised as a series of powerful layers diminishing the original notion of the pyramid but the building's position at the centre of Communist iconography and the enforced pilgrimages to its precious contents (for a while Stalin lay here too until his fall from grace in the wake of Kruschev's condemnation) ensured that of all the buildings in the twentieth-century architecture of death, this was perhaps the most potent.

Although none matched the impact of Schusev's Lenin mausoleum, the Soviet period saw a number of other highly influential memorial designs. Vladimir Tatlin's design for a Monument to the Third International of 1920, although not within the scope of an architecture of death, constituted a memorial to an idea which was to prove at least as influential and revolutionary as Boullée's cenotaph to Newton; while Yakoulov's similarly unexecuted Monument to the six commissars killed in Baku also employed an Expressionist/Constructivist approach to the construction of a new Tower of Babel.

The Revolutionary architects quickly fell out of favour under the Stalinist regime and only those capable of quickly converting to Socialist Realism were given commissions. Melnikov, long out of favour, slightly resurrected his career with a project for a Lenin–Stalin Mausoleum on an artificial island in the Moscow River, designed on Stalin's death in 1953. A jagged piece of sculptural monumentalism based on a star-shaped plan, this unexecuted scheme proved one of the last major events in a Soviet architecture of death.

XIII. ITALY
Modernism, Classicism, Monumentalism, Rationalism

No other Western country has developed such a variety and depth of modern architecture devoted to death as Italy, and it is because of this special position that I have decided to treat this brief introduction to Italian funerary architecture in a separate chapter.

Italy entered the twentieth century in a curious position; in many ways lagging behind the artistic turmoil affecting much of western and northern Europe, there had been no artistic or architectural movement which corresponded to the Arts and Crafts, the Secession or the other impulses towards radical simplification and rethinking of architectural principles, yet the ideas generated by these developing artistic trends would have deep and profound repercussions on Italian architects.

When a radical new impulse did emerge it proved to be the most iconoclastic and brutally radical of all European artistic movements – Futurism. Partly a reaction to the perceived laziness of Italian artists relying on the classical, Renaissance and Baroque glories in which the country still revelled, Futurism was anti-museum and anti-preservation, it was a fresh start attempting to drag Italy into the industrial revolution a century after it had taken hold elsewhere. Vittorio

Gregotti has written: 'Nearly the whole history of the relationship between modern Italian architecture and Italian culture is linked to the Futurist movement.'[29] It is a curious paradox then that, having its roots in iconòclasm and the glorification of a new machine age, Italian architects should also be the first to recognise the importance of classicism, the use of architectural archetypes and the idea that architecture is dependent on its meaning and symbolism on the area in which it stands, the roots of critical regionalism, the antithesis in many ways of an international style.

Twentieth-century Italian architects have been more able to acknowledge a continuum of history, to allow what has gone before to influence the new. It could be said that post-modernism dates not from the work of Robert Venturi but from Gio Ponti, acknowledging Italian precedents half a century earlier; post-modernism merely added the literary conceit, a hint of irony and self-consciousness. In all Western countries the tomb tends to be designed in a manner which embodies tradition: radical modernism is fine in the architecture of the living but in death the outlook seems to universally revert to the conservative. A stroll through Père-Lachaise, Highgate, or any newer cemeteries will seem to confirm this thesis; there are very few avant-garde tombs. However, in Italy a series of circumstances in the early twentieth century contributed to the development of funerary architecture as a laboratory of radical design ideas which both pushed modernism forward while asking serious questions of its most basic precepts.

From the visionary sketches of the Futurists through to Rationalism and beyond, it became apparent to Italian architects (as it did to the Expressionists in Germany) that the monument was an ideal vehicle for experimenting with form and narrative in a way which was not always possible in buildings that had to serve a function and were therefore limited. If we accept Gregotti's assertion about the far-reaching effects of Futurism on Italian architecture then we can perhaps trace the genesis of this phenomenon of the monument as avant-garde building type extraordinaire to the powerful designs of Antonio Sant'Elia.

Sant'Elia's dramatic visions were images rather than buildings; they were a development of the *architecture parlante* of the French Revolutionary architects in that they tended to be of types of buildings, structures which expressed the activity housed within. Naturally these were usually dynamic activities; it was a world inhabited by stations, power-plants, bridges or unnamed thrusting banks of terraced structures which would only come close to being realised in science fiction, notably in Fritz Lang's film *Metropolis*. Undoubtedly these images had been influenced by photographs of New York, a wholly man-made landscape of steel, concrete, and glass, but there was another consistent feature of the sketches of Sant'Elia and his contemporary Mario Chiattone: huge towers, the function of which was sometimes unspecified, sometimes labelled 'monument'.

These were fantasies of form, aesthetic scribblings of shapes which were dynamic and powerful, often heavily (and traditionally) buttressed. The form of these buildings was usually reliant on the fanciful designs which emerged from the Vienna Secession and in particular from the drawing boards of the younger members of the Wagnerschule, and these influences are particularly clear in sketches for tomb and gravestone designs.

The German Expressionists also found the arbitrary title 'monument' or 'monumental edifice' an attractive one where no other reasonable function could be housed in a fantastic construction. Thus, the monument as a building type became a powerful image in the hands of avant-garde architects who used it as a vehicle to express their most deep-seated visions of a new architecture. When the devastation of the First World War swept Europe it obliterated many of the architects who had created the avant-garde and ensured that their vision of a new monumental architecture embodying the new aesthetic could be realised in the form of memorials to those who had perished.

The 1920s and 1930s began to see a crystallisation of the new modernism in Italian architecture as young architects built on the legacy of Futurism while learning the lessons of surrounding architecture. That Fascism arose in Italy in the years following the war was also critical to the emergence of the new style, both in fostering it and later, to some extent denying it. Mussolini's self-aggrandisement and his desire to create an empire to match that of the Romans proved a fantastic boon to both monument building and monumental building. The willingness of the Fascist government to embark on colossal public works schemes (partly to provide employment for the hundreds of thousands of returning soldiers) provided further impetus for the monument building programme. Thus

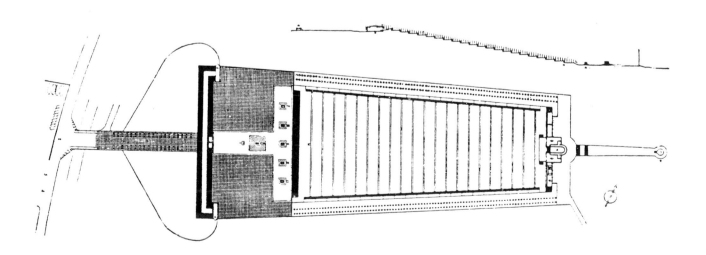

Sacrarium, Redipuglia, Italy, 1938, views and plan, G Greppi and G Castiglioni

was set in motion a series of building projects to commemorate the dead of the Great War.

Similar programmes were set in motion around Europe and its colonies and many very fine buildings resulted, but in Italy a coherent architecture began to emerge and a body of monuments was created which formed one of the least known links in the chain of the development of modern architecture. These monuments were blatantly political; they were intended as memorials to those who had died, but also to the glory of the state which erected them.

The Exhibition of the Fascist Revolution, held in Rome in 1932 to celebrate the tenth anniversary of the Fascist Party's legendary March on Rome, was centred on a Martyr's Shrine, one of the finest examples of the architecture of death in the service of a political cause, equal in power (if not permanence) to the Lenin mausoleum. Designed as a circular, tempietto-like shrine to the martyrs of the Revolution by Rationalists Adalberto Libera and Antonio Valente, the space pivoted around a stark, attenuated metal cross which rose from a pool of blood (a striking theatrical effect achieved by reflecting red light from a central pool of water) and bore the words *Per la Patria. Immortale*. The space was illuminated by bands of light emanating from thousands of tiny repetitions of the word *Presente* that were glazed and back-lit to induce the effect of a vast roll of honour, each of the absent warriors responding with a 'present'. Although theatrical, this simple shrine exuded an immense atmosphere of power and respect.

The repetition of the word *Presente* recurs on the risers of the steps of another powerful memorial, the remarkable sacrarium at Redipuglia, designed by Giovanni Greppi and sculptor Giannino Castiglioni. The structure takes the form of a huge, seemingly endless stair framed by rows of cypress trees which frame the huge expanse of the steps with a stark verticality. The steps are both monument and tomb; the bodies of 40,000 Italian soldiers are buried below them. The commanding officer at the battle lies under a dark stone cube towards the base of the monument. Like a stairway for a colossus, the monument rises with the hillside, its culmination above in the bright Mediterranean sky, almost invisible in the glare. It is also to be read as a deliberately daunting climb, the completion of which is an act of homage to the dead, in effect a sacrificial stair. It is an awesome reminder of the scale of the casualties incurred in the war, and one of the most eloquent of all memorials which seemingly transcends questions of style; as classic as the pyramids, it seeks to evoke the scale rather than the look of the greatest ancient architecture.

On a similar, almost Babylonian scale, is the Sacrario del Monte Grappa by the same architects. Like so many First World War memorials, this monument commemorates a hopeless campaign in which little was achieved at a great cost in life. The setting is almost impossibly theatrical: the monument is placed atop a peak in the Italian Alps and seen against a craggy, harsh landscape which itself seems to express a bleakness and existential *angst*; Man fades away into an ant-like miniature against its unforgiving, rocky vastness. The building is one of the century's greatest expressions of the origin of the temple as the sacred mountain. The memorial becomes an extension of the peak of the mountain upon which it sits, a great crown which was not, in fact, where the soldiers fell (this was nearby in a less dramatic setting lower down).

The memorial takes the form of a kind of inverse colosseum; a series of concentric rings culminates in a circular sanctuary at the highest point. The layers are constructed of roughly hewn but regularly laid blocks of stone, each ring pierced with rows of semicircular openings so that the effect is of a huge columbarium, although the holes are symbolic and do not represent individuals. It is not insignificant that the openings are the same shape as bakers' ovens (ovens in this area tended to be made of stone). The idea of an opening in the mountain also evokes the symbolic presence of the earth spirit, the presence of which is traditionally celebrated in the grottoes later adopted as Christian shrines. From the peak of the monument a processional route (*Via Eroica,* or 'road of heroes') leads across the plateau to the Austro–Hungarian cemetery. The route is built in false perspective, reducing in width as it progresses to increase the sense of grandeur and scale, a typically Baroque touch in a supremely theatrical memorial.

Other important architectural monuments by Greppi and Castiglione exploit their mountain settings as a backdrop to the drama of the built form. The monument at Caporetto is composed of a series of steps rising through a solid mass of dense stone blocks, the building itself representing an overscaled stairway. At close view the composition is a haunting blend of the dream-like metaphysical structures and arcades with their long, melancholy shadows and the impossible architectural

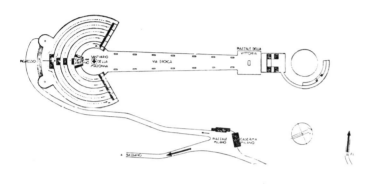

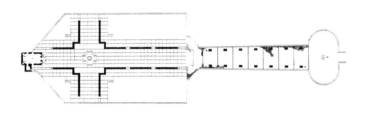

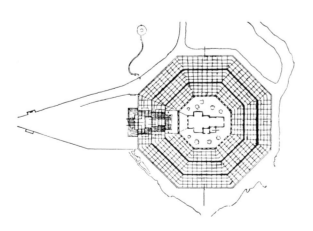

Sacrariums, 1930s, G Greppi and G Castiglioni
FROM ABOVE: Monte Grappa, view and plan; Pian di Salesei,
plan; Caporetto, Milan, plan

sequences of Max Escher. From a distance, the octagonal form of the structure becomes clearer, again the image of the sacred mountain is evoked, made more explicit here by the positioning of a traditional church at the top of the structure, with its asymmetrically placed spire curiously out of place in the rigidly symmetrical scheme.

The memorial at Pian di Salesei displays another grand processional route emphasised by false perspective. Here, pilgrimage of the sacred way culminates in an unassuming chapel, again with a belfry to one side deliberately destroying the careful symmetry which defines the plan. Thick walls pierced by the characteristic semicircular holes outline the edges of the path and a piazza is created in front of the chapel, its centre defined by a single cross. All paths converge on this piazza, one path continuing the main axis to the chapel to create a bold cruciform plan. The form of the chapel is striking, set against the deep green forested hillsides.

A monument at Colle Isarco displays a more subtle approach. Here the reference point is the Alpine grotto; the memorial is placed simply into the craggy rock and uses the same semicircular motifs that can be seen at Monte Grappa, both oven and columbarium. The monument is at once a scar in the surface of the rocks, as the loss of the soldiers is an emotional scar on the nation. The rock above seems to be healing the intrusive panel as great chunks cast heavy shadows on to the retaining wall below.

The ossuary and sacrario in Montello, the work of Felice Nori, is one of the few monuments to match Greppi's ambition. A brutally stark, blocky mass rises out of a low perimeter building atop the now familiar monumental steps. A brooding, dark entrance penetrates the elevation below a stripped classical pediment. The elementality of this scheme seems to presage Aldo Rossi's later neo-Rationalism, while the El Alamein memorial designed by Paolo Caccia Dominione in the 1950s echoes the sheer power of the unadorned mass as memorial. As a body of work, these buildings are an imposing and thoughtful collection of memorials; they begin to express the transition from the Novecento to the outright modern but the new phase would be left to other architects.

Conceived in the same spirit and using very much the same dramatic architectural vocabulary is the war memorial at Erba Incino, near Como, designed by Giuseppe Terragni in 1928 and completed in 1932.

Terragni regarded this monument as the first Rationalist monument in Italy but in fact it bridges the preceding Novecento style and the Rationalism which Terragni would play a crucial role in defining. Rather, it is a piece of theatrical monumentalism closer to Greppi's great memorials in feel, and its form is perhaps closer to the work of Michelangelo or Bernini than it is to his own work of a few years later.

The monument is based around a sacrarium at its centre, a structure which appears circular but is in fact composed of parts of circles, the centres of which are not the same. On plan this gives a crushed, lemon shape which lends the experience of the building dynamism. The sacrarium is carved out of the centre of the great stair, an empty gaping hole at the heart of the memorial signifying the loss of life and affirming that this is a cenotaph not a tomb. The stair spills down the side of the hill like a flow of lava and ends in a semi-circular pile of overflowing steps at the base of the structure.

As if to confirm Gregotti's assertion about the powerful influence of Futurism on the new generation of Italy's architects, Terragni also designed a monument to the First World War dead which was based on sketches by Sant'Elia. As such, it does not represent a true stage in the architect's own career but it is a fascinating project in its own right. The original Sant'Elia sketch had in fact been a design for a power station and its skyward thrust is retained in the executed design. The monument consists of twin volumes which rise from a buttressed base containing the crypt. At once dynamic and rooted solidly to the ground, it is a curious structure which embodies many of the paradoxes of early Italian modernism; monumental and light, modernistic and dated by the time it was built. Nothing dates as fast as the future.

The handful of private sepulchres which Terragni designed are less monumental and more important architecturally than these two relative curiosities. A pair of mausolea at the Como cemetery allowed the architect to practise his sculptural version of stripped classicism. He played the same formal games as those he indulged in at Erba with these Mannerist aedicular structures, and again the tombs are strangely modern or, rather, timeless, and blend in exquisitely with the classical tombs which surround them.

More influential than these, however, was his design for a tomb for the Sarfatti family. Terragni's sketches

from 1935 show a monument of asymmetrical composition which develops in later sketches into a smaller, symmetrical and yet more monumental scheme, undergoing a drastic process of radical simplification. The built version is an elemental composition, T-shaped in plan with a single stair leading to a cubic stone which crowns it. The tomb has a brutal, almost primitive simplicity to it; forbidding and stark it retains elements of the Novecento but signals a lurch into the architect's later mature Rationalism.

Terragni's final sepulchral design, for the Mambretti family (1937–39), was never executed, but it is one of his finest and most mature designs. It begins to explore ideas he developed more fully in the designs for the Danteum, which was roughly contemporary with the tomb design. Two distinct and different schemes emerged from Terragni's many sketches. The first of these consists of a blocky tomb based around the golden section in plan and elevation, which is fragmented into a series of large planes, while the second is a composition on a square plan, utilising a complex series of planes and levels to create a microcosmic, self-contained world. Although tiny, there is a great deal of thought and meaning in these intricate and thoroughly worked designs which are monumental yet diminutive in scale. The narrative architecture which Terragni explored in the Danteum designs can be seen taking shape.

The Danteum designs could easily fall within our scope here as the building was to have been a purely monumental structure with no specific function beyond commemoration of Italy's greatest figure by the man who considered himself so. In its design, Terragni created a twentieth-century equivalent to the works of Boullée and Ledoux, the enigma of which is maintained by their very confinement to paper.

The Danteum would undoubtedly have been among the century's great works, introducing a level of meaning and narrative lacking in most modern work, but it falls a little beyond the scope of this book as I have tried to omit memorials to national heroes. However, as an abject lesson in the planning of a building as memorial, and the ultimate realisation of Loos' dictum about true art belonging only to the tomb as the building type which has no function, it remains unsurpassed.

There are certain similarities between the sturdy classicism of Terragni's early tomb designs and those of his contemporary, Gio Ponti. As has been mentioned, Ponti, was one of the first architects to acknowledge

*ABOVE: Pino family tomb, Parabiago, G Mucchi;
CENTRE: Design for war memorial at Erba Incino, Como, 1932,
G Terragni; BELOW: Sketch for Mambretti family tomb, G Terragni*

the importance of local traditions in architecture. His Borletti tomb of 1932 in the monumental cemetery in Milan is a satisfying piece of sculptural architecture. Designed in the form of a tiny chapel with a family crypt below, it allows escape from the frenetic aesthetic activity in the cemetery which surrounds it.

The desire for grand monuments and auspicious mausolea in Italian cemeteries often makes them visually confusing and tired places. In Ponti's chapel, only the soft grain of the marble which faces all the walls distracts the mourner. There is something of the stripped functionality of Loos in the interior, an effect which retains the symbolic quality of the space but rejects ornament for its own sake. The crypt is an exquisite space, illuminated by a single tiny window and with curving, almost Art Deco steps carved out of the marble surfaces. The tomb is like a distilled essence of a chapel: the superfluous has been removed and the sacred and the private is all that remains.

The approach of Marcello Piacentini (often seen as Mussolini's Albert Speer figure – the approved architect) in his Marconi tomb in Pontecchio, near Bologna, was similarly elemental, though he chose the ancient archetype of the tomb chamber and *dromos* (the passageway to a burial chamber carved into the side of a mound). The sarcophagus lies in a circular chamber under a stepped vaulted roof so that its section is of an inverted ziggurat. Semicircular niches surround the space and are left empty as an indicator of the presence of the absence. The building awakens the deepest notions of the archetypal tomb, the circle, the long passage through the walls of the *dromos* and the single light source from above. It is a form embedded in a collective unconscious which needs no explanation other than the built form.

The innovative architectural approach to sepulchres continued to be characteristic of Italy in the post-war years. Another internalised world, set apart from the visual chaos of the cemetery setting was created by Gabriele Mucchi for the Pino family in Parabiago. A separate world is set up within walls of heavy stone just tall enough to give complete seclusion. The first enclosure encountered is a garden planted with a pair of cypresses and shrubs and an upright monumental slab.

The next stage is entered through an opening in another wall, the curve of which sucks in the visitor with considerable power and conveys the mourner up some steps to the final destination of the twin tombs, which cannot be seen from either the garden or the cemetery outside. It is a work of great subtlety and creates its own narrative in a manner not dissimilar to Terragni's Danteum designs: the architect maintains tension and a powerful desire to follow the building through to its conclusion by the composition of space and mass alone.

In the same Milan cemetery as Ponti's Borletti tomb stands the attenuated vertical mausoleum designed by A Cassi Ramelli for the Turkheimer family. This remarkable building is not out of place among the ostentatious mini-skyscrapers of this cemetery but its forms are stripped to the minimum. The elevations are relieved only by windows and by the flat stone banding that merely suggests the presence of engaged columns. The simplest doorway is capped by a semicircular arch, and a pyramidal roof crowns the structure. It is as much beach hut as mausoleum and the architect plays games with solidity and depth in the paper-thin quality of the facades.

This is a rationalist architecture which borrows both from the classical and from Milan's Gothic heritage yet is firmly placed in the twentieth-century architectural context; it augurs in the rationalism of Rossi and his contemporaries which did not begin to emerge until a generation later but formed the continuum that has made Italian funerary architecture such an incomparable source of interest throughout the century.

XIV. MODERNISM AND THE FUNCTIONAL LANGUAGE OF DEATH

Between the First and Second World Wars there was a remarkable development of the crematorium as a building type, mainly in Central Europe and Scandinavia. Elsewhere, the reticence about expressing the function of these buildings of death generally led to a continuation of a historicist and vaguely ecclesiastical architecture which displayed a reluctance to acknowledge the elemental and sombre activity on the inside, other than that it was something loosely connected with religion – an attitude which still prevails today.

The Expressionism and Cubism which briefly flowered in post-war Europe gave birth to a number of powerful crematoria; bulky buildings with an imposing presence and a frank acknowledgement of the finality of the act of cremation. Without doubt the most expressive of these was Clemens Holzmeister's Vienna Crematorium (1921–22). Placed within the walls of an ancient castle, the new building retains the daunting impenetrability of

the fortress; a single, gaping door waits on axis to swallow the procession. It is massed into an almost pyramidic structure, like some ancient temple echoing the form of the sacred mountain, while spiky castellation evokes the spirit of the castle which once stood on the site.

A huge, daunting plaza is created by walls which embrace the space before the building and draw the cortège to the terrible inevitability of the ogee door. The walls are punctured by an endless series of arches which form the columbarium and echo the shape of the main entrance with its flattened Gothic form, as if the burden of death were compressing the arch into the ground. The same squashed Gothic arch reappears as the vaulting which defines the main ceremonial space at the heart of the building, a Greek-Cross plan with the bier located directly opposite the entrance. The interior is the equal of the powerful Expressionist churches which sprang up in Germany at the same time, an expression of the mystical and the sacred but with a powerful undercurrent of pagan symbolism imbuing every part of the design.

Kuehn's Forst Crematorium of the same period shares the terrifying, blank walls (evoking the spectre of Boullée's representation of the sublime) and the spiky Gothic arches of Holzmeister's building, while Dominikus Böhm's crematorium chapel in Neu Ulm, Cologne, displays the same powerful Gothic imagery in its heavy, rough stone facade. Böhm's triptych of arches is more reminiscent of the attenuated spikiness of Gothic, and his building forms a bridge between the medievalism which had dominated European ecclesiastical design over the past century and the monumental, expressionistic modernism which was emerging throughout Germany.

The other German architect working to create a structural language to express the tragedy of death was Fritz Schumacher. The interior of his cemetery chapel in Ohlsdorf (1929–30) is defined by the same Gothic spirit which imbues the work of Holzmeister and Böhm; a lofty, vaulted chapel with a circular plan forms the centrepiece of the building, a return to the themes he explored in his Dresden Crematorium of 1907. Its tall windows and curving ribs evoke perpendicular Gothic. However, there is none of the delicacy or intricacy of that period; rather, an unbearably heavy burden of bricks and mortar.

The building pivots around the circular chapel, the ancillary spaces, forming wings to either side. From

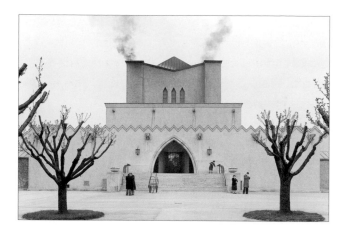

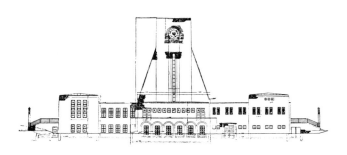

without, the importance of the cylindrical chapel is expressed in its volume, a huge gasometer which towers above the cemetery and the side wings. The twelve columns which support the roof are expressed powerfully in the dark clinker of the facade. The elements of the building remain strongly articulated and reek of symbolism, but this is a stripped architecture; the monumental symmetry remains but the roots of a functional, unsentimental approach show through.

The same symmetrical organisation around the imposing ritual space at the heart of the building can be seen in Schumacher's Hamburg Crematorium. Here a huge tower rises from a plaza like a headstone looming over a tomb, a clock at its apex: the ultimate in *memento mori*. Behind the tower a lofty hall is sheltered under a great parabolic roof structure. Curiously, this building manages to successfully combine elements of a number of the strands of contemporary architecture: the ominously stripped arcades are functional yet they presage the developments of Nazi architects, the tower and its great battered buttressed gable invokes the spirit of Futurist visions of monumental urban landscapes, while the parabolic roof sets the building firmly within Expressionist trends. It is a stark and brutal piece of architecture which does not shirk its responsibilities, a building which eloquently addresses the functional and symbolic requirements of the architecture of the dead.

At the same time, the newly formed Czechoslovakia was the scene of burgeoning architectural experimentation, and the Czechs, too, were coming to terms with the genesis of this new building type. Arnost Wiesner's crematorium at Brno (1925) is another stark building which blurs the borders of classification of inter-war architecture. A long stair rises up to a rigidly symmetrical building which is entered through a heavy plinth. A pair of port-hole windows, one to either side of the door, gives a vaguely anthropomorphic feel to the facade. Above the plinth, the main hall is caged in by piers which culminate in vicious spikes, seen like a crown of thorns against the sky beyond. Internally, the arrangement is simple: a single hall houses the ceremony, top-lit and with plain whitewashed walls – the influence of both Wagner and Loos is apparent in its clean simplicity. To the back and sides the symmetry begins to melt away. One wing houses a columbarium, the niches arranged in a labyrinthine pattern around a central court, the spiky crown of the crematorium always remaining visible.

The same year that Wiesner built the crematorium in Brno, Alois Mezera began work on Prague's own monumental crematorium. Mezera had been a pupil of Plečnik, and the classical influence and language is visible in the building. However, its lean, stripped monumentalism foreshadows the ominous works of Fascist architecture. In the Prague crematorium, the expressionist element has disappeared and given way to a blend of functionalism and classicism which was to define many of the great works of modernism's canon of the architecture of death. Again, this is a stiffly symmetrical building, a great hall rising out of a low-lying plinth-like structure. A colonnade wraps around to form plaza in front of the building and functions as a cloister columbarium. As at Holzmeister's Vienna crematorium, the mortuary and ancillary facilities are located in the basement and the public and ritual space above ground.

Mezera's creation remains one of the most haunting of crematoria; its blankness and monumentality speak of the existential void of death in the modern era. Its classicism is a stripped language of pagan sacrality, a deliberate rebuke to Christian and ecclesiastical symbolism and a clear attempt to christen the new state with a secular route to an uncertain end. Yet it is also a supremely functional building; a theatrical plaza and a grand symmetry confront the cortège and impress the visitor with their respect for the dead, but the rational plan, the modernity of the functional aspects of the building, the clear expression of structure and the light, airy interior are highly advanced for a public building in the age of an international revival of Beaux-Arts classicism. Profound and silent, a mystery, gloom and a grand inscrutability worthy of Kafka himself lurk in the shadows of the arcades to Prague's new crematorium.

The 1930s experienced a dramatic increase in the building of new funerary facilities, particularly crematoria, and witnessed a concerted effort by architects across Europe and in a few cases the USA and Japan, to create a new modernist building type – the hygienic and efficient crematorium – a building to dispel the images of massive, sombre structures redolent of death and grief. Scandinavia was in the vanguard of these efforts and is featured elsewhere. The zenith of this wave of modern funerary architecture undoubtedly came with Asplund's Woodland Crematorium, Stockholm, but this brilliant work has overshadowed other significant examples of funerary modernism which have faded quickly into obscurity as representatives of a poorly covered field of modern architecture.

It is interesting to note that liturgical and structural technological advances had begun to revolutionise ecclesiastical architecture but the effects of these momentous changes would not be felt on a significant scale until after the Second World War. The change from the traditional church plan, which derived from Gothic models and from the original inspiration of the basilica, began to be questioned by theologians and architects who sought to break down the barriers and the physical distance between the clergy and the congregation. Altars and communion tables were shifted into the body of the church, into the midst of the people, and the congregation became as much (or more) the 'House of God' as the church building.

Yet modern architecture was slow to make inroads on church design; the idea of the 'functional' church proved hard to grasp and ran into entrenched conservatism from lay and clergy alike. New materials were also allowing a greater openness and light inside ecclesiastical spaces and facilitating a final realisation of Abbot Suger's Gothic exhortation to dematerialise the walls of the church and mystically illuminate its interior.

Ecclesiastical architects were generally slow to react to the new advances and after an initial spurt of activity in the wake of August Perret's advances in France and those of the late Expressionists in Germany, the atmosphere of extreme conservatism in Europe and the USA virtually halted architectural progress. It was left to those working in the field of funerary architecture and specifically the crematorium builders to advance and realise some of these new ideas. As a relatively new building type the crematorium lacked the associative and symbolic baggage of the church building. Its singular purpose could be more easily refined into a functionalist brief than the mystical rituals of the mass. Its function was hygienic and definable; as much as people were now born into the efficient, clean modernism of the hospital, they would depart within a similarly rational building.

The finest examples of these buildings are in the Scandinavian countries where state encouragement of cremation was an incentive to the building of many fine crematoria. The 1930s witnessed the construction of Otar Hökerberg's crematorium in Eskilstuna in Sweden; Fritz Schlegel's crematoria in Sondermark and Mariebjerg in Copenhagen, Denmark; Rolf Prag's crematorium in Hamar, Norway; Erik Bryggman's exquisite mortuary chapels in Abo and Parainen, Finland; in addition, of course, to Asplund and Lewerentz's masterpieces and a host of others. Elsewhere, Alois Sajtar's Olomouc Crematorium in Croatia (then Yugoslavia) was a fine piece of modern understatement, and further afield the Tokyo Municipal Office of Architecture created a fine building as the city's main crematorium in a country which continues to sponsor some of the very best crematorium architecture.

With the notable exception of the Scandinavian countries, the age of a functional architecture of death came to an abrupt end at the close of the 1930s with the outbreak of the Second World War. Expressionistic elements were reintroduced, as they were elsewhere in modern architecture and specifically in ecclesiastical design, and the optimistic modernism and faith in technology, the high quality and consistency of many of the best inter-war buildings, was lost and has never truly returned. The innocence, optimism or naivety which made possible a search for a solely functional architectural language of death has faded away to be replaced with an attitude that is inquiring and questioning in the best cases or blindly accepting of received tradition and expectations in the worst. The latter category dominates modern funerary architecture.

XV. THE PARADOX OF THE MODERNIST MONUMENT
A New Approach

A series of paradoxes is contained within the notion of the modernist monument. On the one hand an iconoclastic movement concerned with a new beginning and preoccupied with the idea of the functional alone as the driving force behind architecture must inherently oppose the very idea of the memorial. However, Loos, the prototypical early functionalist, asserted that only the monument can be true art as only the monument is released from the burden of function. His own tomb is a cube of stone set upon a plinth, a design fittingly extrapolated from the architect's own sketches after his death. Massimo Cacciari seeks to clarify Loos' often over-simplified position:

> If sepulcher and monument were to be understood
> thematically, they would not in any way escape the
> universe of functions. What Loos means to assert is that

art takes place where it is the idea of sepulcher and monument, the idea of a place of exception that life has led up to, but that transcends or reopens life's functions . . . In this age, the possibility of exception lies in the sepulcher, one can also say that existence has always been 'collected' there.[30]

There is a certain nihilistic or existentialist fascination with death, and in architecture this attention is focused on the memorial as a symbol of hopelessness. Yet apart from a few examples this fundamental Heideggeran notion of only being able to appreciate life through an acute awareness of death has not filtered down into the mainstream architecture of death. The architectural responses to the First World War were diverse and moving, the last great outpouring of a fundamentally Renaissance humanist architecture. The responses prompted by the Second World War were far less secure in their convictions. To some extent Nazism had become synonymous with monumentality and, once the terror of Stalinism was revealed, that regime too would tar the reputation of classical grandeur. Consequently, the task to memorialise the victims of the dictatorships in what was deemed an appropriate manner became more politically fraught.

Modernism had taken a firmer hold on the world by the end of the Second World War and many fine memorials would emerge. However, the most profound monuments already existed as ready-mades. No memorial can match the eloquence of the empty death camps in Poland; the partially destroyed gas-chambers constitute one of the most powerful of all aids to memory, and they cannot easily be added to. The building left standing in Hiroshima which was situated beneath the ground-zero of the first atom-bomb attests powerfully to man's inhumanity to man. Now, with the last remaining victims of the Holocaust and the atom-bombs reaching old-age and death, new monuments are being erected and the antipathy towards monumentalism is receding. Holocaust museums and centres are vast monuments to the victims: in effect, a new building type devoted to memory.

Yet despite modernism's denial of the past, a number of interesting memorials did emerge in the immediate post-war period. As had been the case after the First World War, the most radical and challenging designs emerged from Italy. Architects Belgioioso, Peressutti, Rogers were commissioned to design a number of memorials after the war and the results constituted a

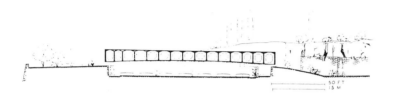

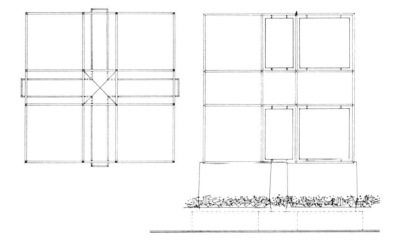

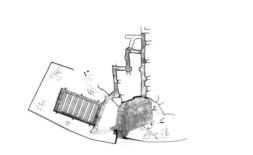

LEFT: Exterior, section, plan and interior of Fosse Ardeatine Monument, Rome, designed 1945, M Fiorentino and G Perugini;
RIGHT: Exterior, plan, elevation and detail of Monument to Those Fallen in Germany, Milan, designed 1946, Belgioioso, Peressutti, Rogers

reassessment of ideas regarding memorialisation. The best known of their memorials was in Milan, dedicated to Those Fallen in Germany, designed in 1946.

This memorial is the diametric opposite of the heavy, dense stone mausolea and tombs which litter the traditional Italian cemetery. In essence, it consists of a steel cage defining a cube. From a distance, the lines merge and only the outline cube is legible. But on closer analysis it can be seen that both the plan and the elevations of the memorial are based on a Greek cross, the proportions of which are derived from the golden section. The outside planes of the framework are hung in places with marble sheets inscribed with the words 'Blessed are those who suffer persecution for the cause of justice'. The disposition of the black and white marble sheets gives the effect almost of a De Stijl painting, yet with a curiously ordered framework in the background.

At the heart of the cage rests a glass bowl full of earth within a glass case. The soil was taken from Mauthausen concentration camp in Austria. Some straggling strands of rusting barbed wire are wrapped around the struts at the centre of the monument, giving the effect of a crown of thorns, a viciously spiky and disordered offence to the clarity and purity of the simple frame. As a response to the tragedy of the concentration camps and the existential crisis they provoked in twentieth century culture, this seems an almost painfully poignant and simple monument.

Another memorial by Belgioioso, Peressutti, Rogers which alters many preconceptions about cemeteria is the odd little Pasquinelli Memorial in Milan's monumental cemetery. Here the architects revert to the sarcophagus form and elevate the memorial entirely off the ground so that it appears as a piece of moveable furniture. If one of the modernist obsessions was the idea of detaching a building from the ground, whether this be to rid the house of notions of attachment to place, or whether to dispose of heavy foundations and a dark cellar with its Freudian overtones of a repressed and dark subconscious, this monument represents one of the rare opportunities to see this philosophy applied to funerary architecture. The sarcophagus was, after all, a freestanding piece, but one so heavy that it was unlikely to be moved too often.

The same effect is employed here; the family vault is raised on five legs but the stone of its construction implies that it would be foolish to attempt to move it.

A depression in the profile of the monument accommodates space for a niche to house a bronze statue, while a canopy is formed above it with the inscriptions of the tombs' occupants beneath.

Giuseppe Pizzigoni used the Bay family monument in the cemetery at Bergamo to explore similar themes of a more fragile architecture of death. His structure is essentially a frame, reminiscent of the purity of De Stijl, a curious mix of asymmetry and a surprising underlying symmetry which becomes clear in the plan. The empty frame, the void at the centre, is a powerful motif which eloquently expresses a modern existential *angst* about death, and questions notions of permanence and solidity in memorialisation.

Another ground-breaking Italian monument was placed firmly in the historical context of Roman memorial building by its placement outside the Via Appia Antica. Commemorating the death of 335 Italians who were murdered in reprisal for the killing of a group of German stormtroopers (all the men were innocent and picked at random as an act of revenge), the monument stands outside the entrance to the cave in which the men were shot. The design, by Aprile, Calcaprina and Cardelli, was finally completed by architects Mario Fiorentino and Giuseppe Perugini after winning a national competition in 1945. It consists essentially of a huge concrete canopy which seems to float above the graves of the deceased (a motif which would be closely echoed in the Yad Vashem Memorial in Israel, 1961) leaving only a narrow slit of light between the tombs and their covering. The entrance to the caves is left open, a black gaping void, while the entrance to the monument itself is via an opening in a sculptural steel wall composed of jagged, twisted elements which recall tangles of barbed wire and a kind of crown of thorns constituting a powerful gesture of penetration of the solid structure. It is a powerful and oppressive monument.

XVI. HOLOCAUST MEMORIALS

The Holocaust is inconceivable and consequently indescribable. Even the words of horror which have been used to describe it have become platitudes that no longer convey any true sense of shock, merely the repetition of standard phrases. No monument can convey the sense of what happened and any monument that succeeded in coming near would probably be decried as too horrible, an insult to the survivors.

Holocaust memorialisation has consequently become a paradox: it is the representation of that which it is impossible to represent. At the same time, the very idea of memorialisation clashes with a post-modern condition unwilling to see history in a single, unchanging interpretation, which is what a memorial must inevitably do.

Thus the quiet remains of the Nazi death camps have become the only real memorials to the Holocaust, for despite the enormous quantity of art and literature devoted to the theme, nothing but the specific sites of these millions of brutal killings can hope to convey anything of the scale and the organisation with which the slaughter was executed. This has led to the death camps becoming quasi-religious places of pilgrimage. The material presence of the venue of this great suffering becomes as important as a place of martyrdom; the museums on the site and, more importantly, the original buildings themselves become reliquaries and shrines. A tourist industry has grown up around the camps. They have become obligatory stops on the map, not only for Jews, but for all Europeans; in Poland, for instance, schoolchildren are taken as part of their education.

In a late-twentieth century, in which cyberspace is becoming the information-gathering zone, physical, dimensional space is charged with an extra force. Auschwitz has become Poland's most popular tourist destination. But it stands for things other than the Holocaust alone. For many Jews, it provides the ultimate justification of the Zionist goal, the event which made the founding of Israel an inevitability. To Western civilisation as a whole, it reverberates with meaning as the place at which Western Capitalism, and with it modernism, ground to a halt; if this could happen and be allowed to happen in the civilised West, then where was there for civilisation to go? Indeed, the proliferation of Holocaust monuments, as Andreas Huyssen has pointed out, is a symptom of the emergence of a post-modern culture, a culture of memory with the memorial and the museum at its heart.[31]

At the same time, Theodor Adorno, in stating that there could be no poetry after Auschwitz, in effect suggested that art is impossible after the Holocaust.[32] How much more then must the notion of attempting to represent the unrepresentable horror of the Holocaust in memorial form seem an impossibility, and an undesirable one at that? Henry Moore, when adjudicating the competition for a memorial at Auschwitz in 1957,

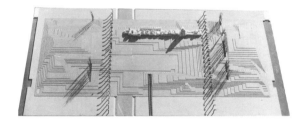

Auschwitz-Birkenau, Poland
FROM ABOVE: Memorial; model; remains of the incinerator

also questioned the wisdom of creating a monument to the emotions engendered by the camp. It was more than a question of whether to choose an abstract or figurative design, it was a question of whether the idea of memorialisation itself was not misguided.

Holocaust memorials are being built around the world at an accelerating pace, yet there is great debate about the very idea of erecting memorials to the Holocaust when Hitler's Germany has become synonymous with monumentalism. This debate rises partly out of modernist orthodoxy: the Modern Movement thrived on a positive break with the past and the idea of a modernist monument seems itself a paradox for a movement obsessed with breaking with the past.

The whole point of a memorial is, as its name suggests, memory. But as the generations who suffered in the camps and survived come to the end of their lives, a new memory has to be constructed and implanted in the younger generations. This is one of the reasons why memorial building has become so widespread in recent years. It has also much to do with Jewish traditions of memory. Judaism is a culture soaked in the memory of collective suffering; its principal religious monument is the Wailing Wall, the fragment of a great temple which was destroyed, and at Auschwitz the most poignant memorial is not the statuary but the ruins of the crematorium, a building which was deemed too terrible to survive.

In his novel *The Book of Laughter and Forgetting* (1981), Milan Kundera described totalitarian politics as a battle between memory and forgetting, and indeed writes that, 'what terrifies us about death is not the loss of the future but the loss of the past. Forgetting is a form of death ever present within life.'[33] The cult of Holocaust memory, which is a concerted effort to not allow people to forget, to keep alive the memory of death, has reached dramatic proportions.

Cities across the USA, which remained distant from the Holocaust until its troops liberated some of the camps, and many European cities, host Holocaust centres, libraries, museums and educational facilities. The Holocaust has become so much a part of the Jewish experience and so inseparable from Jewishness in the eyes of outsiders that Jews have become known for a few years of terrible suffering over and above the thousands of years for which they existed before the camps.

In an age when the museum has often been touted as the replacement for the temple, where people go to spend their weekends worshipping at the altar of (valuable) artefacts, the Holocaust museum takes on a special quasi-religious status which sees the creation of a new building type, part memorial, part library, part school and part museum, all bound together by an atmosphere of compulsory pilgrimage and sacrality. If the museum has become the metaphor for a post-modern culture of memory, then the Holocaust museum has a special place.

Earlier, I devoted a chapter to John Soane (chapter VII), whose own house is a kind of museum of death, a monument to himself and a vehicle to express his fears, *angst* and loneliness. Although to some extent all museums celebrate death and the belongings of the dead (our modern version of the cult of ancestor worship) Soane's house is perhaps the closest parallel to the idea of a museum commemorating death itself, in which the artefacts are there for what they represent rather than what they are; thousands of spectacle frames have no intrinsic value and it is only their number which represents the attitude of worthlessness towards human life and which breaks taboos about the personal possessions of the dead becoming untouchable, thus representing the cruelty of the regime that created the pile and, more importantly, the organisation and ruthless efficiency of the Nazi death machine.

The Anne Frank House in the Netherlands is one of the most poignant of Holocaust memorials, yet similarly it is a building type not connected with the monument, linked tangentially to the tragedy by the girl's diary which has become a standard school text: house becomes memorial becomes museum through book; book becomes standard text because of its irresistible and sentimental appeal and the identification with an innocent individual. It is the ultimate post-modern paradigm.

The issue of how to commemorate the Holocaust is one which has raised many questions, and now that we are entering a wave of unprecedented memorial building, it is becoming ever more pertinent. In an age of artistic and architectural pluralism, modernism has become the unchallenged language of Holocaust commemoration, partly because of the Nazi associations of classicism but partly to do with the internationalist aspirations of the Modern Movement and the very notion of an 'international style', exactly the ideas for which modernism was condemned by the Nazis; modern art and architecture was seen as a Jewish/Bolshevik plot to deprave and demean pure Aryan culture.

In the Soviet Union, where state-sponsored art and architecture was defined by Socialist Realism, a close relative of Nazi monumentalism, there was no real memorialisation of the Holocaust as the systematised killing of Jews was seen only as a constituent part of the 'Great Patriotic War' (in which, it has to be said, millions of Russians also died in camps), seen exclusively as an anti-Fascist war in which the Russians were cast as liberators. Therefore, for the Soviet authorities there was no real question of commemorating the Holocaust separately. At Buchenwald, where the Soviets did make an effort to create a lasting memorial, the solid, monumental pylons with torches atop their monolithic forms bore a disturbing similarity to the work of Hitler's architect, Albert Speer, while the huge clock tower, although an appropriate *memento mori,* seems eerily misplaced and too keen to draw attention to its colossal form.

Other monuments erected on the sites of the camps tended to be similarly overbearing or otherwise inadequate. The defence of figurative sculptural monuments as opposed to abstract designs was encapsulated by Nathan Rapoport, the artist responsible for the 1948 Warsaw Ghetto Monument, when he said, 'Could I have made a rock with a hole in it and said "Voila! The heroism of the Jews?"'[34] It was at Rapoport's monument that German leader Willy Brandt sank to his knees in one of the most memorable moments of modern politics. The argument was almost unnecessary for architectural style because the buildings of the camps themselves still stood.

If a truly modern architecture of death has emerged, it could be said to be exemplified by the buildings of Auschwitz-Birkenau and the other death camps. But it is paradoxically the least monumental of all architecture. The functional architecture of death, the buildings of a killing complex are the most faceless and banal of all monuments, and it is partly from their inauspicious nature that there true power derives.

Panic disrupted the organisation of a camp, so crowds were not to be frightened by their surroundings as they stepped off the wagons (although once there, brutality and fear were a critical part of the regime). The signs on the gate, *Arbeit Macht Frei* ('Work Sets You Free'), were designed to engender hope from the outset. Once the programme of orchestrated killing had begun, the machinery of death was to be disguised as something else; the weak and infirm, those who could

Views of Auschwitz-Birkenau, Poland

not be put to useful labour were herded into shower-rooms which turned out to be gas-chambers where Zyklon-B came instead of water. It was the ultimate metaphor for the Nazi racial cleansing programme.

The crematoria were partially submerged to become less conspicuous. The wall against which inmates were shot was put away from view. A curious coyness was employed throughout the camps which otherwise reeked of death from every corner: despite communal graves and inmates being forced to cremate and dump bodies, the camps' Nazi organisers were averse to a display of the true function of the buildings and, indeed, attempted to destroy the evidence with explosives when the Allies approached, as if somehow the memory could be erased.

Yet the most effective memorials are these structures themselves, those which were destroyed and left as ruins and those which remain or were restored. The buildings of Auschwitz remain the most compelling of memorials. Much of the camp was built by the prisoners themselves, who similarly were to dig their own graves. The buildings were adapted from designs developed for the quick erection of stables. There was a proliferation of primitive forms, almost archetypes: the timber guard towers with their pyramidal roofs and weather-boarding powerfully evoke the primitive hut, while the entrance building is designed using a kind of primitive *architecture parlante*, the single gateway with railway-tracks approaching, and the clock at its centre, either reminiscent of a rural station building or a reminder of man's limited time on earth. The crematoria are half-submerged and passages are cut into the mound to give access, the effect closely echoing the *dromos* of ancient burial chambers.

Despite these associations (most of which I would think are at least partially accidental), the most striking aspect of these buildings is their sheer banality. Once the grass and weeds have grown around them, once the emaciated figures and uniformed guards have disappeared there is no real evidence of the inhumanity which pervaded these camps, and everything has to be labelled for real emotive power to be exerted once again. Like all buildings concerned with the functional aspect of death – with the disposal of the physical remains of the body – there is little room for expression. Once it is known that these are the remains of the crematorium, or that this is the wall where prisoners were shot, only then do the buildings regain their power to disturb.

It is the implanted memory of what went on in these buildings which makes them memorials; images spanning from photographs and books, from films such as Alain Resnais' definitive documentary *Nuit et Bruillard* (Night and Fog) to Spielberg's exploitational but undeniably powerful film *Schindler's List*, memories which come from secondary sources. The aim of the rash of memorials, museums and libraries which are currently being built is to reinforce these cultural memories, the idea being that an awareness of the events of the Holocaust will diminish the likelihood of anything similar happening again. In the light of a growing proclivity among right-wingers to deny the existence of the Holocaust as historical fact, these monuments grow in importance; they contribute to what James E Young has termed 'the creation of public memory'.[35]

XVII. THE HOLOCAUST AND THE CREATION OF MEMORY

Visions of the past are inevitably tainted with the attitudes and concerns of the present. The memorial contains within it not only the superficial gesture towards remembrance and the dead but a wealth of information about the priorities, politics and sensibilities of those who built it. A memorial will tell us more about its builders than about those to whom it is dedicated.

Bearing this in mind, Holocaust memorials have to be seen against a background of the politics and the memorial tradition of the nation in which they are built. These factors present us with a complex web of criteria and it is hard to remain objective and neutral as a critic should when faced with a memorial to something as unquestionably worthy of memorialisation as the murder of some six million Jews, gypsies, homosexuals and Communists by the Nazis and their collaborators.

Different nations concentrate on different aspects of the Holocaust; some memorials are firmly in the tradition of the celebration of heroism (of those who resisted and fought the Nazis) while others are intended spuriously as anti-monuments, gestures which attempt to realise new forms of the representation of memory. At the same time, a new building type has emerged; the Holocaust museum and library.

Again this form is prompted partially as a response to the attempts of a few historians and academics to deny that the Holocaust ever happened. It is a paradox that many of those who supported the idea of the Holocaust now claim that it was a hoax. The notion of Holocaust denial has led to a new vitality in memorial building and those memorials have become interactive buildings rather than urban monuments. The allocation of a plot in Washington DC's mall to a monumental Holocaust Museum (James Ingo Freed, 1993) is the ultimate recognition of the outrage provoked by the proposal that the Holocaust never happened.

The history of Holocaust memorials begins with the buildings themselves. Before the end of the Second World War the Soviets had already created the first memorial museum at the camp at Majdanek in Poland in 1944. After the war, in 1947, the Polish authorities decided to maintain the buildings and ruins at Auschwitz-Birkenau as a memorial. A decade later, an international competition was launched to design a memorial for Auschwitz. The brief was fraught with problems – the design had to respect the memory of the dead and the views of the survivors, to represent unimaginable suffering yet not offend its site, which had become an unmarked cemetery, and so on. No clear winner emerged and the decision reached by the jury (headed by Henry Moore) was to engage three of the best entrants into a collaborative design.

The monument now stands in line with the entrance to the camp, at the end of the long, straight railway track which remains in place. It is the decidedly unmonumental gateway, however, which is the image one remembers; the other image is the mass of concrete and steel of the ruined crematorium. It is a monument in the finest tradition of the ruin as a symbol of a lost civilisation. Hitler and Speer had planned their buildings to leave glorious ruins, evidence of the magnificence of the Third Reich for future generations. The most famous ruin they left behind was at Auschwitz.

Of all the memorials at the sites of extermination, perhaps that at Treblinka (designed by Franciszek Duszenko and Adam Haupt in 1964) is the most successful. Destroyed and buried by the Nazis to hide the evidence of their atrocities, the site displays no evidence of the camp. What is to be seen today is a huge stone memorial, which approached through woods stands in a great circular clearing. The monument resembles a megalithic temple, set within a paved circle. It could once have been used for sun-worship, instead it commemorates Western civilisation's darkest period. The randomly shaped natural rocks that surround the central monument recall the Jewish custom of placing stones on the grave, or a landscape of rough-hewn headstones.

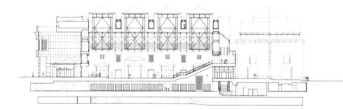

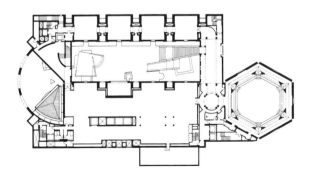

US Holocaust Museum, Washington DC, 1993, J Freed
FROM ABOVE: Interior; section; second-floor plan

Yad Vashem Memorial, Mount Herzel, Israel, 1961,
A Elhanani

Another significant memorial was created at Buchenwald, where the huge tower and monumental works by Ludwig Deiters, Hans Grotewohl, Horst Kutzat, Karl Tausendschon, Hugo Namslauer and Hubert Mathas contain within them wholly inappropriate echoes of Nazi monumentalism and spectacularly demonstrate the pitfalls of monumentality in commemorating the Holocaust. On the site of the Warsaw Ghetto, Nathan Rapoport's Monument to the Ghetto Uprising became one of the best known of Holocaust monuments. Executed in 1948, it is one of the few monuments to approach the subject from the traditional iconographic position of heroism rather than suffering.

Rapoport's sculpture, 'Liberation', executed in 1985, stands in Liberty State Park, New Jersey. The background to the figure of the American soldier carrying a concentration camp victim is formed by the Statue of Liberty and Ellis Island, the symbols of immigration and freedom which the USA sees itself as representing. The emphasis is on the US soldier as liberator more than the Jew as victim – it is a telling indicator of the way iconography varies from country to country.

The recent Holocaust Memorial Museum in Washington DC is the most significant example of attempts to engender Holocaust memory; however, many other Holocaust museums and libraries have emerged in the last couple of decades. One of the finest memorials never to have been built was Louis Kahn's 1966 proposal for a Memorial to Six Million Jewish Martyrs in Battery Park, New York City. A series of glass blocks would have created an enigmatic monument – the idea may have influenced Stanley Saitowitz's design for the New England Holocaust Memorial.

Holocaust memorial building began to pick up momentum during the 1960s although most examples were sculptural rather than architectural, and many were sentimental and mawkish, proving how difficult it is to commemorate genocide in anything like an appropriate manner. Of the few architectural monuments, Israel's Yad Vashem Hall of Remembrance of 1961, an unbearably heavy and mute structure which speaks of the terrible burden of grief which the Holocaust imposed on the Jewish people, is perhaps the best known of this wave of building. But others also exerted considerable impact in an age where the memory of war and genocide was beginning to fade under a new prosperity.

One of the finest and most enigmatic memorials of this period graces the Ile de la Cité, in the shadow of

Notre Dame Cathedral, Paris. Designed by Georges Henri Pingusson and completed in 1962, the monument is almost invisible from the island itself. It is reached by descending a stairway jammed jammed between two thick walls. An enclosed plaza is focused on two openings, one of which affords a view to the water of the Seine below and to nothing else; the other giving access to a chamber of hexagonal plan-form. Off this, on the main axis, lies a lengthy corridor which is inaccessible but visible though a grille. In the walls of this corridor lie immured the ashes of a number of French victims of the Nazi camps. The structure is embellished with gratings and grilles of jagged, spiky ironwork reminiscent of the barbed wire boundaries of the camps.

The intense, subterranean isolation of this prominent memorial, a space in the heart of tourist Paris which remains eerily silent and empty, and its rigid symmetry and claustrophobia-inducing spaces, make this one of the few memorials which evoke feelings of grief and pain purely through the experience of space. It is a sublime monument, close to classicism and perhaps to the *architecture parlante* of the Revolutionary era, and at the same time, the Dantesque descent into a realm of darkness evokes the narrative architecture of Terragni. Pingusson is one of the few architects who has achieved such a powerful effect though the manipulation of space rather than simply using mass, monumentality or sculpture.

After the 1960s, the next great wave of memorial building occurred in the 1980s. This new impetus can be partly attributed to the fear of the first-hand experiences of Holocaust survivors dying out and leaving a dearth of irrefutable experience of the genocide, and partly to the emerging post-modern *museal* and memorial culture which retains a firm grip on the world's great cities. Whatever its genesis, the new-found momentum has led to the erection of memorials throughout the Western hemisphere, and an increasing recognition of other groups who lost their lives in the Holocaust: the Homomonument and Gypsy Monument in Amsterdam, memorials to murdered Communists and a host of other fine sculptural memorials in Père-Lachaise, and the designs for a memorial to victims of the Gestapo in Berlin which remains unexecuted.

In more recent years, much of the most thoughtful Holocaust memorialisation has emerged in Germany; perhaps it has become easier for new generations of artists to broach the subject after a gap of half a century.

In Harburg, a suburb of Hamburg, Jochen Gerz and Esther Shalev-Gerz erected a twelve-metre-high, lead-clad column upon which people were encouraged to scrawl their anti-Fascist comments. As a section of the column filled up (between 1986 and 1993), it was lowered into the ground and the process was repeated until it was entirely submerged.

Horst Hoheisel's 'Negative Form' monument in Kassel (1987), similarly exploits ideas of submergence and the nether realm of darkness to which the Holocaust belongs. Designed as a replica of a fountain donated to the town by Jewish businessmen and subsequently destroyed by the Nazis, the structure inhabits a subterranean realm and is visible only as a pattern in the paving. Closer inspection through a series of openings and grilles reveals the whole, submerged structure, twelve metres in depth, with water flowing down its sides in a perverse parody of the original fountain.

Despite this rash of construction, the two most poignant and powerful memorials to the devastation of the period are unintentional monuments. In Japan, the building left standing under ground-zero of the atomic bomb, and which has been preserved in its ruined but miraculously still standing condition, is the most eloquent reminder of the tragedy of war, while at Auschwitz it is the fearful mouth of the gateway to Birkenau which sticks in the memory. In his film *Nuit et Bruillard*, Alain Resnais commented on 'Architects who calmly designed doorways to be entered only once'. There can be no more powerful monument.

XVIII. EPILOGUE

Like Laudomia, every city has at its side another city whose inhabitants are called by the same name: it is the Laudomia of the dead, the cemetery . . . On fine afternoons the living population pays a visit to the dead and they decipher their own names on their stone slabs: like the city of the living, this other city communicates a history of toil, anger, illusions, emotions; only here all has become necessary, divorced from chance, categorized, set in order. And to feel sure of itself, the living Laudomia has to seek in the Laudomia of the dead the explanation of itself, even at the risk of finding more there, or less: explanations for more than one Laudomia, for different cities that could have been and were not, or reasons that are incomplete, contradictory, disappointing.[36]

'Everybody dies.'[37]

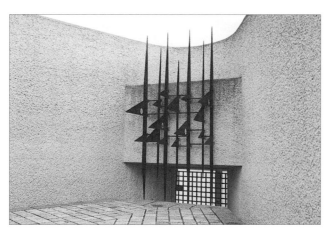

Holocaust Memorial, Ile de la Cité, Paris, 1962, G H Pingusson

Everybody dies. Every body leaves a memory, that is the simplest form of memorial. Paul Auster has written, 'Reach a certain moment in your life, and you discover that your days are spent as much with the dead as they are with the living.' But man has found a need to construct concrete adjuncts to these memories, markers, dwellings and entire cities to the dead throughout history. The architecture of death is an ideal architecture: in it is expressed man's *angst*, insecurity, vision of the next world, fear of or desires for the afterlife. Yet at the end of the twentieth century only a few artists and designers are truly considering the depth of these questions and producing work which reinterprets these archaic expressions of the collective unconscious. I have tried to include some of these in this book but this is not a cross-section through the world of funerary architecture, it is a portion of the cream off the top.

There has been a sharp decline in the consideration of the architecture of death as a subject worthy of attention for designers and artists during the twentieth century, although a few figures have had some success in reinvigorating it as a field of serious consideration and among them are Aldo Rossi, Carlo Scarpa, Imre Makovecz and a few others. The recent boom in Holocaust memorialisation has reintroduced the subject to a number of younger artists and architects often through the competition format, and has produced a few excellent works and many mediocre pieces which add little to the city, to memory or to the subject as a whole. But it has led to a rediscovery of the place of memorialisation in an increasingly sanitised city.

As our city centres increasingly become memorials themselves, untouchable shrines of heritage, paradoxically the architecture of memorialisation is dying. The museum and the listed building have become holy grails and yet new expressions of commemoration are becoming ever rarer. Italo Calvino has recognised the mythical place of the necropolis at the heart of our consciousness and as the necessary mirror image of our own cities, the place where we can contemplate our past and our future. Calvino's living visit the dead to find out and ask questions about themselves. Laudomia's necropolis is a mirror. The city of the dead is the archetype of the city of the living; its reflection and its negative. If, as Heidegger has said, it is the awareness of impending death which makes us truly alive, then the architecture of death should be the most considered and thoughtful aspect of our cities; *memento mori*, ray of hope and existential barometer.

The few buildings illustrated in this book attempt to show the results when the importance of an architecture of the dead is realised at the end of the twentieth century. It is fascinating to consider these forms and designs and to imagine whether there really are archetypes; is there an architecture of death in some kind of Jungian subconscious? We seem to inherently recognise some of these symbols – Rossi's empty windows and blind house, the garden of contemplation with nature

and water as the symbol of life and eternity, which appears frequently in Japanese architecture and in Scarpa's Brion Cemetery, the descent into the underworld, the ascent to the sky.

These eternal themes and motifs continue to exert considerable power on our imagination and our existential being. I hope that this book's brief examination of their reoccurrence and longevity can have some impact in fostering an awareness of the critical and pivotal importance of the role played by the architecture of death in understanding ourselves, our cities and our buildings – those of the living and those of the dead.

Notes

1 Lewis Mumford, *The City in History*, Secker and Warburg (USA and London), 1998.

2 Italo Calvino, *Invisible Cities*, Secker and Warburg (London), 1974.

3 Oswald Spengler, *The Decline of the West*, George Allen and Unwin Ltd (London), 1961, reprint, p104.

4 Ibid.

5 Adolf Loos, *Architecture*, 1910, reprinted in Arts Council Exhibition catalogue, (London) 1985, p56.

6 Fritz Lang, *Metropolis*, Universum Film AG (Germany) 1927.

7 Danilo Kiš, *A Tomb for Boris Davidovich*, Penguin (London), 1980, p74 (original translation 1978).

8 Jean Jacques Rousseau, *Confessions*, 1765, first published 1781.

9 Erwin Panofsky, *Meaning in the Visual Arts*, Doubleday Anchor Books (New York), 1955, p295.

10 Jean Jacques Rousseau, *La Nouvelle Héloïse*, 1761.

11 Petronius, *Satyricon,* translation published 1965, Penguin Books (London), p85.

12 Etienne-Louis Boullée, *Architecture, essai sur l'art* (edited by Jean-Marie Perouse de Montclos), Hermann (Paris), 1968.

13 Quoted in Richard A Etlin, *Symbolic Space, French Enlightenment Architecture and Its Legacy,* University of Chicago Press (Chicago), 1994, p197

14 Richard A Etlin, *Symbolic Space*, op cit.

15 Mircea Eliade, *The Sacred and the Profane: The Nature of Religion*, Harcourt Brace and Co (New York), 1959.

16 William Godwin, *Essay on Sepulchres*, 1809.

17 John Summerson, *The Unromantic Castle*, Thames and Hudson (London), 1990; contains the essay 'Sir John Soane and the Furniture of Death'.

18 Charles Baudelaire, 'Posthumous Regret', *Selected Poems*, Penguin (London), 1975, p77.

19 Maurice Maeterlinck, *Death*, Methuen (London), 1911, p58.

20 Oswald Spengler, *The Decline of the West*, op cit, p105.

21 Karel Teige, *Modern Architecture in Czechoslovakia*, Czechoslovakia Ministry of Information (Prague), 1947, p60.

22 Erich Maria Remarque, *All Quiet on the Western Front*, first English edition 1929; Triad/Panther Books (London), 1977, pp41–42.

23 Vincent Scully, *Architecture: The Natural and the Manmade*, St Martin's Press (New York), 1991, p159.

24 William Lethaby, *Form in Civilisation, Collected Papers of Art and Labour*, Oxford University Press (London), 1922, pp56–65.

25 Franco Borsi, *The Monumental Era, European Architecture and Design 1929-1939*, Lund Humphries (London), 1987.

26 Richard A Etlin, *Symbolic Space*, op cit.

27 Quoted in AD Profile 23, *Neo-Classicism*, Academy Editions (London), edited by Geoffrey Broadbent, vol 49, 8–9, p40.

28 S Frederick Starr, *Melnikov, Solo Architect in a Mass Society*, Princeton University Press (Princeton), 1978.

29 Vittorio Gregotti, *New Directions in Italian Architecture*, Studio Vista (London), 1968, p9.

30 Massimo Cacciari, *Architecture and Nihilism: On the Philosophy of Modern Architecture*, Yale University Press (New Haven), 1933, pp197–98.

31 Andreas Huyssen, *After the Great Divide: Modernism, Mass Culture, Postmodernism*, Indiana University Press (Bloomington), 1986.

32 Theodor Adorno, 'Valery Proust Museum', in *Prisms*, MIT Press (Cambridge, Mass), 1981.

33 Milan Kundera, *The Book of Laughter and Forgetting*, Penguin Books (London), 1981, pp234–35; edition includes interview with the author by Philip Roth.

34 Quoted in James E Young (ed), *The Art of Memory, Holocaust Memorials in History*, Prestel Verlag (Munich and New York), 1994, p24: the best book on holocaust memorials but the pace at which they are being built has dated it very quickly. The essays collected here are concise and informative and this remains a good work of reference.

35 James E Young, *The Art of Memory*, op cit.

36 Italo Calvino, *Invisible Cities*, op cit, p11.

37 William Conrad addressing boxer John Garfield in *Body and Soul*, United Artists film, 1947.

ABOVE: Approach to Gunnar Asplund's Woodland Crematorium (1935–40), Stockholm; view of exterior; CENTRE: Dromos of mortuary building; Asplund's Woodland Chapel (1918-20); BELOW: Sigurd Lewerentz's mortuary and Chapel of the Resurrection, 1925

GUNNAR ASPLUND AND SIGURD LEWERENTZ
THE PRIMITIVE HUT AND THE CLASSICAL TEMPLE

Of all the buildings which comprise the modern architecture of death, one particular grouping, Gunnar Asplund's Woodland Crematorium, Enskede, near Stockholm (1935–40), has become pre-eminent as the definitive example. Its instantly recognisable, stripped down forms are symbolic of modernism; almost a new classicism, a building expressed in a seemingly perfected, elemental modern language. Probably more has been written about this building than about any of the other schemes in this book, and it is worth examining exactly what it is that makes the Woodland Crematorium such an enigmatic place and an enduring architectural icon.

The first step is to clarify the relationship of the crematorium to the site, the other buildings and the landscape which form the cemetery. Just as the ancient Greeks placed their most sacred temples in the midst of a landscape imbued with sacral meaning and mythological associations, the Woodland Crematorium derives its power and status from the Nordic forest and the landscape of which it is an integral part. A curious but powerful blend of pantheism, Christianity and twentieth-century Rationalism combine to create the enigma of the most powerful landscape of death from the era.

Its roots lie in the movement for burial reform which was sweeping through Europe at the beginning of the century, and in the new society being energetically forged in Sweden. The introduction of an international architectural competition (the first ever in Sweden) to determine the form of this largely new cemetery for Stockholm attests to the status it was given and to the importance associated with the reforms of burial and the rituals which would accompany the relatively new process of cremation.

Sigurd Lewerentz, a young Swedish architect, had been involved in the development of new ideas about an architecture that would accommodate changing rituals of burial and cremation, and had proposed an interesting and innovative design for a crematory chapel in Helsingborg. Gunnar Asplund, another young architect, first saw the model of this proposal at the Baltic Exhibition in Malmö in 1914. It was at this point that the two decided to collaborate on an entry for the Stockholm Cemetery competition.

The result of their efforts was a remarkable design which took the landscape as its inspiration and revolved around imbuing the forest with powerfully primitive associations and which enhanced the existing landscape to create a new conception of the cemetery as a narrative landscape, not in the often whimsical sense of the English garden but more as an embodiment of archetypal Nordic forms and associations. The landscape itself became the architecture and the features within it the sites upon which the atmosphere of the design was created.

The forest was left intact and only a few paths were left to meander through its verdant darkness while graves were shown scattered seemingly as randomly as the growth of the trees themselves – an organic part of the landscape. Lewerentz's often reproduced sketch of the *Way of the Cross,* a kind of pilgrimage path through the cemetery, framed by a leaning, expressionistic cross, captured the intended atmosphere of the scheme: a blend of the Roman road of tombs (the Via Appia for example) and the mystery of the Nordic forest. The buildings remained relatively unimportant at this early stage.

As parts of the design began to be realised, it was evident that at this early stage there was not enough money available to create the centrepiece the architects desired, and it was decided to begin with a smaller chapel. This first building, designed by Asplund between 1918 and 1920 and christened the Woodland Chapel, took the form of a kind of primitive forester's

Woodland Chapel interior

Detail of Woodland Chapel doors

hut, but one articulated in a curious but striking mix of classical and vernacular architectonic elements, in many ways similar to the language used by Asplund's contemporary Jože Plečnik.

Despite the fame of the main crematorium building, it is this little structure which best embodies the spirit of the original design, and which evokes most fully the atmosphere of death in the heart of the forest. It is approached through a narrow gateway, a simple, rather primitive structure with thick walls and a shallow pitched roof which gives it an aedicular appearance. A plaque above the opening depicts a simplified classical temple and an oak tree which seems to be hovering between life and death, a few leaves still clinging to its sparse branches. The words of a Latin *memento mori* serve to introduce the theme of the crossing of the world of the living into another darker realm.

The entrance is constricted and claustrophobic; a route of shadows and shade introduces the visitor to the forest on the far side, as if to reinforce the notion of the forest itself as a symbolic setting, from the open landscape to the dense darkness of the pines. From the gateway, the visitor is cast into the woods and a long straight path leads to the chapel. The forest floor is dappled with sunlight which has found its way through the foliage. The chapel appears as a pyramidal roof at the end of the path, with the curious doric columns supporting it as slender and vertical as the trunks of the trees which envelop the structure. The visitor is drawn into the sheltering space beneath the low eaves; it is a space of preparation and protection.

The key to the doors is inserted into the eye-socket of a skull (now removed due to vandalism), a piece of wrought ironwork which complements the richly worked inner doors, replete with skull and cross-bones,

snakes and cinerary urns, their upper halves revealing a more optimistic set of symbols including a sun and the Lamb of God bearing a cross.

Opening these doors reveals a somehow completely unexpected space: a shallow dome hovers over the area, which is defined as a circular temple. An oculus at its centre admits light but reveals no depth of structure – it sits flush with the ceiling so that the roof appears weightless and insubstantial – quite the opposite of the solid vernacular of the steeply pitched, angular roof seen from without. However, the space beneath the dome is square, creating murky, dark corners at the edges. The dome is supported on more correctly pro-portioned Doric columns defining the central space, and the chairs (also designed by Asplund in a simple vernacular style) are laid out in a circle focusing on the stone slab situated on the floor directly opposite the entrance. This is the catafalque, behind which an altar stands in an odd compressed arch that resembles a misplaced fireplace and perhaps represents the furnace doors – the entry to the next stage. Asplund had origi-nally planned the exit on a different axis so that there would be a clear narrative route involving the mourners in a linear process, rather than one in which they merely double back on themselves, but this was never implemented.

On leaving the chapel, however, a striking difference in the quality of light between its wooded surrounding and the open space beyond the gateway becomes apparent. The visitor is drawn towards the entrance once again by a bright aura of light and sunshine beyond the dark confines of the tunnel-like gateway. This finally confirms one of the themes which is most consistently elaborated in this spatial progression, the move from light to dark and back again, a metaphor

Chapel of the Holy Cross

Interior of one of the smaller chapels, Woodland Crematorium

for the journey undertaken by the mourners who must emerge from their grief into the embrace of nature and the outside world – a way to put their problems into perspective.

To one side of the chapel stands the mortuary, an ominous mound entered via a passage reminiscent of the *dromos* of ancient tombs. The inferral is of the tumulus, the primitive burial mound; heavy iron doors guard the entrance to this other realm, a type of fanlight type window indicates that those who might enter this space still have need for light. To the other side of the chapel, a tiny circular enclosure (the 'urn grove') leads to terracing and the path to the children's cemetery, while a well in the chapel courtyard echoes the form of the gate through which the visitors arrive, and the wall of water behind Doric columns announces the entrance to the whole cemetery; it is a reminder of the symbolism of entry and exit to this mysterious realm compounded by water as a symbol of life.

Asplund's original sketches for the chapel illustrated a completely different conception. Having just returned from his honeymoon in Denmark, where he was inspired by the vernacular of the cottage he stayed in, it appears that he abandoned his original ideas in favour of the final version. This featured similar ruralised versions of a classical language: the low, deep eaves supported on classical columns, for instance, and the steep pitched roof. His first ideas show a severe classical temple in the northern tradition of Neoclassicism; an imposing portico, massively thick walls and a crypt beneath, the building was almost the opposite of the enigmatic lightness and ethereality of the primitive-hut-in-the-woods that was finally realised. However, it was close in feel to Lewerentz's designs for the Chapel of Resurrection, which stands at the far end of the cemetery.

Built three years after the Woodland Chapel, Lewerentz's principal built contribution to the cemetery is a severe and imposing piece of nordic classicism. Its odd, unbalanced form is due to a conflict between the architect and the authorities: the latter had wanted a traditional east-west orientation to the chapel, but the architect had insisted on the entrance as the culmination of the long, drawn-out ceremonial path (the Way of the Seven Wells).

The result is a compromise – a grand portico, visible from far away, heralding the entrance and then a ninety-degree shift in axis on entrance to the long, narrow and very high ceremonial hall. A single window on the wall opposite the entrance illuminates the catafalque; it is an odd, disembodied opening, asymmetrically placed, Michelangelesque in its Mannerist detail and overbearing scale. The sharp white classicism of the building is intended as a direct contrast to the dark green of the woods, a glimpse of a Platonic world of order. The other buildings which make up the grouping consist of a waiting room of semicircular plan and a long colonnade which gives access to the mortuaries. A great affinity with the architectonic language of Plečnik can be seen in this latter structure.

However, the building which has become synonymous with the architecture of death, if indeed not with modern architecture as a whole, is Asplund's crematorium building. Lewerentz was apparently awkward and troublesome to work with and was consequently dropped from the project. Asplund was asked to continue the work at the cemetery without him, although Lewerentz did reappear to continue with a number of landscape interventions.

This break proved the end of the architects' partnership and friendship but Asplund's solo effort was a spectacular success. Despite the modesty of the Woodland Chapel, when the authorities finally raised the money, they funded a real architectural showpiece. There was much propaganda attached to the building: it was seen as an advert for cremation, a paradigm of burial reform, and as an early manifestation of the huge social programme upon which the Swedish state was about to embark. The opportunity was also seized to attempt to shape a new ritual, the creation of an architecture which would foster the development of new forms of celebration and commemoration.

To this end, Asplund's building is composed with a narrative language; the routes are planned and deliberate, each stage as carefully considered as the next. From the entrance to the cemetery, with its semicircular enclosure and the cascade of water set into massive masonry retaining walls, there is an undeniably powerful draw towards the crematorium. A long wall and a wide stone path guide visitors uphill towards the massive granite cross. To one side, the wall (overhung and shaded by trees) shelters the columbaria. The path is decidedly uphill and the looming black cross reinforces the notion of the route as pilgrimage or Calvary.

The great portico of Asplund's crematorium looms into view on approach as the final stage in the long series of buildings, and beyond it only the woods are visible. On the visitor's right is the sequence of small chapels and waiting rooms protected by a continuous stone wall (the extension of the columbaria) in which periodic breaches form the entrances. At the very end of the wall a bizarre clock hangs from a metal stand, a final *memento mori*, a reminder of our finite time on earth. Lars Lerup has compared this view of the building to Giorgio de Chirico's 1914 painting *Gare Montparnasse*.[1] It is a perceptive comparison: in the painting there is a strange uncertainty as to whether the train has been missed by the two shadowy figures or whether they have disembarked. A clock creates the focus of the scene while a building with blind arcades, very similar to Asplund's crematorium, dominates the centre of the picture, and a steep path leads uphill along it in an absurdly exaggerated perspective.

The deep shadows cast by Asplund's building, the oddly cantilevered lamps and clock, and the reflection of the building in the calm water of a pond are all elements that would fit into De Chirico's silently surreal and disturbing world. For the mourners, the ritual journey begins before the great portico; they deviate

from the path into one of the waiting areas and thence to either the small chapels or to the main ceremonial hall, the Chapel of the Holy Cross. As with his earlier Woodland Chapel, there is a discrepancy between the harshly angular exterior and the gentle, embracing curves of the interior space. The focus is again on the central catafalque, beyond which a mural suggests another world through a kind of proscenium arch.

The coffin rests on a catafalque and is lowered into the basement for cremation only once the mourners have left. Although this seems to be a fine gesture with which to complete the ritual, apparently it was too redolent of the idea of a burial from which the original aim was to escape. When the ceremony is finished, a huge glass screen, which stretches the whole length of the main elevation, slides down into the ground and the mourners pour out into the light and the green of the landscape with the view of the hill and the woods beyond. It is a supremely optimistic and pantheistic gesture. The screen is presently not in use and the guests file back the way they came, completely destroying the poetry of the original conception.

Standing under the portico, one looks out on to a cluster of trees atop a steep hill which appears like some great burial mound. The effect is deliberate; the architects tried to create a focus in the landscape, a kind of sacred grove. In-between the crematorium and the hill, another catafalque stands upon a lower mound, surrounded by a ring of lamps. A large paved area allows very well-attended funerals to be held here within the landscape itself, using the mound, the woods and the temple-like portico as a suitably dramatic backdrop. From here the architecture is at its clearest; it is an odd kind of modernism. Asplund had gone from Nordic classicism via the associations of the primitive to functionalism, and with the building of the crematorium, he seems almost to have progressed to post-modernism, all in a couple of decades.

Part of the building's enigma is that it fits easily into histories of Rationalism, functionalism, neo-classicism and monumentalism while anticipating neo-Rationalism and post-modernism. It has also become the building which defines the relationship of modern architecture to death and it remains unsurpassed. But the landscape as a whole, I believe, has fared yet better.

Asplund and Lewerentz's original entry was named *Tallum,* which is a Latin version of the Swedish word for pine-tree, and it exemplifies the mystical-mythological status with which the architects wanted to imbue the scheme from the outset. Their efforts are a culmination of ideas which reach back to the beginnings of the narrative garden in Mannerist Rome and Georgian England and encompass Rousseauesque notions of the primitive, Nordic mythology and archaeology and the modern existential *angst* of Kierkegaard and its resultant northern European Expressionism and Romanticism. These elements are combined to create something truly modern which embraces all the ideas that have slowly and irrevocably made the modern position inevitable. Asplund himself was one of the first to be cremated at the cemetery. He is commemorated with a plaque which reads 'His work lives on'.

Aside from the Woodland Crematorium, Asplund and Lewerentz were also responsible for many other works which have contributed to the formation of a convincing modern architecture of death. Lewerentz's design for a crematory chapel in Helsingborg showed a linear building reached via a long flight of stairs, in which a Hall of Death (dimly lit and oppressive) was followed by a Hall of Life (brightly painted and light) and thence by a courtyard and arcaded columbarium culminating in a Temple of Remembrance. The building described a narrative and cathartic route, echoes of which re-emerged in the various elements of the Woodland Crematorium.

Lewerentz's plans for Malmö Eastern Cemetery also presaged the classical architectural and landscape elements of his later collaboration with Asplund. At Valdemarsvik he created a remarkable chapel with a drawn-out cone roof which seems to anticipate organic architecture, while designs for cemeteries at Forsbacka, Stora Tuna, Kvarnsveden and for the poetically simple Burial Chapel, Enköping, confirmed his position as one of the key European figures working in this oeuvre. In the chapels of St Knut and St Gertrude at Malmö

Eastern Cemetery, Lewerentz created architecture that equalled Asplund's contemporary design for the crematorium, a building in which every detail is considered, deliberate and articulate, and one which is defined and known by its exquisitely simple portico. Asplund was also to return to the genre with designs for crematoria at Kviberg and Skovde but neither attained the status of his work at the Woodland Crematorium.

It is the Woodland Crematorium more than any other complex which continues to function and inspire as the great paradigm of the meeting of mortality and modern architecture. It is dramatic without being theatrical, functional without being overtly functionalist, and about death without being morbid or depressing. The architects succeeded in creating an archetypal landscape which can both encourage and accommodate the formation of the new rituals necessary to accompany the rise of cremation, and yet despite this largely secular impulse, the cemetery and crematorium managed to paradoxically accommodate and embody Christian, pantheistic and social democratic ideals.

We recognise something mysterious in this landscape and in these buildings. John Donne wrote that, 'We have a winding-sheet in our mother's womb which grows with us from our conception . . . for we come to seek a grave'. His implication is that our death is implicit in our being; not imposed from without but growing from a germ within. Heidegger wrote that it is an awareness of death which makes us alive. The Woodland Crematorium seems to eerily awake these visions of death from a source deep within us: somehow we recognise these forms and their significance. The images are disturbing and comforting by turns, but either way they have an undeniable power.

Note
1 Lars Lerup, *Lotus International*, no 38, Electa (Italy), 1983.

JOŽE PLEČNIK
THE CITY OF THE DEAD AND THE GARDEN OF ARCHETYPES

There can be few cities where the influence of a single architect has had such a profound effect on the urban fabric as that of Jože Plečnik on his home town of Ljubljana in Slovenia. His touch and his endless invention can be seen everywhere, his architecture defining the city; from buildings and monuments to handrails and street lamps.

For an example of a city created totally by Plečnik, rather than the series of sophisticated interventions which embody the Slovenian capital, it is necessary to move to the edges of the city to Žale Cemetery (1938-40) where Plečnik created a necropolis to balance the city of the living of which it is the negative. This is one of the few instances of a necropolis realised almost entirely by a single man in a single vision, and it constitutes one of the key funerary masterpieces of the twentieth century.

From his beginnings as one of Otto Wagner's finest acolytes and as one of the most promising and original of the architects associated with the Secession movement, Plečnik did not pursue his career in cosmopolitan Vienna but returned to his Slav roots coming home to Ljubljana via a long and fruitful interlude in Prague. As intensely proud of his homeland as he was fervently religious, Plečnik made it his mission to create a truly Slovenian architecture to celebrate the tiny country's recent independence gained from the Austro-Hungarian Empire at the end of the First World War. To do this he attempted to form an architecture which he saw as timeless, composed of elements which he identified from the local vernacular and the area's ancient classical and Etruscan roots.

The Žale necropolis can be seen as a sketch-book toward this end. The buildings show the architect working through ideas, motifs, archetypes and an approach which is simultaneously religious and humanist, mindful of the intensity of the sacred and the compassion of the detail.

The genesis of the cemetery lies in the edicts of the old Austro–Hungarian Empire which had decreed that the treatment of the dead was to be standardised throughout its territories to conform with central notions of hygiene and the colossal bureaucracy for which the empire was noted. These changes coincided with a period of population growth in Ljubljana and it was decided that the cemetery site on the outskirts of the city was to be provided with a complex which would bring the procedures and handling of the undertaking process into line with the new regulations.

A new building type, the *Leichenhallen* was developed to accommodate the new procedures and it consisted essentially of a single long hall in which the bodies of the dead are placed prior to burial (for a small, modern example of this building type see Heinz Tesar's building on page 214). Severely functional, the single space was divided into public and service access routes and the relatives were able to visit their dead who were laid out on biers in the hall, though there was no privacy and little room. Plečnik's design should be seen partly at least as a reaction to the indignity and impersonality of this building type. His intrinsic humanism, feeling for the sacred and for ritual, and respect for tradition made him question the brutal anonymity of the *Leichenhallen* and formulate a more humane solution which lay somewhere between a city and a garden of the dead.

The complex is entered through an imposing propylaeum, immediately emphasising the importance of the procession, the *cortège*, and of arrival in another world – the world of the dead. As the procession passes through the gate the columns seem to embrace the mourners, drawing them into the garden and on to the main chapel which is situated on the main axis. Instead of receiving the procession through a door placed on this principal axis, a huge Doric column breaks-up the

Žale Cemetery buildings (1938-40), Ljubljana, Jože Plečnik

procession into a series of individuals before access is gained into the chapel behind.

For Plečnik, the single column was more than a Mannerist architectural device, it was a built representation of the human form, a powerful upright exerting its presence, existence and individuality on the landscape. It is the symbol of the lone body being brought into the garden. A catafalque stands before the column with a simple canopy forming an intermediate zone before the finality of the chapel and the forthcoming service. The chapel itself is a remarkable and powerful structure: the walls are dematerialised into a grid of niche-like glazed openings like a great columbarium, and in the centre of each opening in the grid is placed a symbolic cinerary urn so that the light which enters the chapel from outside is filtered through the containers of the dead themselves. The shape of these urns is based on ancient Egyptian ointment jars and thus the architect expresses the timelessness of the ritual: the eternal notion of the journey to the next world.

The chapel is set in a landscape of temples. The garden resembles an archaeological site, an ancient forum where the buildings of different ages have grown together and been rediscovered as a city of the dead. The Pompeiian symbolism of the lost world of the dead (see page 17) is very much in evidence here. Yet this is not folly; it is a symbolic landscape in some ways related to the cemetery of Père-Lachaise in Paris, but without its pomposity and formality, and heavily influenced by Italian cemeteries crowded with tiny temples in a timeless chaos.

Rather, Plečnik's work at Žale is a humane attempt to personalise death. His experiences in Vienna had alienated him from the rigidly impersonal inhumanity of central municipal mortuaries and his response was to create a garden in which small-scale chapels are large enough to hold the closest family only, in which relatives are able to express their grief in private. This was an approximation of the local custom of setting out the dead the night before burial in the family home so that mourners can pay their respects in a private domestic setting. Although the new laws concerning the handling of the dead could not accommodate this custom, Plečnik conceived each chapel as a house, a private space of grief and mourning but each within the broader context of the garden and related to the landscape of trees, shrubs and birdsong as a symbol of paradise and the afterlife.

Fourteen individual chapels were planned for the site. This number corresponds to the Stations of the Cross and allows the separate districts of the city to be allocated a chapel each, leaving a single chapel (designated the Adam and Eve building) for use by the families of atheists, non-Christians, suicides and others normally excluded from the Christian mainstream. By creating a grouping of small individual chapels, Plečnik also achieved a sense of equality in death, opposed to the spirit of the original brief which had called for a distinction in classes and therefore in the treatment of the corpses.

In order to maintain the sacred feel of the central grove the architect placed the functional buildings at the extremities of the site. The offices and mortuary are placed in the wings beside the propylaeum which forms the entrance, and the workshops and ancillary buildings are at the rear of the site. Plečnik's desire for democracy and equality of the parts across the whole site led to each element within the garden being given equal consideration and detail, and the monumental workshop is in fact one of the finest buildings in the whole composition. Its elevations are decorated with panels inlaid with a combination of materials held to be Plečnik's homage to Gottfried Semper's ideas about the origins of the wall as textile covering: the patterns become symbolic draperies protecting the interior world. Above these, a frieze of golden saints on a black background is placed under the dark shadows of the deep, overhanging eaves.

Each of the chapels is a little masterpiece of timeless architecture, blending Plečnik's elements from eccentric architectonic vocabulary into odd, sculptural sepulchres. Perhaps the most successful and enigmatic is the tiny chapel of St John. Like the main chapel, its elevation is defined by a single, centrally placed column, capped with Plečnik's characteristic version of the Ionic capital, however unlike its grander counterpart, the column divides the facade between solid and void. One half of the elevation reveals the deep black recess of the entrance while the other is simply rendered in white, with a simple urn placed against its surface. It is a startling evocation of the coexistence in this place of the worlds of the living and the dead.

This little building has been compared to some of the ideas of René Magritte who similarly used startling juxtapositions of darkness and light, of bizarre objects and physical phenomena to create a dream-like world of subconscious recognition. Magritte was fond of the inclusion of night and day in a single scene (for example, *The Empire of Lights*, 1954, and other paintings on a similar theme), and Plečnik's building seems to do just that. The single column representing man stands on the borders of the two realms of darkness and light.

The profound influence on Plečnik exerted by the ruins of Rome when he was a scholar there, is evident in some of his other chapels. Indeed, his sketchbooks reveal his keen interest in the Roman architecture of death. One of the chapels takes the form of a beehive-shaped tumulus built of rough stone; the most primitive of the chapels yet one of the most evocative, it seems a remnant from a past age and is deliberately overgrown. Another of the tiny buildings has more the feel of a bandstand than a funerary chapel, surrounded as it is by slender columns and topped with a delicately billowing pavilion-style roof. Other examples include a chapel based loosely on a Byzantine model, with horizontally banded stonework, and a chapel which displays a stripped classical form of tall, undecorated arcades in a manner which recalls the blind buildings of De Chirico.

It is worth considering that Plečnik's Žale Cemetery is an exact contemporary of Asplund's Woodland Cemetery in Stockholm. It seems hard to imagine two more different schemes but there are more similarities than a first glance would reveal. Both architects can be seen exploring similar themes: ideas of death and landscape and a re-examination of classical architecture and the national vernacular versions of classical forms on a level deeper than the purely aesthetic or stylistic.

They were also concerned that architecture should provide a dignified setting for those close to the dead; a sympathetic and humanist architecture at all levels from the overall design to the details.

Plečnik devoted much of his time to funerary architecture; his prolific output was crammed with fascinating sepulchral designs. For Plečnik the sepulchre represented a tool for experimentation in sculptural form and architectural language. From the early tombs of his Vienna Secession period to his late designs using an eclectic and eccentric classical vocabulary, the architecture of death remained fertile ground for the Slovene architect. Among his last designs were a reinterpretation of the primitive hut as shelter for a monument to those who died in the Second World War, and another memorial to those same fallen, consisting of a sphere on a cube echoing Goethe's Altar of Good Fortune.

The breadth and the classical architectonic language of Plečnik's work has assured that he has been left out of modernist assessments of twentieth-century architecture but has made him attractive to the postmodernists as a spurious ancestor of a new eclectic classical language in a modern idiom. That Plečnik never intended his work to be ironic in any way must be made clear; he believed that he was using an eternal architectural language embedded in a collective unconscious. It is perhaps his work on memorial architecture that has most fully vindicated his view, and that leaves us one of the most striking architectural legacies of the modern period.

Propylaeum and one of the chapels at Žale Cemetery

TAKEFUMI AIDA

Takefumi Aida's memorials to the dead of the Second World War are among the most powerful of architectural memorials, using the landscape and the setting to define an idea of the connection to the land and the nation for which these people died. The Tokyo Memorial Park (originally 1960, Aida's work dating from 1988) is a scheme which rationalises a series of buildings and memorials which already occupied the site in the centre of Japan's capital city. It serves as a memorial to the 160,000 Tokyo residents who died in the war but also as a monument to the peace which has ensued since then. Its curious site is surrounded by the blocky, modern buildings of downtown Tokyo, the wavy lines and ferris wheel of the funfair and a band of greenery which uncharacteristically wraps itself around this part of the city.

Aida's scheme derives from his ideas on 'fluctuation', a concept which he has appropriated from science, which is concerned with the tiny irregularities that punctuate seemingly stable patterns. He gives the variations in the rhythms of the human pulse or the motion in the flame of a candle as examples of the principle. He sees contemporary architecture settling into a more or less stable pattern, despite the myriad styles and approaches, and the element of fluctuation is introduced into the architectural realm through a series of displacements and 'tremors' (in which he borrows a metaphor from Japan's profound consciousness of the possibility of earthquakes and their dramatic effects on the architectural fabric).

Aida combines the notion of fluctuation with Hans Sedlmayr's observation of the loss of a centre in contemporary architecture and his own idea of Japan as a culture with a 'weak centre', one which is able to adapt easily to Western cultural tradition and as a diverse contemporary culture in itself.

The park is conceived as a public space where the internal spaces are created through extensions of the grids and symmetries which govern the external space so that the whole area, inside and out, is opened up to public participation. A

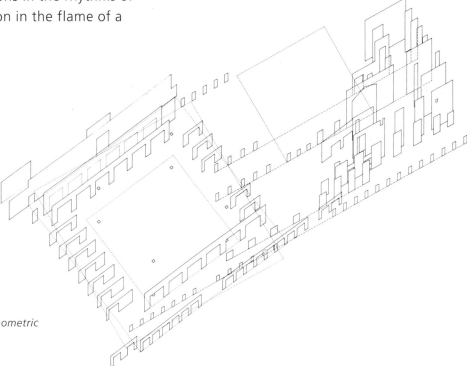

Tokyo Memorial Park, *1988*
OPPOSITE: Exterior views; RIGHT: Axonometric

series of gates and openings refers to the Japanese tradition of *Torii*, the symbolic archways of the precincts of Japanese temples, and creates a narrative landscape representing a journey through various stages. Consequently, the public space is fluid and encourages movement (the sense of movement is further emphasised by the displaced, rotated grids), quite the antithesis of the tradition of the memorial as a single object in space.

The two grids were derived from the siting of two of the original buildings in the park – the crypt and the rest area – and these were extended across the site to emphasise the subtle shifts between them and to create distortions at the junctions where the grids meet. The park area is punctuated by the penetrable gate symbols running parallel to one axis, while the rest area is dotted with fragments of walls that resemble slabs left over from an ancient monument. Aida explains the interior spaces created on the site as simply the addition of roofs and extra walls to these fundamental parts of its organisation.

The open public space itself becomes a theatrical series of stage-sets: the complex geometries create sequences of distorted perspectives and a complicated layering of space. The architect compares this sequence to that of the experience of film, where the director is able to create effects by moving the angle of the camera to transform the vision of space and create a new context.

Aida sums up his ideas as the unification of a series of opposites to achieve a new freedom:

A number of words were in the back of my mind as I designed this project: life and death, regeneration and preservation, stability and instability, permanence and contemporariness, invisible context and clear geometry, closedness and openness, consciousness of the west and things Japanese, architecture and nature. These pairs of ideas need to be united, if we are to free ourselves of fixed notions in architecture. An architecture of fluctuation can help us achieve such a unification.[1]

In the earlier Iwo Jima Memorial (1983), Aida created a similarly intriguing wedding of landscape and architecture. But whereas the Tokyo Memorial Park celebrates complexity and creates an internal order and geometry, the Iwo Jima Memorial relies on severe and formal symmetry to contrast with the grandeur and beauty of the encompassing landscape.

The island of Io, which the Americans named Iwo Jima, was the site of a hard-fought battle during the Second World War. It sits atop a hill with fantastic views to the ocean and to Mount Suribachi, the highest point on the island, which in fact provides the focus for the main axis of the memorial. Along this central spine are placed a podium and an open space for the visitors to the memorial. A pillar at each of the four corners of the podium defines it as a sacred space in reference to the ancient Shinto shrines. The pyramidal caps of the pillars evoke the primal forms of the obelisk or of a grave-marker.

At the centre of this space is a pool with a memorial stone rising from its heart. A channel

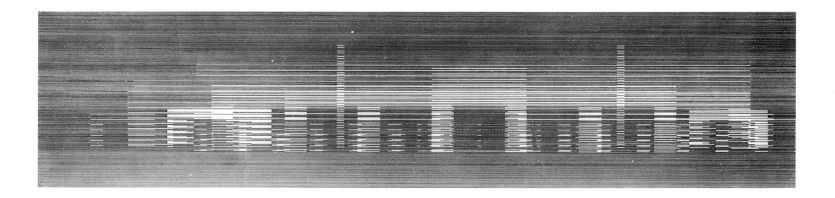

OPPOSITE: Exterior and interior details; ABOVE: Yuragi drawing

cut into the stone paving leads from the memorial through the public spaces which precede it. These are defined as a sequence by two pergolas expressed in oversized, heavy elements, which create frames for the views and the sky above. This is a memorial which focuses almost pantheistically on the landscape; its emphasis is outwards rather than the rigid internalisation of Aida's Tokyo Memorial Park scheme. The water channel culminates in a circular pool which denotes the beginning of the sequence and provides water for a flowering hibiscus.

Aida's most recent funerary work is the new Funeral Hall in Saitama Prefecture. The building's dramatic plan follows a subtle but dynamic curve which wraps itself around two pentagonal ponds at the heart of the structure. One of these ponds is contained within the entrance hall, the pentagonal plan form of which echoes the shape of the pond at its centre; the other lies at one edge of the crematory hall. The rest of the facilities, ritual and administrative, are spread to either side. The slight curve gives a powerful dynamic to the circulation spaces which contrasts with the more restful forms and intimate size of the sacred and ritual rooms.

Note

1 Takefumi Aida, *The Japan Architect* (Japan) 1989, p20.

Iwo Jima Memorial, 1983
OPPOSITE: Memorial in its island setting; ABOVE: Sequence of pergolas; BELOW: Site plan

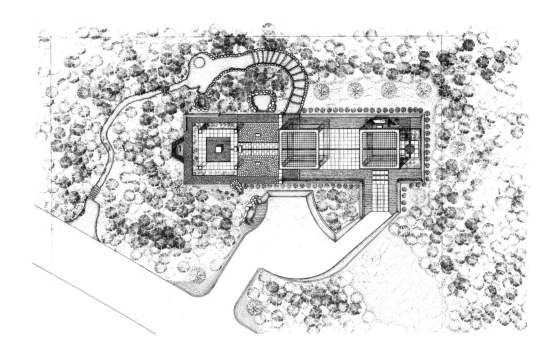

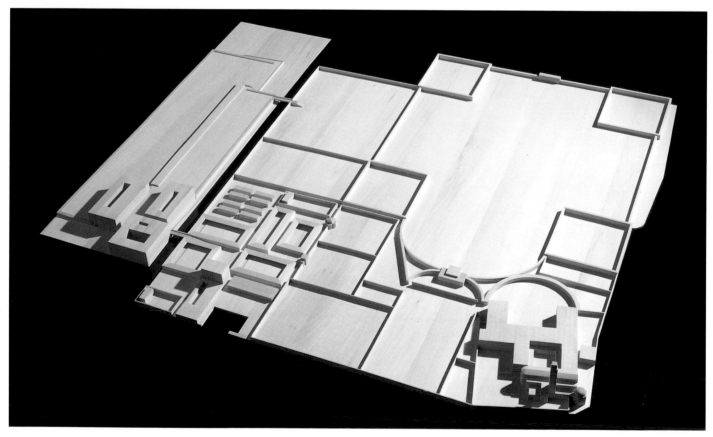

DAVID CHIPPERFIELD ARCHITECTS

The chronic lack of space in Venice encouraged the cities' inhabitants to build a cemetery on a nearby island, and Venice became one of the first major European settlements since the Romans to separate the cities of the living and the dead. The cemetery of San Michele, with its fifteenth-century church, is placed on an island between Venice and Murano but, like most other Italian cemeteries, it is entirely surrounded by a wall so that its spectacular location and views cannot be exploited. Inside the cemetery there is no indication of the proximity to Venice. David Chipperfield Architects' successful entry for an international competition held by Venice City Council in 1998 is based around a proposal which attempts to address exactly this problem.

Two distinct phases are proposed for the cemetery. The first is the building of the crematorium and associated facilities – ossuaries, columbaria and a plot for burials – all of which will be sited on the western corner of the island. The existing cemetery buildings are located on the other side of the same edge of the island so that all the tectonic masses will be distributed along the one

side. The second phase of the design is separated from the main island by a canal, thus reintroducing the surrounding water into the cemetery. It will be linked to the existing island by two bridges. This new section of the cemetery is designed as a series of horizontal planes which build-up towards the north-east of the island where they culminate in a grouping of columbaria which complement the massing of the buildings on the other side of the canal.

The built elements are positioned to create a system of streets and plazas between their volumes to give the scheme a tightly-knit, urban feel, which contrasts with the large terraces of open gardens stretching out towards the south of the island. The blocks are solid and cubic, reminiscent of great medieval palazzos, at once domestic and fortified – the minimal articulation of their facades consisting merely of random open slits between the building blocks, revealing the massive thickness

Cemetery of San Michele, Venice, 1998
OPPOSITE, FROM ABOVE: View of San Michele; model of David Chipperfield Architects' proposal (seen on the left); elevation view of proposal from Venice of whole island; RIGHT: Site plan

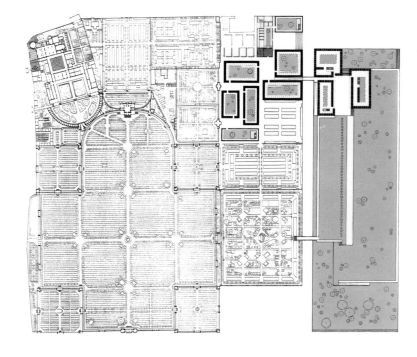

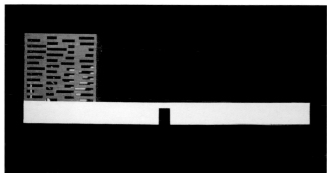

*FROM ABOVE, L TO R: Model interior; elevation; sections;
OPPOSITE, L TO R: Elevation of church; sections through site*

of the walls (which must accommodate tombs) and also affording views to the outside. The mass, the lack of tectonic articulation and the white stone which creates the shell of these buildings, reinforces the idea of an eerily mute city of the dead.

The dense fabric of these tightly arranged blocks gives way to generous expanses of gardens arranged on two lower levels. Chipperfield conceived these gardens as a response, or a critique, of those in the existing cemetery. Whereas the original gardens are formal and insular, closed off from the city they serve, the new gardens are designed to allow reflection on the island's relationship to the city as a separate world related by the omnipresent water. Their organisation is looser and more romantic than the rigidly symmetrical gardens of the old cemetery (perhaps a more English approach to the idea of landscape), and this openness helps to define the compact, urban nature of the built-up area of the island.

The only building which is executed in a colour other than white is the chapel. It stands above the other buildings, the red colour of its blocks raised on a plinth of white which knits it in with the surrounding structures. The structure is simple and striking: light filters in through a series of random gaps in the blockwork courses, creating a dramatic play of sunbeams and dappled patches of light on the interior. Its height and colour mark

the building out as the most sacred block, a special building among the houses of the dead.

Behind the chapel is the business end of the complex, housing the crematorium, workshops and mortuaries. These are served by an existing dock which deals with the traffic arriving on the island. For ceremonial burials, the body arrives with the mourners at the western corner of the scheme, where all are received into a piazza approached by a series of steps leading from the water's edge. The water is allowed to lap up to the edges of the island, to the extent that some of the gardens are expected to flood during high tides in an erosion of the boundaries between the water which is slowly engulfing the city and the island constantly threatened by the fear of becoming another Atlantis.

In this book I have referred to Calvino's *Invisible Cities*. Calvino uses Marco Polo to describe a multitude of exotic and absurd cities which transpire to be allegories of Venice. One of the 'Cities of the Dead' is Adelma, a place where all the faces one sees are reminiscent of friends who have died: 'Perhaps Adelma is the city where you arrive dying and where each man finds again the people he has known. This means I, too, am dead.'

Chipperfield's designs for Venice's new city of the dead evoke this notion of an alternative city, a Venice of the dead which affords mournful views across the water to a city of the living which is sinking under the weight of its own memories.

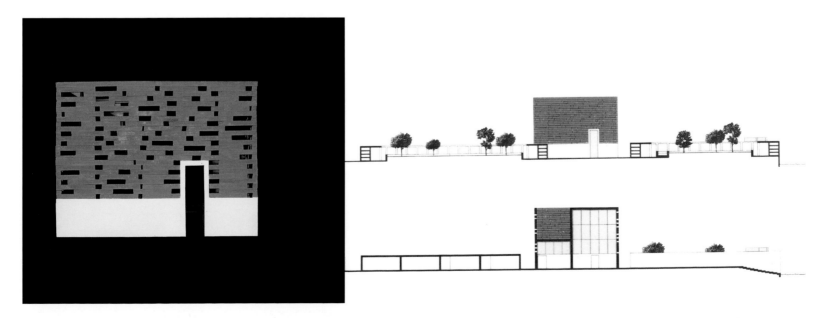

WIM CUYVERS

Wim Cuyvers is fascinated by caves. He has been involved in exploring and mapping uncharted cave systems, together with speleologists, from Spain to the Far East. It is interesting to note that the earth as womb is an image which seems to have existed since the beginning, a fecund mother-god in which the spirits dwell. The sun was thought to set in a cave where it spent the night and in 'The Caves of the Sun', Adrian Bailey argues that almost all mythology is based around these archetypal notions of worship in the cave to invoke the sun to rise again.

The Oracle at Delphi is perhaps the ultimate legend of the supernatural power of the earth to impart knowledge. 'Delphi' is probably derived from the word for vagina and here the sexual aspect of the myth comes to the fore. Caves are associated with an entrance to the womb, with penetration, they are mysterious but equally, erotic spaces. They also have a close affinity with the idea of a subterranean realm of death, a fear of an unknown world of darkness, a world which is a version of hell, a nightmare venue of the after-life.

In architectural terms, the cave is the cellar, the subterranean realm of darkness and the repository of unwanted relics from a half-forgotten past – the subconscious of Freud and Bachelard.

In an excellent essay about Cuyvers, Bart Lootsma points out that the architect works in his basement, a 'labyrinthine space, where daylight hardly penetrates'. It seems that this nether realm exerts a profound pull on the architect's imagination. His work is a fascinating exploration of the themes of death, eroticism, the subconscious and the subterranean.

Cuyvers' grave for his father (1993) consists of two slabs of white stone of different sizes but with the same proportions, arranged like bed and pillow. Between the two slabs, a sheet of glass

has been inserted vertically. This was to enable the architect's children to maintain the illusion that they could peer into the glass and see their grandfather's body, 'To arouse their desire to look at death. To show death'.

His 'Coffin for Donald Judd' (1994–95) is a prospective retrospective addition to the works of the sculptor, the one piece which Judd seemed to have failed to design. Using details, techniques and proportions lifted from Judd's work, Cuyvers designed a timber coffin. The idea of seeing the deceased through glass reappears here in the form of a fully glass lid to the coffin and is compounded by a hole through which the smell of the decaying body is able to escape, allowing the viewer to smell the presence of death as well as to see it.

His installation 'Brothels of Death' at the de Singel Gallery in Antwerp (1995) was a remarkable investigation of eroticism and death: the foyer was brilliantly lit in red while the space was inhabited by a series of ready-made concrete coffin casings (made for use in mausolea). The building exuded a seedy brothel-like glow at night. His 'Lion from Vietnam' simply consists of a souvenir brought home at the time of his father's death; a poignant example of the transformation of object to memorial.

Cuyvers has reinterpreted Loos' dictum about the removal of art. He states, 'Architecture is only art when it emphasises the transition from life to death'. His work is the most complete critique of attitudes to death in terms of waste disposal, robbed of its symbolic and human content.

OPPOSITE, FROM ABOVE: **Grave for George Cuyvers**, Eksel, Belgium, 1993; **Brothels of Death**, de Singel Gallery, Antwerp, 1995; FROM ABOVE: **Coffin for Donald Judd**, 1995; **Lion from Vietnam**, 1993

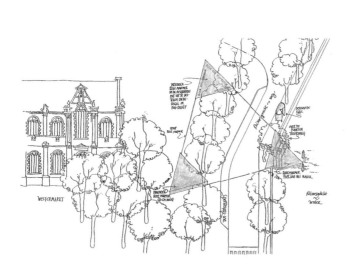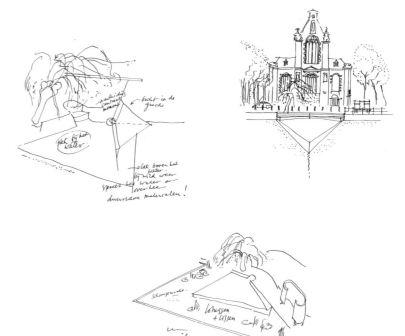

Homomonument, *Amsterdam, 1987*
ABOVE: Monument in context; BELOW: Sketches;
OPPOSITE: Homomonument with Westerkerk in background

KARIN DAAN

The pink triangle which homosexuals were forced to wear in Nazi camps (like the Star of David worn by Jews) became a defining symbol, one worn with pride later as a recognition of the martyrdom of homosexuals persecuted for their sexuality. It has been adopted as a universally recognisable badge of gay pride and its iconic significance is recognised in Karin Daan's competition-winning entry (1981) for a monument to homosexual victims of the Nazi Holocaust in Amsterdam – the Homomonument (1987).

This subtle monument occupies a position which embraces sculpture, architecture, landscape and urbanism, a scope which is only rarely to be found in modern memorials. It consists of a large equilateral triangle outlined on the banks of the Keizersgracht Canal. Its shape is demarcated by pink stone set into the existing paving and the surface of the road. At each of the three corners of the triangle is a smaller triangle. At the point at which the triangle intersects the bank of the canal, the waterway kinks slightly. This change of direction is used as a kind of anchor for the intervention so that the part of the triangle which juts out into the water is seen as a pivotal point around which the canal itself changes its direction. The kink in the quay wall is reflected in a set of angled steps, like a series of internal fractures, leading down to the water's edge and created out of the pink granite which also defines the other corners.

The southernmost corner of the triangle is manifested as a raised plinth which becomes a kind of bench. This is the closest element to the grand Westerkerk that exerts its imposing presence on the surrounding area, a vertical monument with which the subtle horizontality of the Homomonument does not attempt to compete. The third corner is a triangle of marble set flush with the street level, upon which is inscribed the poem *Such an Unlimited Longing for Friendship* by Jacob Israel de Haan.

The monument, and in particular the steps leading down to the water's edge, has become a place of contemplation for the gay population and for gay tourists, a place to pay homage to all those who have been discriminated against and persecuted for their sexuality, and as such it has become a place of wider significance and greater meaning than a memorial to the Holocaust alone. Its lack of bombast or monumentality and the subtlety of its intervention in the urban fabric make it one of the most poignant and satisfying of all urban memorials. Its position close to the Anne Frank House, the ultimate example of a piece of mundane architecture turned into a shrine and memorial through its history of habitation and memory, reinforces the idea of the memorial as a work which takes in a scope wider than homosexual persecution alone and which embraces victims of all forms of intolerance.

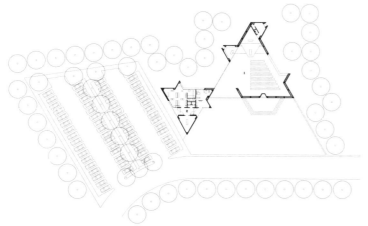

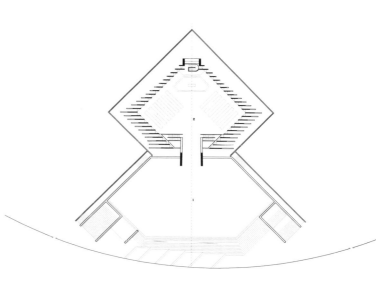

*LEFT: **Montesacro Chapel**; views and plan; RIGHT, AND OPPOSITE: **Chapel of the Assumption**, Fields of Peace Cemetery, Medellin, 1973; views, plan and section*

LAUREANO FORERO

Both the Chapel of the Assumption and the Montesacro Chapel, two cemetery chapels by Colombian architect Laureano Forero, are based around triangular geometries. Forero takes this shape to represent the Trinity, one of the cornerstones of Catholic belief. The interior of the Montesacro Chapel is a pure triangular plan form from which a series of smaller triangles unfolds to house the sacristy, choir and the opening of a window. The triangular geometry is continued in the landscaping and the forms outside, and the entrance is created by a break in the continuity of the wall which breaks down the barriers between exterior and interior. The craggy form created by the swooping roof above the altar echoes the rocky mountains which provide the dramatic backdrop to the cemetery and give the chapel its name.

The Chapel of the Assumption at the Fields of Peace Cemetery (1973), located south of Medellín, is similarly based around a theatrical structure which rises sharply to a point above the altar. The building is entered at its lowest point from a grand plaza which sweeps outwards from the building to embrace the mourners. A dramatic glazed rooflight creates the backbone of the rigidly symmetrical building and ascends from the entrance, creating powerful horizontal and vertical axes. The steel bars which bind the two sides of the structure continue along the length of this rooflight and powerfully evoke the image of Jacob's Ladder, a stairway to the heavens. A series of concrete ribs forms the structure of the chapel, each rib taller than the last; these thin elements give the building a visual lightness, as if it were constructed, like a fan, out of a careful mathematical pattern of regular folds of paper. Between the ribs, glazing increases the brightness of the interior and compounds the visual effect of physical lightness. The focus is laid firmly on the altar, which stands at the apex of the building and behind which a huge full-height window rises to meet the rooflight and provides a view of a slice of the wooded landscape and the blue of the sky.

The interior is sparse, the visual interest provided by the structure itself and the flood of light which streams in from the plethora of glazed openings. To maintain the purity of form outside and within the interior, the ancillary facilities and a smaller chapel are located in the basement. The building is left to stand alone, a powerfully sculptural, symbolic representation of ascent and resurrection amidst the verdant South American landscape.

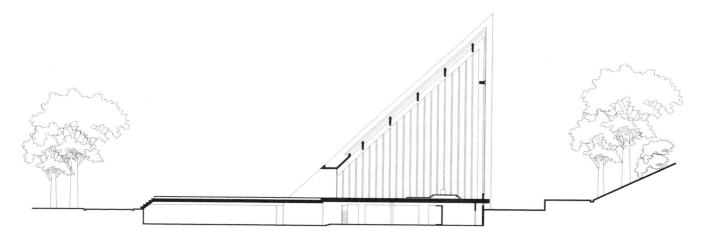

HERMAN HERTZBERGER

On October 4, 1992, Amsterdam's Bijlmermeer estate was hit by one of modern technological society's worst nightmares: a Boeing 747 cargo plane fell out of the sky and crashed into the Groeneveen and Kruiberg apartment buildings. Immediately after the tragedy, the area became the venue for thousands who came to mourn the dead and see the devastation wrought by the crash. The focus for this early, spontaneous grieving was a single tree, positioned very near the epicentre of the crash, which miraculously remained standing. This tree became the symbol of the tragedy: a single, living vertical marker among the destruction, and when it was decided to create a memorial at the site, the tree was naturally to remain the focal point of commemorative activity.

Architectuurstudio Herman Hertzberger was commissioned to create the memorial and it was decided to create a place for grief and commemoration without resorting to the means of a conventional, formal monument. Its location was the site of the ten-storey apartment blocks destroyed by the plane, and the space between them which already functioned as a small urban park. As part of a larger complex of buildings and interconnecting spaces, the site had to be differentiated from the surrounding structures.

The tree remains at the centre of the scheme, surrounded by a mosaic floor which consists of 2,000 individual smaller mosaics made by the local inhabitants, who were profoundly affected by the tragedy. This acted as a kind of cathartic exercise but also, unusually, allowed the local

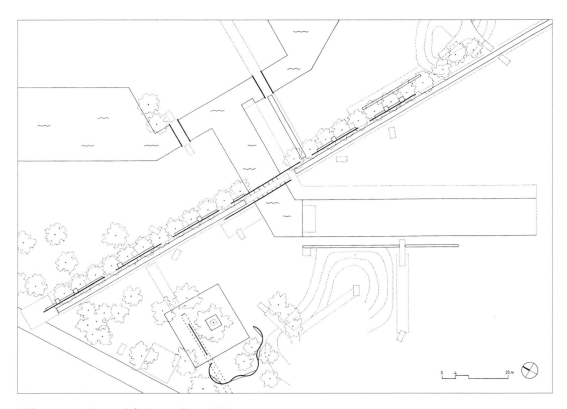

Bijlmermeer Memorial, *Amsterdam, 1993*
OPPOSITE: Wall of Inscriptions and mosaic floor; ABOVE: Site plan

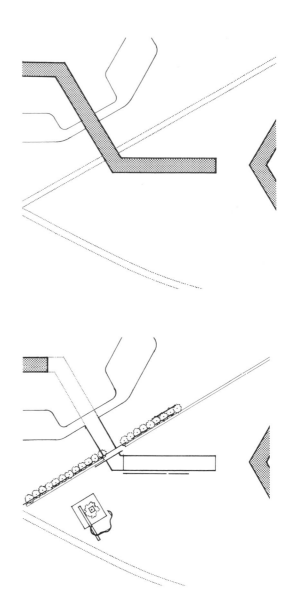

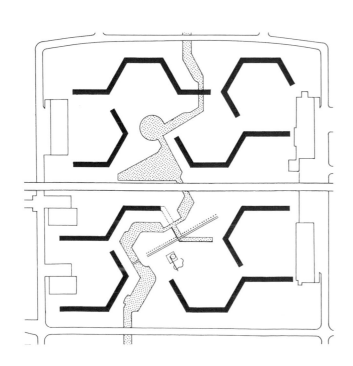

population to participate in the act of creating the permanent memorial and thus, the opportunity to tie the scheme closer into the community and ensure its continued functioning as a place with real meaning.

The tree is also bounded by a glass wall inscribed with the names of the known victims of the tragedy, a text by Herman Hertzberger, information about the events and the comments compiled by individuals as they were making their contributions to the mosaic floor. An organic, undulating wall of seating bounds the far corner of this part of the commemorative area and defines the edge of the memorial. The ghost of the buildings which were destroyed in the crash is demarcated by a wall outlining its original boundaries and an avenue has been created through the site, dramatically cutting through the buildings' original footprint.

OPPOSITE, LEFT AND ABOVE: Wall of Inscriptions and plans; LEFT: Detail of wall; BELOW: Local children with their contributions to the mosaic

OVE HIDEMARK

Rising from the green slopes of a hill, the solid brick mass of Ove Hidemark's Lilla Aska Crematorium and Chapel (1990) in Sweden evokes the image of a fortified monastery. The illusion of defence is reinforced by the building's base, a powerful, battered stylobate which seems to rise like a rocky outcrop from the gentler slope upon which it sits. Like a monastery, it contains an interior world with clearly delineated spaces, each of which has a deliberately defined atmosphere appropriate to its function, and is arranged around a central cloister. But while the monastery may serve as a useful architectural metaphor, Hidemark's fine building belongs firmly to the clear and open world of Swedish protestant tradition and is architecturally close to the work of his illustrious, pragmatic antecedents, particularly to the thoughtful ecclesiastical work of Sigurd Lewerentz.

Like all the best Swedish modernists, Hidemark employs an unassuming architecture in which the quality of space and material is able to create atmosphere without resorting to expressionistic or theatrical devices. The building sits in a landscape which is artificially natural, an idealised version of the local scenery. In addition to embracing the building and shielding it from the intrusion of local roads (achieved by the placement of trees and the creation of woods), the landscape is allowed into the heart of the building where a cloister surrounds a garden which provides greenery year-round and is focused on a

Lilla Aska Crematorium and Chapel, *Sweden, 1990*
OPPOSITE: View of complex from pond; ABOVE: Site plan

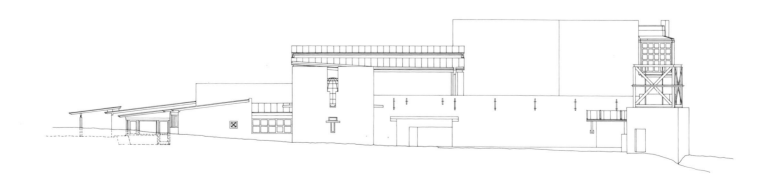

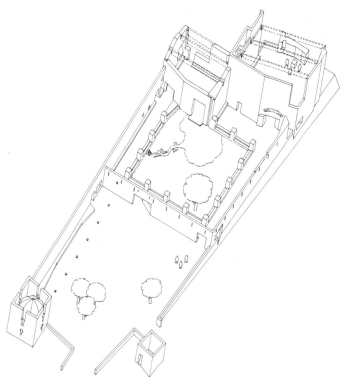

OPPOSITE AND ABOVE: Views of exterior;
BELOW LEFT AND RIGHT: Elevation; axonometric

ABOVE: View of courtyard; OPPOSITE, FROM ABOVE: Chapel of Stillness; Memorial wall; ground-floor plan; first-floor plan

picturesque pond, while the tops of trees are visible beyond the long, low walls.

The building is approached through its landscape setting and the visitor is greeted on one side by a squat open-work bell-tower on a stocky brick base and by the Chapel of Stillness opposite, which embrace the visitor like the hands of two great arms. The Chapel of Stillness terminates a long wall, off which a lean-to roof with broadly overhanging eaves supported on slender timber columns provides a defined route and physical shelter for mourners and for wreaths placed on the wall itself.

Access to the complex is gained at the end of the wall; in this way, the memorial wall itself is penetrated. At this point the building divides roughly into a long block along the north-south axis. This contains the functional aspects of the building and a series of spaces disposed around the cloister which cater to the spiritual and ritual needs of the mourners.

The cloister provides an ambulatory space for contemplation; massive brick piers and timber roof trusses give a deliberately solid, almost Roman feel to the building, offering a restful preparatory space for the services which are conducted in a pair of chapels of considerably different character. The smaller of the two chapels, the Chapel of Hope, is a more internalised,

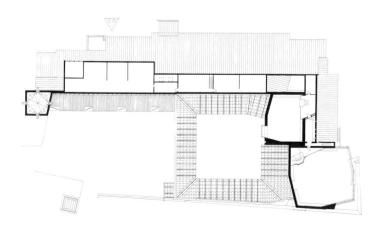

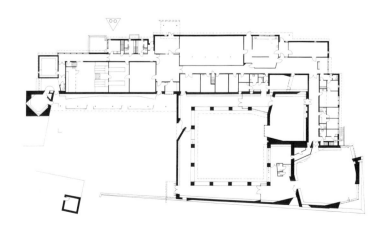

protective space set into the heart of the building, although a large bay window allows a view of the garden within the cloister, and light is reflected back into the chapel from the constantly changing surface of the pool of water outside.

The larger space, the Chapel of Light, forms the north-east corner of the building. A huge, full-height glass curtain-wall allows northern light to flood the interior and encloses one end of the chapel, while the view to the landscape is obscured by a section of curved wall only at a point directly behind the bier to help focus attention on the coffin. A solid horizontal band, which runs across the middle of the glass wall, features an interpretation of the landscape by Par Andersson, whose rendering of a sheltering sky also embellishes the ceiling.

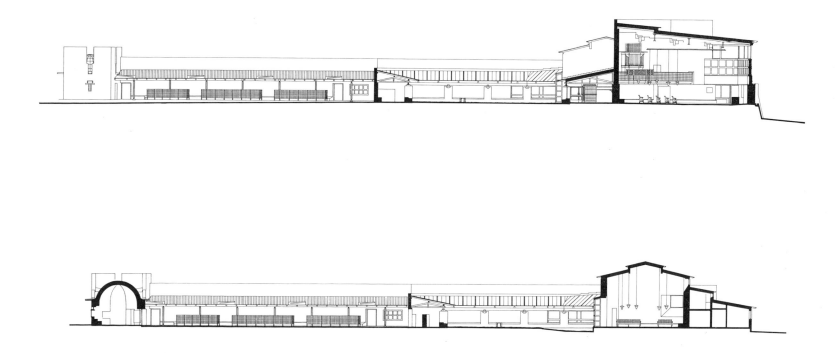

OPPOSITE: Chapel of Light; FROM ABOVE: Interior of chapel; sections

Streaks of marble criss-cross the timber floor to resolve the chapel's subtle asymmetries and angled walls, while an organ gallery helps to counter-balance the powerful pull of the off-centre funeral bier. Both chapels are preceded by ante-rooms which echo the characteristics of their final destinations; the Chapel of Light is preceded by a large, airy waiting-room with large windows on to the courtyard, while the room which gives access to the Chapel of Hope is a more secure and intimate space.

The parts of the building allocated to the pragmatic requirements of the crematorium complex are expressed in a simple, functional architecture and distributed rationally around the structure, serving all sections of the building. This area houses the incinerator, mortuary and all ancillary accommodation. The journey of both the body and the mourners culminates in the point of entry, returning to the tiny Chapel of Stillness. This is where the relatives receive the urn containing the ashes of the deceased – the final destination and a space for an ultimate reflection on the nature of death. It is articulated as a small chapel enclosed by massive, fortress-like walls, but slots in the solid brick surfaces allow a view into the lead-covered dome which surmounts the chapel.

Using the traditional iconography of the vault as the representation of the heavens, this final space is capped with a cupola constructed of brick, as if the earth, rather than the sky, is enclosing the mourner in the way that it will soon enclose the dead. The space is also used for small and intimate funeral services. The solidity and internalised isolation of this last piece of the building fabric is reassuring with its sheltering massiveness. Walls of up to a metre thick, and the robust, traditional brick of the sheltering vault, create a fitting culmination to a solid, austere, yet fundamentally humane building.

The exquisite detailing of the scheme helps to reinforce the innate humanism of Hidemark's architecture and the tradition of Scandinavian modernism to which he belongs. The variety of texture and colour of the brick upon which dance the shadows of pine trees, the grain of the heavy oak doors and windows, and the lead and zinc roofs, create a subtly changing background to the drama of the ritual. The furniture and fittings are every bit as considered and deliberate as the architecture itself: from the external light-fittings which are set into the walls (a necessity for long winter nights), to the waffle-backed benches which accommodate the mourners, the architecture achieves the status of an all-embracing *gesamtkunstwerk*, a building which is about death, but created to alleviate its burden on the living.

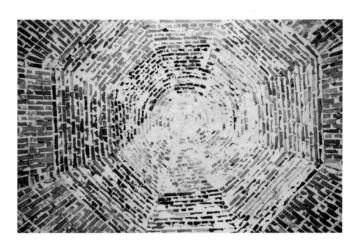

OPPOSITE: Chapel of Hope; ABOVE: Brick vault of dome in Chapel of Stillness

ISHIMOTO

The cities of the living and the cities of the dead feed off each other and influence each other's growth and development. The metropolis needs its places of burial and its memorials to root it to its site, while the necropolis takes the city as its model, the dead dwelling in plots which are bought and sold and arranged in streets and houses. The crematorium represents a departure from the relationship of earth to body; in burning the body is passed into the air.

This transition from the physical to the ethereal necessitates a complex which can take the place of the necropolis or the graveyard for those fleeting moments of cremation. An internalised world is required which accommodates the ritual and the physical needs of the mourners, the pragmatic requirements of the physical process of cremation and proposes a new type of world: one which is both of this realm and affords a glimpse of the next. It must be separate from the realm of the living yet function as a critical adjunct to the city, a functional and spiritual cog in the machine of urban living.

In Japan, cremation was officially encouraged and has become widespread. The growth in cremation required the building of vast crematoria to cater for a number of surrounding towns and cities. They have not only to deal with a substantial volume of traffic and provide a sympathetic setting for the mourners (avoiding the impression of a production line) but also accommodate the complex rituals enshrined in Japanese tradition.

Ishimoto Architectural Engineering Firm Inc has created one of the most impressive funerary complexes of recent years. The building takes the oriental mythical world-view as its inspiration; a reproduction of an Eastern archetype not merely of the city but of the cosmos itself. The Tone complex (completed in 1987) stands in the midst of the paddy fields which embrace the banks of the Tone River. Its monumental scale and low

The Tone Complex, Japan, 1987
OPPOSITE: Main entrance; ABOVE: Exterior

The Tone Complex
*FROM ABOVE: Entrance hall; elevation; OPPOSITE, FROM ABOVE:
First-floor plan; ground-floor plan; ceiling detail; OVERLEAF:
Entrance hall*

walls give the impression of an ancient walled settlement, and the disposition of the elements within the walls further evokes the notion of a self-contained world.

The plan is based around the disc which contains the elements representing the boundaries of the physical world. Within the circle, areas are allocated roles in accordance with an ancient Chinese system of divination in which the four cardinal points of the compass are associated with corresponding divinities. The northernmost point of the scheme (which houses the cremation facilities) is associated with a symbolic zone of darkness, while the other points are allocated to three animistic divinities: a white tiger to the west, a crimson bird to the south, and a blue dragon to the east.

The hugely impressive, cavernous entrance hall is positioned at the southern end of the building and paved in a yellow stone which is taken to represent the world of the living – the present – while the crematory hall further along the central axis at the northern end of the building (the symbolic zone of darkness) is paved in polished

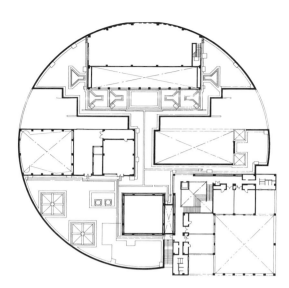

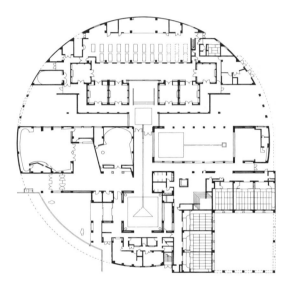

black granite. The ceiling to the entrance hall provides a theatrical focus to the space; its billowing form recalls the roof of Le Corbusier's chapel at Ronchamp and the desired effect is similarly that of a weightless fabric, evoking the lightness of a tent rather than the physical burden of a weighty roof.

The route that connects the entrance and crematory halls governs the circulation to the facilities to either side of the main concourse and is demarcated in a pattern in the stone floor which resembles the watercourses in a courtyard opposite. To the west, are the building's ceremonial halls: related to the mythical white tiger, these spaces are characterised by light-coloured materials and dramatic, expressionistic forms.

To the east of the main concourse lie the waiting rooms and lounge, for which great efforts have been made to achieve lightness and openness. A series of generous circulation spaces and exquisite courtyards eliminates any sense of the claustrophobia which might otherwise have resulted from the spaces in such a dense complex. A water-garden centres on the form of an eye-shaped pool and fountain and provides the view for the lounge through a huge picture window. The space feels almost like a verandah, rather than an enclosed internal room. A square courtyard at the southern end of the building breaks into the fabric of the circular wall and allows views into and out of the complex, creating an intermediate zone. The rooms around this zone are decorated using the blue colour associated with the dragon symbol; these are calm and simple spaces laid

with traditional *tatami* mats and they contrast with the red colour used throughout the administration accommodation which occupies the western part of the complex.

Throughout the scheme it is the combination of natural light and vivid colours which gives the spaces form and character and differentiates their physical and ritual functions. All the ceremonial spaces are illuminated from above and deny their occupants views to the outside world, thus increasing the sense of concentration on the ritual and final communion with the deceased. The 'farewell hall' of the crematory features clerestory lighting. This is further filtered through gauze sheets to ensure an unseen and mystical source of light which is bright but never distracting. The enshrinement rooms and oratories surrounding this main part of the building provide an intimate space for the mourners and the families of the deceased. The details are reminiscent of a blend of Art Deco and of Carlo Scarpa's meticulous work on the Brion tomb, yet also of the absurd, visionary world created by Terry Gilliam in *Brazil* – monumental spaces which look both to visions of the past and the future for their inspiration.

Exactly contemporary with the Tone building is the Sanbu Regional Crematorium (1989). This is a much simpler structure based around a more orthodox plan, but it contains a series of spaces which are easily as poetic and certainly more subtle than those at Tone. The building is organised around a core of gardens and a courtyard in which water features heavily. The source of the main watercourse is a small round pool which bridges

Sanbu Regional Crematorium, Japan, 1989

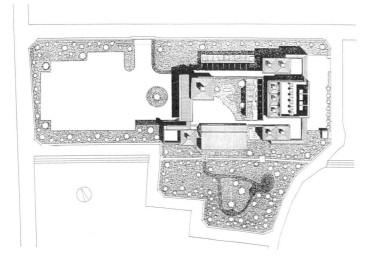

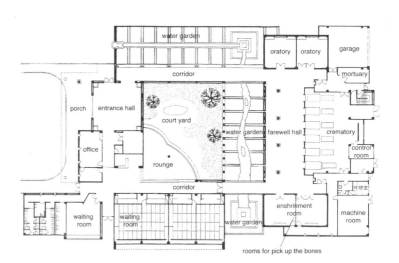

FROM ABOVE, L TO R: Courtyard; site plan; ground-floor plan; OPPOSITE: The Farewell Hall

the realms of the exterior and the interior, and is seen through a gap in the thick wall surrounding the garden. The wall is suspended above in a gravity-defying act of architectural bravura.

The watercourse culminates in another pool, this time of square form, from whence it changes direction and becomes a meandering brook that traces its pattern through the far end of the courtyard, demarcating the business end of the operation – the grand hall of the crematory. The building's entrance hall opens from the shelter afforded by the deep eaves and reveals the garden at the centre of the structure placed diametrically opposite the entrance. Another spectacular concrete roof crowns the entrance hall and seems

to suck the soul up towards the sky (a metaphor for the smoke which rises into the sky during the cremation); it reveals itself through the light from an aperture at its centre. Here, too, the roof is elevated so that light can penetrate beneath, creating an eerily light effect in what is evidently a heavy concrete structure.

The courtyard facing the entrance space at the heart of the building acts as a cloistered garden. Glazed corridors provide circulation space around its circumference while it also functions as a mediator between the waiting rooms and the ceremonial parts of the complex. The cloud-like lines of the lounge intervene in the square walls of the courtyard to create a soft, billowing space

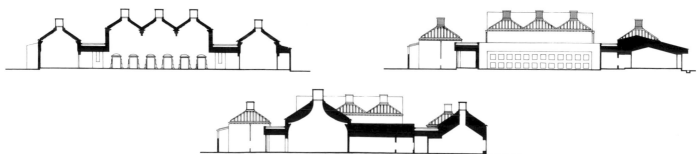

which responds to the flowing curves of the stream facing it across the open space.

In the same way as the Tone building, the large 'farewell hall' of the crematorium contrasts with the modest simplicity of the waiting rooms. This grand space culminates in a series of doors leading to the individual burners. Tall narrow windows afford views over the water-garden and cast dramatic streaks of light across the polished stone floor of the hall. The space leaps up in height as it approaches its final stage, a row of columns dividing the single- from the double-height space. Stepped, pyramidal ceilings extend the space into the infinity of the sky as they culminate in a lantern at the apex. Similar ziggurat-like ceilings crown the enshrinement rooms and highlight these as the spaces in which the ritual reaches its climax.

The enshrinement rooms accommodate the traditional ceremony of transferral of the remains to a box – what is left of the bones after cremation is passed between the mourners via chopsticks and finally encased. Again, the fine concrete work which creates the stepped surfaces of the walls and ceilings recalls the work of Carlo Scarpa; the inspiration for these rooms may well have been the interior of the chapel at the Brion cemetery.

OPPOSITE, FROM ABOVE: Ceiling detail; elevations; ABOVE: Interior details

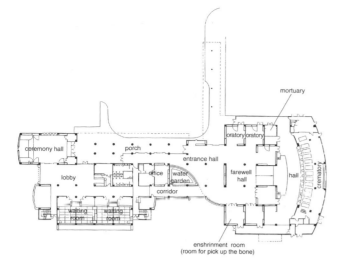

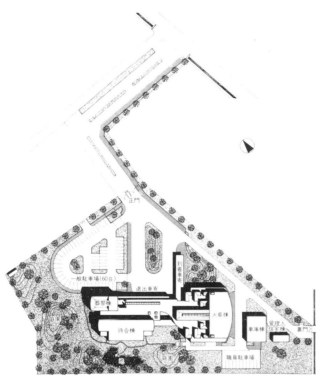

Ishimoto's other significant crematorium is the complex at Urawa (completed in 1980). The building follows a similar arrangement to those of the later schemes, in that a long, ceremonial route from the waiting rooms incorporates the ceremonial hall and culminates in a grand, well-appointed crematory and 'farewell hall'. The waiting rooms are simple, elegant spaces employing traditional Japanese joinery and translucent screens. In contrast, the 'farewell hall' and crematory are finished in lavish, gleaming marble. The culmination of the building occurs in the curved wall of the crematory itself, where the entrances to the individual burners are visible as a long bank of doors along a wall which curves and wraps around the communal space.

Ishimoto's contribution to a modern architecture of death is one of the most comprehensive and fascinating in the oeuvre. His work is imbued with a consistency and quality of space and light which illuminates the physical, spiritual and ritual processes of the celebration of death and is both extraordinary and rewarding.

Urawa Crematorium, *Japan, 1980*
*FROM ABOVE: Ground-floor plan; site plan;
Farewell Hall; OPPOSITE: Entrance hall*

FOR NURIA   ARATA ISOZAKI '93

TOMB OF GIGI   ARATA ISOZAKI '93

Luigi Nono Memorial, *San Michele, Venice, 1993*

ARATA ISOZAKI

At the time of his death, Italian composer Luigi Nono had been discussing a collaboration with Arata Isozaki in which he would compose a piece of music to which Isozaki would create a specific architectural setting: a coming together of space, sound and performance. Nono died before the collaboration could come to fruition and his widow Nuria (daughter of Arnold Schoenberg) asked Isozaki to design his memorial on Venice's cemetery island, San Michele.

The resulting memorial is without doubt the simplest work featured in this book, but also one of the most eloquent. By reducing the idea of the plot and the gravestone to its most elemental, Isozaki blends the Zen tradition of the stone as object of beauty and catalyst of contemplation with the orthogonal, rectangular bed of the tomb, unmistakable in its rigidity as a burial plot, a piece of land demarcated for burial defined by the frame of granite which surrounds it. The stone is a simple piece of basalt from the Pyrenees which Isozaki picked out from the Vicenza quarry. The bed is now draped with ivy.

If Adolf Loos' tombstone in Vienna represents the ultimate in architectural simplicity; a simple block inscribed with the architect's name but finished into a cube and placed on a plinth so as not to appear unfinished, then Nono's gravestone appears as a marker of a life which was ended prematurely; as if the stone has yet to be carved but is at the same time perfectly eloquent in its rawness. The blend of Eastern and Western aesthetic tradition, where one adds extra meaning to the other is seen here at its zenith.

The notion of the cross-fertilisation of the two traditions also provided the starting point for Isozaki's designs for the tomb of Don Francisco Otomo Sorin (not illustrated). Sorin (1530–87) had been a Lord of Japan's Bungo region and died as a Christian. His memory was honoured by a Buddhist-style grave, which was erected some time after his death, but recently, as part of an effort to commemorate the history of Christianity in Japan's Ohita Prefecture, a reconstruction of Sorin's grave was proposed. Isozaki took the form of the vaulted sarcophagus as his inspiration for the tomb's centre-piece. A curved stone screen forms its backdrop and carves into the sloping earth of the hill behind the tomb. Isozaki rounds off his own description of the tomb with the words:

I can imagine that the vaulted roof made Japanese Christians envision Europe, the distant centre of their faith. In a sense, we are still practising the same imagining; a form embodies sympathy between distant places, distant cultures.

(Translated by Sabu Kohso)

CHRISTIAN KEREZ

The simple, elegant form of Christian Kerez's tiny mortuary chapel in Bonaduz, Switzerland (1992–93), suggests the most archetypal of tombs, the tumulus or Loos' beloved, simple burial mound in the forest. Its presence is denoted only by the oval form of the glazed lantern which protrudes above the surface of the small hillock in which the structure nestles. As work progressed on the excavation of the site, a round burial pit dating from the Ice Age was uncovered, as if to give legitimacy to this reinterpretation of the most primitive and yet most suggestive form of building. Kerez asserts that the building was designed to be free of associations and orthodox systems of symbol and meaning, but he is pleased that the locals react by imbuing it with their own interpretation of its form and the many layers of meaning they seem to detect within it.

The building serves the function for the mainly Catholic community of the domestic room where the body was laid out for three days before commitment to the ground. It provides a space for the mourners to pay their respects to the deceased alone, in complete privacy and seclusion, and it serves as the gathering space for the mourners as the body undertakes its final journey to the grave. Kerez was clear in his intentions to create a space of contemplation and of proximity to the body and to death, in which to confront the finality of death.

The only influence from the outside is sunlight, which is diffused through the glass blocks of the lantern, evenly spread throughout the tiny room

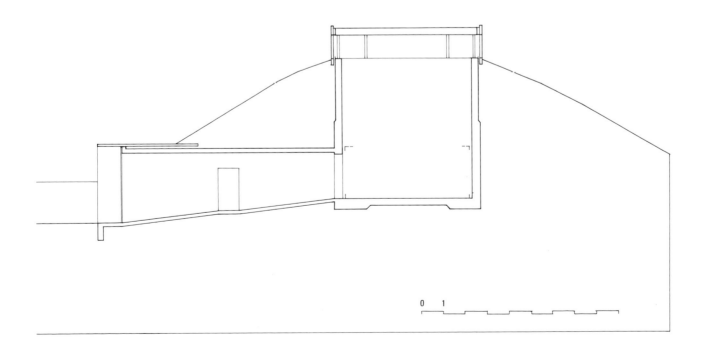

Mortuary Chapel, *Bonaduz, Switzerland, 1993*
OPPOSITE: Entrance; ABOVE: Section

rather than providing a specific directionality. In fact, the inspiration for the space was the white card screens which photographers place in a subtle curve behind their subjects to give the impression of an infinite space and a neutral background that cannot detract from the object on display; here that object is very clearly the body.

Perhaps the photograph which shows the most is that which superficially describes the least. The white of the wall, the barely discernible junction of the floor wall and the sharp band of light give mystical form to a room which seems to fade at the edges, to suggest a bleed to infinity. The bodies are laid out in the two *Totenraum* (rooms of the dead) which are subdivided from the main hall by the simplest of folding doors. Each room contains a funeral bier and a curved bench. Light descends through a circular hole in the ceiling, providing the space with natural illumination.

The building is entered through the side of the mound, via a long, narrow corridor suggesting the form of the *dromos*. The door is pierced with a pattern of vertical slits, within which the shape of a cross can be made out. Kerez notes that the corridor rises from the outside to the main space and that this ascent was a deliberate attempt to offset the notion of descent into some kind of

FROM ABOVE: Exterior; construction site; sketches; OPPOSITE FROM ABOVE: Chapel in context

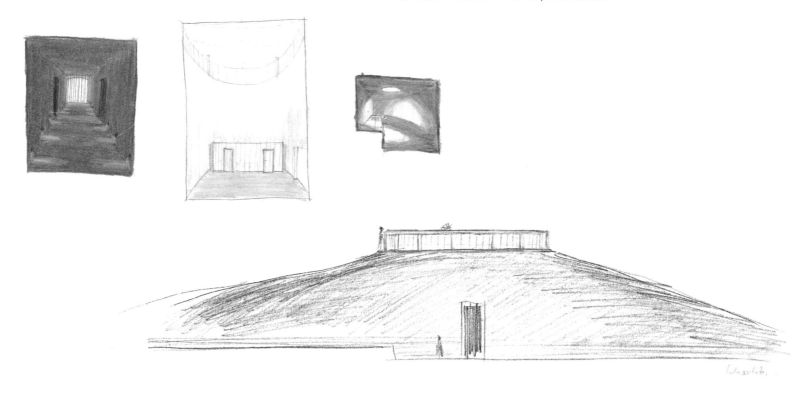

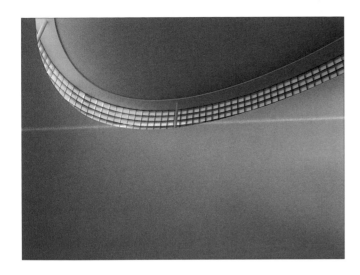

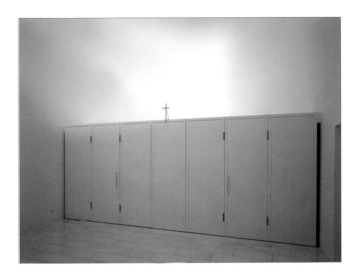

OPPOSITE AND ABOVE: Interior details; BELOW: Plan

subterranean world. Thus, the visitor experiences an ascent towards the diffused light which filters into the corridor through translucent glass doors.

The oval shape of the main space itself is also part of a conscious process of denying the obvious associations of the building's underground siting and a way of avoiding a feeling of claustrophobia. The original sketches had shown a rectangular space but the architect felt that this would have been too reminiscent of the form of a freshly dug grave. To me, the soft, organic nature of the oval with its indeterminate light and its unadorned walls, the sense of security and enclosure, seem to powerfully suggest the womb, a return to the earth, which in turn suggests an almost pantheistic interpretation of the structure.

The photographs of the construction seem to be the most fundamental illustrations of the scheme, clearly indicating the relationship with the land and surrounding landscape. Most architectural photographs address the final product rather than the process, yet here these pictures help to reveal the nature of the structure. The earth was soft and yielding so that heavy equipment or explosives were not necessary; the hole becomes a negative image of the building with which it will ultimately be filled. The new building was inserted into the landscape so that the physical shape of the ground is little changed but its meaning is altered. It occupies a space at the

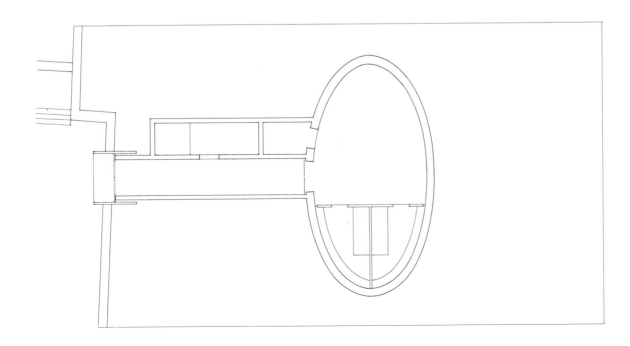

heart of the village between the kindergarten, the school and the church, completing the cycle of life from childhood through ritual to death.

It seems that many settlements were built around burial sites; to bury one's dead is to grow spiritual and physical roots into the landscape, it sacralises the land and provides the reason for choosing one site over another, particularly in the many cultures which thrived on forms of ancestor worship. In this simple, elemental design Christian Kerez has, retrospectively, provided the Swiss village of Bonaduz with a heart which is able to speak a language of the universal symbolism of ascent and descent, burial and resurrection, and the paradox of infinity contained within this tiny temple of death in the Alpine earth.

OPPOSITE AND RIGHT: Interior details; BELOW: Sections

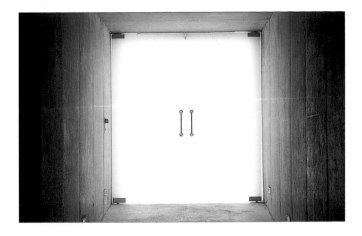

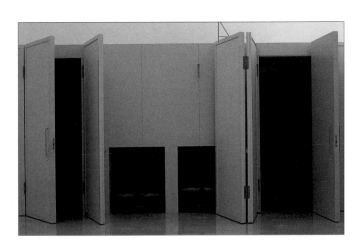

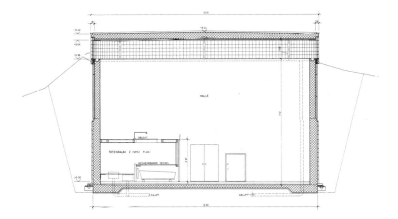

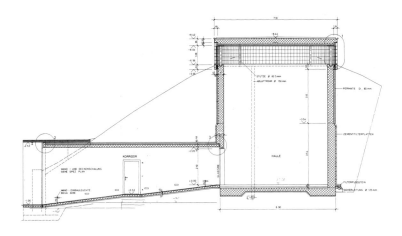

ABOVE AND OPPOSITE LEFT: **Pula Mortuary Chapel**, Hungary, 1993, exterior and cutaway axonometric; BELOW AND OPPOSITE RIGHT: **Vigandpetend Mortuary Chapel**, Hungary, 1993 (design), exterior and plan

ANDRÁS KRIZSÁN

The rise of organic architecture in Hungary has been a remarkable success. Imre Makovecz was among the first to bring this new Hungarian variant to the fore and has been the most successful and internationally recognised of its exponents. Subsequently, it has become a varied and dynamic force in contemporary European architecture exerting an influence beyond the confines of that small country.

Among the younger architects working in this genre is András Krizsán of the Kör office. Like Makovecz, he has made a considerable contribution to the architecture of death with a number of small but striking schemes. Designed for tiny villages in rural Hungary, these buildings are constructed on minuscule budgets yet the architect manages to engender a sense of permanence and gradual growth from the landscape.

The first of Krizsán's mortuary chapels was erected in Pula in 1993. The building is formed around a kind of centrifugal force generated by the powerful squat tower which announces the chapel's presence. A great swooping roof spins off the side of the tower and creates a sheltered

transitional space below, where mourners can rest on carved timber seating.

The interior incorporates parts of an existing structure. It is unassuming, with only the curve of the roof ridge indicating the wilful presence of the architect's hand. The setting also plays a critical role in defining the final place of the coffin before it becomes one with the earth; there is the hint of a fragment of a once powerful, ruined bastion revealed within the greenery of the woods.

The conception of the Vigandpetend Mortuary Chapel is very similar, but more clear. The tower once again generates the plan, drawing the visitor into the deep shade of the porch like a secret entrance to the realm of darkness of the woods beyond, which can be glimpsed through columns. The building is exquisitely simple; only a single space, a perfect circle inside the tower, forms the ritual hall. Illuminated by candles, this is a space of contemplation, the circle and the darkness implying infinity and the renewal of the cycle. On exit, the first view is of the single rubble column, used as Plečnik had done as a symbol of humankind, set against the horizontality of the landscape.

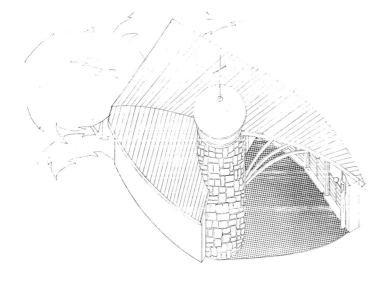

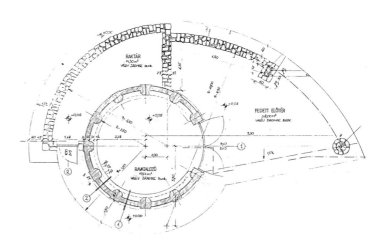

DENNIS LAU AND NG CHEN MAN

There is a poetic appropriateness in the island of high-density living producing a high-rise, high-density building to house the dead. Yet despite the architectural innovation of the placing of ten levels of columbarium, one on top of the other, architects Dennis Lau and Ng Chen Man have in their Tsuen Wan Columbarium (1987) managed to respect local customs and are working within the traditional terracing system which can already be seen elsewhere in the Chinese Cemetery (Kowloon, Hong Kong) in which this structure stands.

The terraces, which are usually staggered into the side of a hill, are simply placed on top of each other. The lack of visible structure means that the cantilevered levels appear as pure horizontal elements while the hanging greenery cascading over their sides further evokes the idea of the hill terrace. At the same time, the building's vaguely pyramidal form represents an interpretation of the sacred mountain, an echo of the hill into which the cemetery is set.

The close-knit relationships of Chinese families are maintained even after death, so it was important for the architects to design a place which satisfied the physical and spiritual needs of the living as well as the dead. The lower levels house a series of 36 family niche rooms which can hold almost 2,000 sets of ashes. Each niche also has a compartment for the storage of ancestral records, so the place becomes a repository of history and memory.

The upper seven levels of the building contain the ordinary niches and are able to store more than 26,000 further sets of ashes, an economic and functional solution to the problem of finding space for remembrance on an island where the authorities encourage cremation precisely because of its space-saving implications.

Despite the building's modern aesthetic, Lau and Chen Man have incorporated many traditional elements and used Chinese architectural symbolism to inform the plan and organisation. The entrance is guarded by a pair of sculpted stone creatures known as 'Chasers of Evil'. These sentinels are composed of the head of a dragon, the wings of a phoenix, the body of a lion and tail of a tiger.

Their totemic presence both guards the portal against evil spirits and represents a mythical world of resurrection and rebirth.

The arch of the portal itself is intended as a modern reinterpretation of the arches which stand at the entrances to traditional Chinese cemeteries, while the red and white colour scheme and the repetitive motif of the square also refer to Chinese traditions.

The entrance reveals a central space around which the building is organised. This takes the form of a six-storey atrium illuminated from above; this well-lit and ventilated space represents a deliberate attempt to move away from the darkness and gloom associated with columbaria and places of death. To compound this image of peace and serenity, the walls of the atrium are adorned with a pair of huge stone murals that depict 'The World of Perfect Happiness' in forms taken from a well-known Chinese tapestry.

Tsuen Wan Columbarium, *Kowloon, Hong Kong, 1987*
OPPOSITE, L TO R: 'Chaser of Evil'; atrium with 'The World of Perfect Happiness' mural; interior detail; ABOVE: Exterior

MAYA LIN

Washington DC is the whitest city I have ever seen. The bright summer sunshine creates an almost blinding glare along its showpiece concourse, the Mall. It is a city of memorials and a city which is itself a memorial to its eponymous American hero and the ideals of the revolution he led. The black stone of Maya Lin's Vietnam Veterans' Memorial sticks out like a scar in the gleaming white fabric of monument city. While the city's other great monuments aim to be prominent landmarks, the Vietnam Memorial is a discreet gash in the landscape: barely visible on approach, all that one sees is crowds to either side, descending into and emerging from the ground. It only becomes clear later that the memorial is sunken into the earth, a single great retaining wall faced with the names of the thousands who died in the conflict.

The Vietnam war became the most intensely unpopular war in US history. It produced no tangible benefits to either side and created a generation of disenchanted conscripts who had fought a brutal war in a far-away jungle and who returned to be received with apathy and even condemnation. The physical and emotional scars inflicted by the war run deep in American culture and have never been exorcised; the stream of films, books and images which continue to be inspired by the experience attests to the impact of the war on what had been the world's most confident power. The memorial is an eloquent expression of the sense of loss and of a deep and profound emptiness which was felt throughout the country at the end of what was seen to be a pointless war.

Like many of the great memorials to those who died in the First World War, the Vietnam Memorial is covered with the names of the fallen and the missing. Unlike those earlier memorials, little more meets the eye apart from the names and the stone surface upon which they are inscribed. Lin has written of her intention to create a monument out of the seemingly infinite list of names so that the overwhelming numbers melt into a single entity, a fleeting impression of the scale of loss. Although the memorial may resemble a huge negative page of text, as a work of reference it has little value and, in fact, has to be accompanied by a series of books to help people find the names of friends and relatives, since the names appear not in alphabetical order but in the order in which their deaths were recorded. Thus the memorial becomes a chronological journey through the now semi-mythical time of the war, measured in units of human life.

When one looks at the memorial there is the curious effect of the high polish of the stone: the reflection of the onlooker is superimposed on the list of names which appear like tattoos on the reflection, as if inscribed on to one's very being.

As much as the memorial is a kind of anti-monument, it is also linked intimately to the network of memorials which describe the physical shape of the city. The Washington Monument, a towering white obelisk, a memorial to clear and precise ideals, can be seen as the diametric opposite of Lin's creation. It is wholly appropriate then that Lin oriented the Vietnam Memorial on the lines which had already been set out by the designers of the Washington and Lincoln Monuments; it is from these that the angles derive.

The new memorial forms both a continuum with the existing keystones of the city's man-made topography and an irreparable break in their fabric and clear-cut idealism. The architects for the Vietnam Memorial, Cooper Lecky, are also responsible for the nearby Korean War Memorial (1995) which builds on the power of the memorial wall.

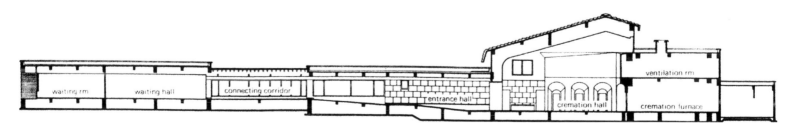

Hirosaki Funeral Hall, *Honshu, Japan, 1984*
FROM ABOVE: Exterior and interior details; section; OPPOSITE: Site plan

KUNIO MAEKAWA

In the shadow of Mount Osore ('fearful mountain') at the northern end of the main Japanese Island of Honshu, Kunio Maekawa's new Hirosaki Funeral Hall (1984) is built into the landscape in a deliberate attempt to suggest the notion of the body returning to the earth.

The long, low eaves of the building provide shelter from the harsh climate and draw the mourners into the embrace of the building. The entrance canopy occurs at the junction of the building's two blocks and its broad, shallow pitch unites the elements of the plan. At the northern end of the site stands the cremation block, which is based around a square plan and built into the side of the hill. The cremation hall is positioned as a diagonal ribbon of space which cuts across the square plan and seems to echo the contours of the hill behind, while the furnace and machine rooms are actually placed in the slope of the richly wooded hillside, suggesting the form of a cave in the rocks.

The form of the space was determined by an attempt to accommodate local custom and ritual: it was customary for the mourners to be near the dead as they were cremated and to place a bowl of water by the furnace during the cremation to maintain a balance between fire and water. The proximity of the cremation hall and the incinerators also ensures the continuation of this ritual.

The building's other wing, at the southern end of the site, contains the waiting rooms and is connected to the rest of the structure via a glazed corridor. The views from this corridor reveal a pair of carefully contrived rock gardens in the sparse Zen tradition. To one side, is the building's forecourt and terrace, while to the other the fecund swelling of the earth echoes the hilly landscape behind, in which the woods are visible further up the slope.

The funeral hall was planned to be visible from the approach road from the city, where it would be perceived instantly as a generous, sheltering roof. It is reached by a road along which stand the thirty-three historic Chousho-Ji Zen temples and rows of cedar trees. Placed between cedar woods on the slopes above it, with the snow-capped mountain above the tree-tops and an orchard forming the foreground, this is one of the most manifestly pantheistic crematorium buildings of recent years. It complies exquisitely with Frank Lloyd Wright's assertion that a building should love the building upon which it stands.

Kaze-no-Oka Crematorium, *Nakatsu, Japan, 1997*
ABOVE AND OPPOSITE: Carved Walkway; concept sketches

FUMIHIKO MAKI

The site of Fumihiko Maki's Kaze-no-Oka crematorium (1997) in Nakatsu City, southern Japan, has historically been connected with rituals of death, as attested by the discovery of third-century burial mounds recently discovered there. The new scheme for a crematorium incorporates an existing cemetery in a public park. The whole site is named Kaze-no-Oka ('hill of the winds').

Approaching the crematorium, the visitor is struck by the impression that it is being swallowed up by the earth around it. The elements form a curious landscape of disparate, seemingly crooked fragments, partially buried in the landscape. It subsequently becomes clear that these fragments are the individual elements which collectively form the crematorium, each distinct in character, use of form, materials and, in particular, an impeccably controlled and subtle use of natural light.

The complex consists essentially of three loosely connected but separate buildings; a funeral hall which accommodates vigils and funeral services, the crematorium itself, which is the fundamental ritual space of the actual cremation and its rites, and finally a waiting area. Between the crematorium and the funeral hall sit the ancillary accommodation and circulation spaces, deliberately planned to enhance an appreciation of the ritual meaning of the individual spaces and laid out in such a way as to create a change of atmosphere, view and light in transit between the stages of the journey.

A long, covered walkway greets the visitor on arrival at the building's *porte-cochère*; walled on one side and facing a garden on the other, it leads into a bare entry porch, its emptiness somehow emphasised by its stark, fair-faced concrete surfaces

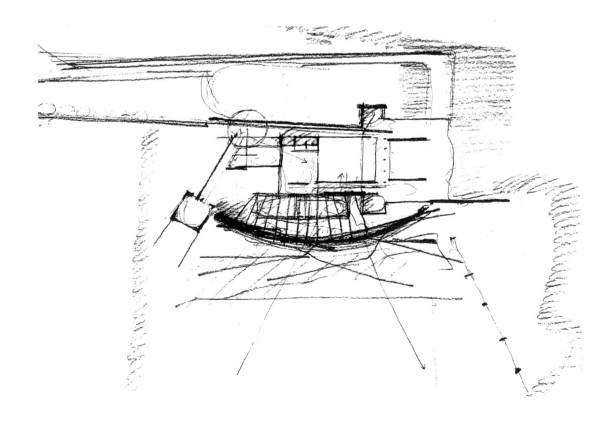

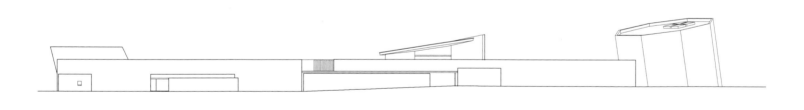

and the single light which is admitted through an opening in the ceiling. This space precedes the next phase of the journey, the entry to one of a pair of intimate oratories, each lit by a clerestory on one side which lets in only indirect light, conveying the effect of a mournful, twilight world. Each oratory is centred on a simple funeral bier of a single block to support the coffin. It is in these spaces that the farewell ceremony begins.

From here, the journey and the ceremony continue in the crematory hall which houses the incinerator. One side of the hall opens out on to a courtyard containing a pool; the water reflects the motion of the clouds above and creates a constant sensation of subtle movements with its rippling surface. This reduces the claustrophobia of the space and allows the mourner to remain aware of the outside world while firmly within the confines of the building.

While the body is incinerated, mourners walk along a sloping corridor to a waiting area overlooking the surrounding garden. This is a freer space, the forms are less claustrophobic and intense, and the increasing softness is underlined by the timber finish defining the interior as a warmer, more comforting space. Visitors then travel to an enshrinement room where the bones and the ashes of the deceased are ceremonially handed over to the family and encased. In this room, as in the oratories, the light is indirect – filtered from above through louvres – while the space itself is hauntingly bare and empty.

The final phase of the ritual passage takes place at the funeral hall. Here, startlingly skewed walls enclose the space in an octagonal plan form, perhaps deliberately reminiscent of the traditional baptistery shape to emphasise the finality. The walls slope towards the entrance,

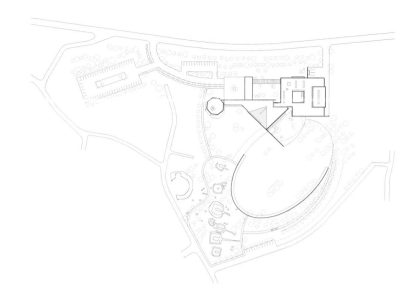

OPPOSITE, FROM ABOVE: View of exterior; elevations; FROM ABOVE: Site plan; courtyard; waiting area; OVERLEAF: Funeral hall

and according to the architect they 'seem to collapse toward the visitor', creating a dynamism which is compounded by the disturbed symmetry of the space and the asymmetry of the lighting. This comes both from above and from the side, where it is reflected into an opening low down in the wall from an adjacent pool. The four circular roof-lights seem to emphasise the notion of ascent from this space to the heavens, and it is here that the mourners make an offering of incense to the dead.

The layout of the scheme suggests the internalised world of the monastery. The elements are tied together by a series of walkways which evoke cloisters, looking on one side towards gardens, but the buildings themselves generally have no conventional windows to afford views of the outside world. This not only reinforces the powerful effect of the internal geometries and the perception of the buildings as abstract sculpture in a landscape of death, but also creates an internal language and referential system. The multitude of effects and moods created by light is particularly striking, and it is the strange quality of light which gives the building its exquisite ethereality and shapes the complex and thoughtful exploration of the architecture of death in a profound way.

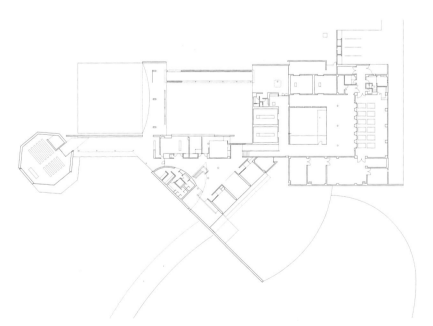

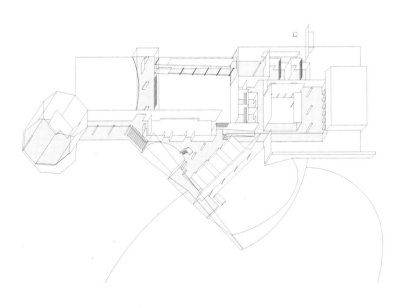

OPPOSITE: Enshrinement room; FROM ABOVE, L TO R: Interior details; plan; cutaway axonometric

Farkasrét Mortuary Chapel, *Budapest, 1975*
Interior of chapel with sculpture of the Tree of Life (by Gábor Mezei)

IMRE MAKOVECZ

Imre Makovecz's Farkasrét mortuary chapel in Budapest, Hungary (1975) is conceived as a huge ribcage, with the bier placed symbolically at its centre, where the heart would be. Just as the human body can be seen as a physical container for the essence – the soul – so Makovecz's chapel is intended as the final ritual receptacle for the corpse; it becomes a place of transition between mourning and burial, between this world and the next.

The great ribcage is a cavernous, melancholy shelter for the mourners, just as it is a spiritual shelter for a soul in limbo. Indeed the walls themselves seem to betray their grief. The effect is deliberately reinforced by seats placed between the timber ribs which take on the anthropomorphic form of ghostly mourners (Gábor Mezei was responsible for the carving), the layering of the backs formed in a series of curving ribs which echo the encompassing structure.

Although the anthropomorphic symbolism is both immediate and profound, it is perverted by the gross scale of the representation of the ribcage so that the effect is as monstrous as it is melancholy. The chapel haunts the subconscious with the fear of being swallowed by a mythical beast and evokes the ultimate biblical parable of resurrection, Jonah and the Whale. The whale represents darkness and chaos; it is the *angst* of Jonah's lack of faith and his renewal of faith which causes him to see the light of the love for God, as the whale vomits him out once more into the world. In *Pinocchio*, the puppet and his maker are ejected from the belly of the shark in a repetition of the same myth.

The juxtaposition of the two worlds is as clear in Makovecz's building as it is in the parable of Jonah. The brooding darkness of the chapel is relieved only by the twin doors which open like the feathered wings of a great bird to reveal the light and the garden beyond. The axis which links the coffin on its bier to the doors is expressed by a central spine undulating along the ceiling like a snake and dipping down into the chapel space at a point directly over the bier. The coffin thus remains the only element within the chapel that is not wedded entirely to the structure or the shell, appearing like an oversized pearl, at once the most precious object in the building and yet set apart from it.

The central axis was originally given more emphasis by a powerful wooden sculpture of the Tree of Life, which combined the characteristics of the crucifix with the pagan overtones of the ancient world-view of the Hungarians of the cosmos supported in the branches of a great mythical tree. The notion of Christ's resurrection from the crucifix and the cycle of life represented by the tree were combined into a single iconic gesture reinforcing a fundamentally optimistic view of the building which, since the removal of the Tree of Life sculpture, has undoubtedly become harder to read.

Although the architect is at pains to point out that the building is based simply on the metaphor of the human ribcage, there is a clear connection with his contemporary work on movement patterns and a series of investigations into the idea of 'minimal space'. These investigations were based around a series of experiments and mappings of the reactions through movement of the human body, depending on its physical and geographical position. Thus a person's movements show differing patterns dependent on the stability or precariousness of the ground conditions below them (for example the edge of a precipice or the middle of a plain), and by mapping these motions a shell can be built,

FROM ABOVE: Sketch of interior; seating by Gábor Mezei; OPPOSITE: Plan

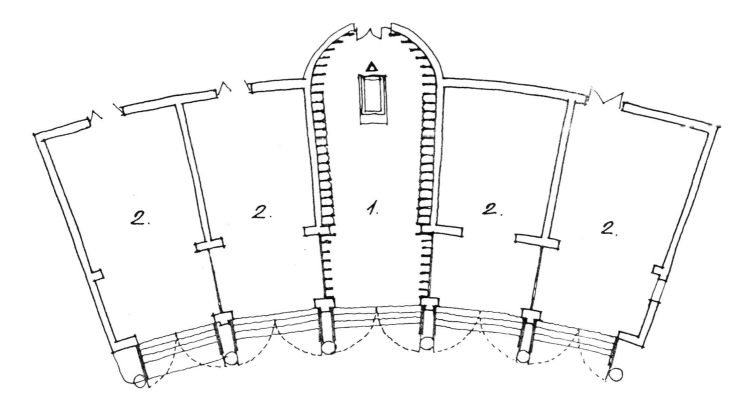

described by the outer extent of the curves of limb movements.

The effect is of a series of stop-frame pictures of the human body. When taken together, these form a series of planes. To relate this idea specifically to this building, we can see each structural timber-rib as the mapping of the movement of a body under certain conditions. Thus, the whole building becomes a complicated documentation of the movements of a body (rather like Leonardo da Vinci's man inscribed in square and circle) through space and time, linking the building's geometry and form to the human body at a more sophisticated level than the simple metaphor of the ribcage, and illuminating the progression through the building as a journey through space, time and the constrictions and physical limitations of the human body.

Makovecz's mortuary chapel was an intervention into a row of existing structures which dated from the 1930s but were damaged soon after their completion by bombing during the Second World War. The architectural language of the existing structures was a stripped modern classicism characteristic of the era, and the juxtaposition of the faceless, white marble of the exterior and the powerful, embracing darkness of Makovecz's interior is profoundly disturbing.

The intervention was made all the more unusual by virtue of the architectural climate of the time.

It was designed and built under the Hungarian Communist regime which generally sanctioned only a debased form of international modernism. The expressive and explicit organicism of this scheme had a powerful impact on Hungarian and European architecture, and was one of the key projects in the early stages of the formation of a Hungarian organic architecture.

Makovecz has subsequently designed a number of other schemes for funerary chapels, many of which engage in similarly profound archetypal imagery. A theme which has run consistently through his cemetery architecture is that of the burial mound as a type. Adolf Loos singled out the burial mound as the most fundamental form of building, that which in a Jungian sense seems to dwell most deeply within us. At the Pusztaszer funerary chapel, Makovecz used this image in its most explicit form. Brick walls and a heavy lintel take the mourner on a journey to the dark heart of the earth. It is an elemental entrance with its genesis in the tombs of ancient Mycenae, where the Tomb of Agamemnon (or Treasury of Atreus) remains to remind us of this ancient archetype.

Characteristic of the Tomb of Agamemnon is the stone-built entrance passage, or *dromos*, beginning as a route carved into the side of the mound and continuing via the entrance to become the tunnel which leads to a vaulted chamber at the heart of the tomb. It is a pattern

that can be found in the megalithic burial mounds of Orkney and the Mediterranean area, and which may have developed independently in these places – an idea which either gives further credence to the Jungian notion of this form as being something deeply embedded in the human subconscious or suggests that this form developed through a common evolutionary process as an ideal shelter, allowing the dead to both return to the earth and be protected by it.

The idea of descent into the earth has become a staple for Freudians, an analogy of the return to the womb. The Roman god Mithras was born of rock and his cult was originally celebrated in underground caverns, perhaps providing inspiration to the early Christians who used the catacombs of Rome as their Church. The idea of the sacred grotto in the rocks has similarly been appropriated from pantheistic cultures, and the oracle at Delphi gained knowledge from the earth-spirit which issued forth from a cleft in the rocks of the Greek landscape. (Delphi, as I have mentioned, translates as 'vagina', which brings us back to the innate sexual symbolism of the cavernous entry into the earth.)

The interior of the chapel is austere and unadorned, a pair of simple, elemental brick vaults arranged consecutively along the central route. Entry is announced by an oversized brick lintel with lion reliefs which hint at the Assyrian genesis of some of the architectural ideas in this scheme. The 'figure 8' plan is deliberately reminiscent of the form of Rudolf Steiner's first Goetheanum in Dornach (1913–22). Steiner believed that this combination of two circles in plan was the only 'restful' building form, without the thrustingly aggressive directionality of the square and rectangle, and any combinations of those, and without the aimless rotation implied by the single circle or oval. It was the one combination which for Steiner could retain implied direction with repose and harmony.

In the Goetheanum, the stage and auditorium meet at the conjunction of the two circles; in Makovecz's chapel the coffin lays at this critical point thus becoming very much the centre of the structure, but it also lies at the point where the two vaults come together and dip uncomfortably low into the space. Makovecz uses similar architectural language in his Forest Study Centre in Visegrad (1981) to explore pantheistic themes, immersing the building in the earth so that it becomes a part of nature rather than an imposition upon its surface.

In his designs for a Church of the Dead for a cemetery in Budapest (1985), Makovecz combines some of the ideas visible at Pusztaszer with the visionary architecture of Boullée. The architect's sketches show a gigantic dome appearing above an earth berm surrounding it. A dense forest of grave-markers covers the sides of the mound. A primitive stone lintel and piers form the entrance to the structure, evoking some great megalithic monument half-buried in the ground. The interior space echoes the monumental sphere of Boullée's designs for a cenotaph for Sir Isaac Newton. The stone altar is placed below an opening in the crown of the structure which admits light from above and gives a view to the sky, while a pair of sculpted angels flank the celebrant behind the altar.

Although unexecuted, this remains one of Makovecz's most powerful schemes, one which manages to express the sentiments of outrage at the pointless deaths of those who had perished under the former regime, and which notionally creates a pantheon for the nation.

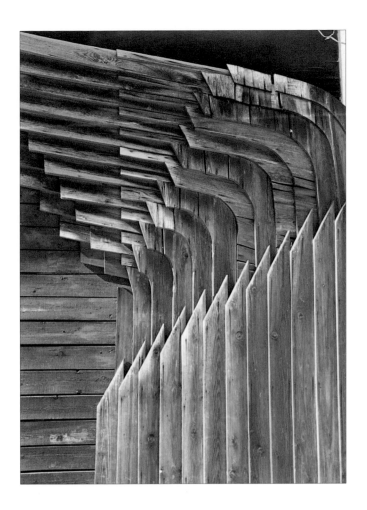

OPPOSITE: Views of interior; ABOVE: Doors details
Church of the Dead, Budapest, 1985; LEFT: Sketch

INGRID MAYR AND JORG MAYR

The original hall of ceremonies of the Israelite religious community at the Jewish cemetery in Graz was burned down by the Nazis after the Anschluss in 1938. The building of a new hall constituted a potent mix of painful memory, optimistic reconstruction and hope for the future. Ingrid Mayr and Jorg Mayr's design is a modern reinterpretation of the destroyed structure, expressed in modern materials and techniques and a modern architectural language, in contrast to the typical Austro–Hungarian historicism of the the original building.

In his critique of the building, Harald Baloch points out that the reconstruction of the destroyed ceremonial hall allows a kind of dialogue through the medium of time as well as through space, mass and symbolic architectural language – a notion which sits comfortably within the Jewish tradition of seeing time and history as the physical site of the sacral.

As in the original building, the ceremonial space is centred beneath the dome. The dome previously surmounted an octagonal drum, however in the new building it is placed on a fully-glazed podium so that it appears to float above the building like the spectral ghost of the original dome hovering over the cemetery site. From within, it becomes apparent that the dome is supported by four slender columns, and from these four points radiates the complex network of timber ribs which forms the structure of the dome itself.

The timber of the dome and the columns and the render of the internal walls seem to differentiate the two structures; the containing walls and the vault of the heavens. This separation is emphasised further by the lifting of the dome above the main structure and the insertion of glass in the space in-between. A lantern at the apex of the dome

Ceremony Hall, Jewish Cemetery, Graz, 1988–91
OPPOSITE: Reconstructed exterior; FROM ABOVE: Original building; contemporary news picture of fire; dome construction

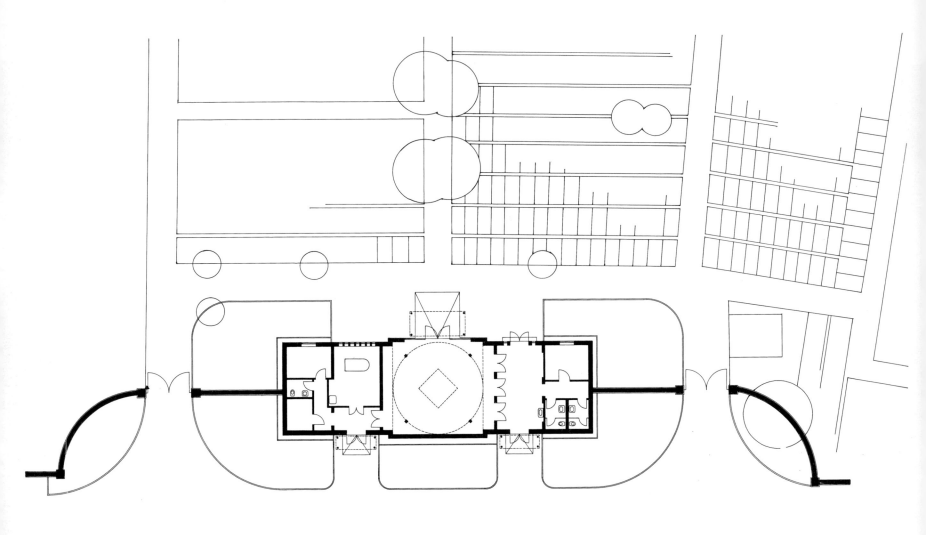

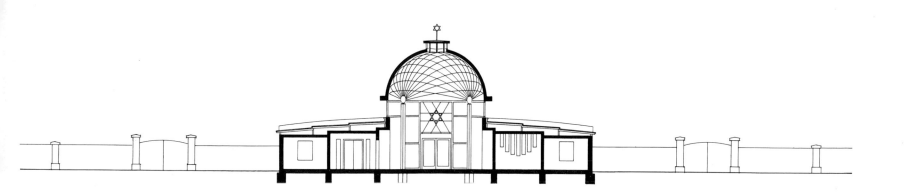

FROM ABOVE: Plan; section

reinforces the building's centrality and further illuminates what is already a very light and airy space. The meticulous construction is put deliberately on display, partly to reveal the stability and permanence of its structure, and partly as an aid for reflection on the Jewish theological teaching of God's 'construction' of the earth and the heavens – how all was created out of the darkness and the seas of chaos. Thus the visible construction becomes the stable point in a world of flux and the turbulent and migratory history of the Jewish people.

Like the original building, the new structure is severely symmetrical with the main ritual space at its centre, the foyer and Tahara to either side and ancillary spaces at the extremities. The Tahara (where the body rests) fulfils the role of the *Leichenhalle*, that of the mortuary hall, seen in other central European funerary buildings (Plečnik's in Žale and Tesar's in Kleinarl). Its light emanates from seven vertical strip windows, their cills staggered into a gentle curve which suggests the seven candles of the Menorah. The floors and the fittings are of dark, polished stone and subtly veined marble which contrasts with the white walls and the blue of the vault above.

From the street, the building appears as a continuation of the long, low cemetery wall and the elevation of the dome to a level above the top of the wall compounds this impression of the unobtrusive extension of the wall element. Only two subtle porches appear to breach the wall at this point; these do not detract from the symmetrical twinned entrances to the cemetery. The building sits half within and half outside the cemetery like a sentinel bestriding the worlds of the living and the dead. Its copper-covered dome appears almost like that of an observatory and suggests the heavens or the contemplation of the sky, as well as evoking the spectre of the past.

OPPOSITE: Entrance; FROM ABOVE: Tahara; foyer; detail of interior

ENRIC MIRALLES

It has been noted that the ancient Egyptians, along with many other ancient peoples, would often ritually break the objects which they put into the tombs of the dead to accompany them into the realms of the afterlife. This served the purpose of ceremonially 'killing' the objects and releasing their soul or essence, thus enabling the dead to take them into the afterlife. It also had the useful side-effect of rendering the objects valueless and therefore useless to grave-robbers.

The jagged, fragmented lines of Igualada Cemetery in Barcelona (1986–90) by Enric Miralles and Carme Piños are reminiscent of the symbolism of this archaic ritual. Indeed, an important part of Miralles' working technique revolves around the idea of cut-outs; the reassembling of shattered and broken images and shapes from drawings and photographs to inspire new forms.

Miralles sees the site as a palimpsest and the building as only one of the layers within it – a single stage in the development of the landscape. This idea becomes clear in the design of Igualada Cemetery which sits firmly within the landscape of the outlying industrial suburb, rather than upon it. The buildings, niches and banks of columbaria reflect the contours of the site, yet their jagged, zigzag forms do not imitate nature; quite the opposite. These are harsh interventions, a very deliberate, tortuous route carved into the landscape. The intervention is very obviously man-made: it brings to mind a quarry, a constructed rift in the earth. From the surrounding landscape it remains largely invisible and unobtrusive, and one is forced to descend into the earth to commune with the dead. Their remains become like the stones left in a disused quarry – a part of the landscape.

In contrast to the sumptuous materials usually employed in the architecture of death, Miralles resorted to pre-cast concrete and a system of reinforcement bars which permeate the artificial landscape like weeds or cobwebs. From the entrance to the site, controlled by a pair of latticework gates which seem to be awaiting a concrete shell to give them substance, the language is of the construction site rather than the finished building. Just as the empty darkness of some of the still unoccupied burial niches appears to long for some content, an air of incompleteness permeates the site. But rather than extra building work which will complete the project, it is the processes of nature which the site awaits.

The rusting of the steel bars is slowly and deliberately staining the surfaces below them, the concrete begins to deteriorate, the trees and shrubs are beginning to shade and cover parts of the site, all acting as *memento mori*, symbols of time and decay. Thus the cemetery itself is going

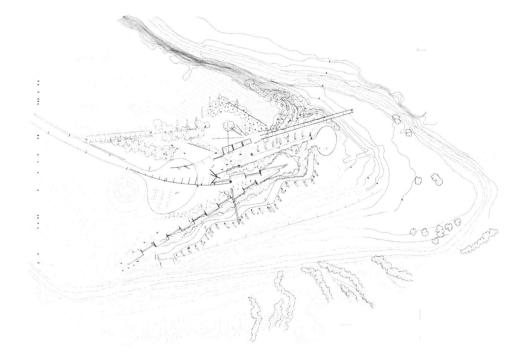

Igualada Cemetery, *Barcelona, 1990*
OPPOSITE: Columbarium; ABOVE: Site plan

ABOVE: *Columbarium detail;* BELOW: *Plan;*
OPPOSITE, FROM ABOVE: *Stairway; columbaria details*

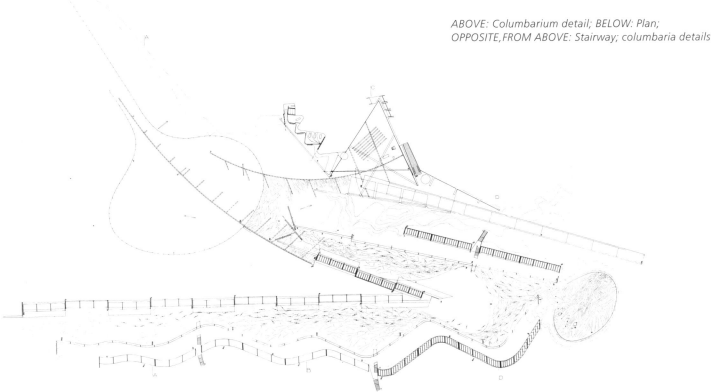

through a process of decay and is declining along with the mourners who visit their already dead friends and relatives.

The cemetery is perceived through a dramatic dog-leg route from the entrance, which is marked by a pair of sculptural constructions of steel members forming the cemetery gates. A steep descent into the earth follows and takes the visitor past screens formed of panels of pre-cast concrete elements which begin to suggest the piercings of the openings in the subsequent structures for the burial niches. The niches are housed in skewed concrete structures crowned with deep overhanging eaves. They slope towards the path at an oppressive angle, as if impinging on the life of the living.

The visitor also passes the mortuary and the chapel, the venues of the physical and metaphysical rituals which accompany the end of life. The culmination of the route is reached via a kind of tree-lined street of the dead, and is denoted by a circular space carved into the ground, the banked walls of which house the mausolea.

The sliding doors giving access to the mausolea display a continuation of the subtle play of two-dimensional forms detectable throughout the cemetery, juggling solid and void, materiality and emptiness. The rusting steel parallelogram-shaped panels of the doors echo the sloping forms of the burial niches to create an internal, self-referential architectural language.

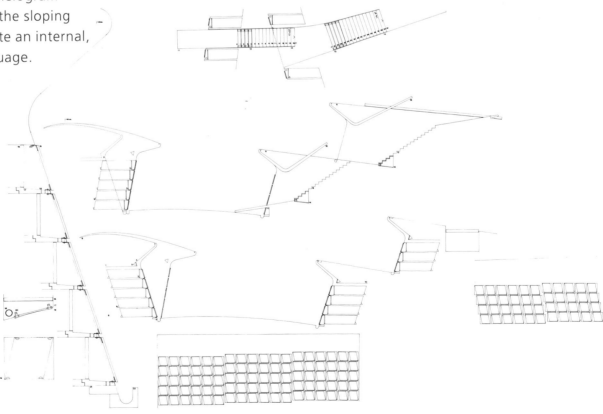

FROM ABOVE: Mausolea; plan; sections

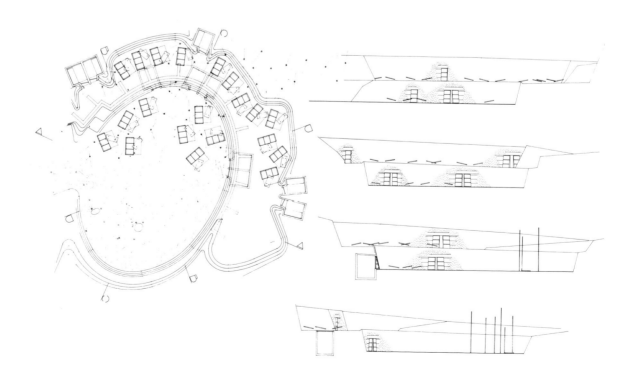

Miralles' 1998 designs for the San Michele Cemetery competition represent a further development of this architectonic language. Here, the fragmented forms of the plan contrast sharply with the ordered formal symmetry of the existing cemetery. While the existing buildings at one end of the island are slightly skewed from the main axes, Miralles' addition at the other end of the island appears as a kind of scrunched-up corner, a dislocated fragment.

However, the more significant part of the scheme is divorced from the main island; appearing on the drawings as an organic mass attached to San Michele by an umbellical bridge. The idea was that this part of the cemetery should be located elsewhere on a new site, away from the island to stop the process of growth and of the irrevocable sub-urbanisation of Venice and the coming together of Murano and the city. The built forms are more substantial than at the Igualada Cemetery but the language is similar; that of long, low banks of tombs and niches staggered and stepped into terraces and capped with curved canopies which seem to suggest a flight from this world to the realms of the heavens.

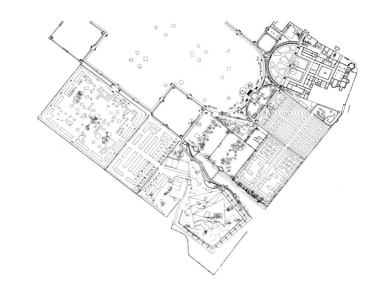

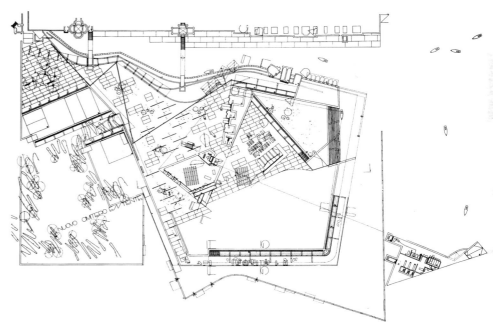

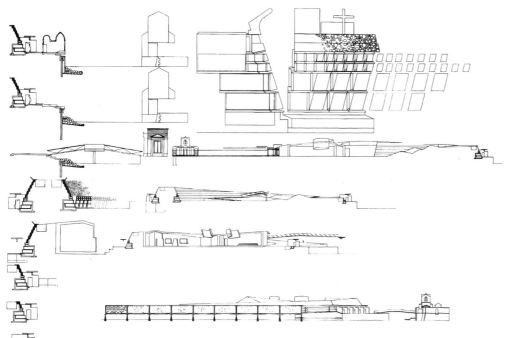

San Michele Cemetery, Venice, 1998
FROM ABOVE: Site plan; detail plan; sections

Voorburg Cemetery Aula, *The Netherlands, 1995, FROM ABOVE: Chapel; aula*

HANS NOUT

Perhaps the most modest architectural scheme in this book, Hans Nout's Aula in Voorburg Cemetery, Holland (1994–95), is also one of the most subtle of interventions. It makes a useful and interesting comparison to look upon Nout's new element for the existing set of buildings as analogous to the huge and monumental porch at the Woodland Cemetery by Gunnar Asplund. In some ways, the scale and massive monumentality of Asplund's porch would seem to make it the diametric opposite of Nout's self-effacing addition, but on the other hand its function is similar.

This is the element of the building which deals with public gathering. The coffin may be at the centre of the ritual but the ceremony is being held for the mourners, and the success of funerary architecture usually relies on the success of the building in accommodating the movements of people in a way that is smoothly controlled and evokes the moods, relief from grief or contemplation which the architect intends. The new element is a long, low porch which wraps around the existing structure while allowing the brick-built central space in which the ceremony is housed to protrude above it and remain the centre of the complex both in plan and in terms of mass.

Four slender columns on the main elevation hold aloft the overhanging eaves and meet a small podium consisting of three steps leading the structure back into the earth. At the centre, where the central column should be, is a gap which announces the principal entrance, placed dead-centre to preserve the building's original symmetrical configuration. The facade is expressed in a complex rhythm of solid panels, transparent and translucent glazing and louvres. The architect's intention was not only to give interest to the elevation but to attempt to express the dual nature of the space, the paradox of the

public ritual and the private grief, the semi-sacred space inside and the profane outside. The transparency is enough to admit plenty of light and allow views of the surrounding landscape but it affords a level of privacy to those within from onlookers outside. It is also used as a device to express externally the nature of the activity taking place on the inside; its public or private nature.

The slight curve of the facade helps to unify the elements of the interior (with the protruding central ritual space and recessed ancillary facilities) and to impart a subtle sense of dynamism to the newly defined area which is, in effect, a circulation zone; a preamble to the ritual parts of the structure. The building also benefits from two new courtyards which bring light into the heart of the structure and open the spaces up, significantly reducing the claustrophobia and confinement of the plan.

This chapter began with the suggestion of a comparison with the great portico of Asplund's Woodland Cemetery. This should not be taken as an aesthetic comparison; in fact, this little structure is an almost perfect opposite to the solemn bombast of Asplund's monumental reinterpretation of the classical. But some of the underlying ideas can be seen to be similar: the idea of a zone of transition, sheltered by a roof yet open to the landscape, the move from exterior to interior zone protected by glazing to create a further buffer, the symmetry and the use of columns to regulate the facade, and the idea of the whole being reflected in a pond outside, suggesting another, somehow inverted realm, which mirrors our own yet remains intangible.

Nout has created an unassuming yet impressive work out of the most ordinary of palettes. Neither overtly sombre nor falsely optimistic, it proves that theatricality or a sentimental vernacular are not the only approaches to smaller funerary schemes.

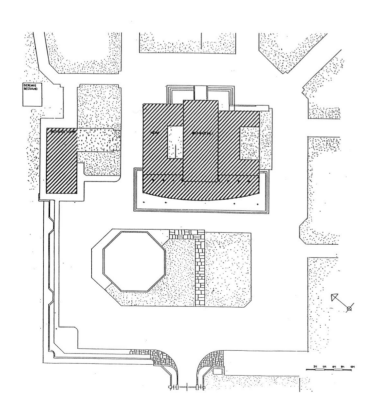

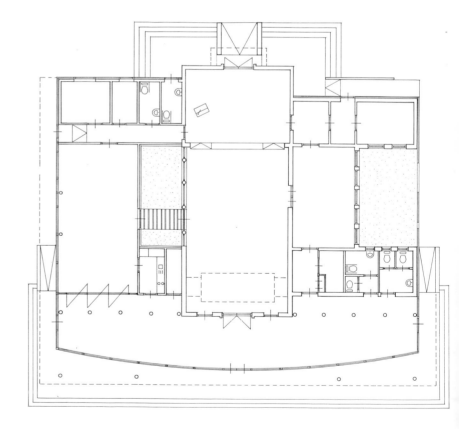

FROM ABOVE, L TO R: Exterior; site plan; ground-floor plan;
OPPOSITE, FROM ABOVE L TO R: Exterior; axononometric;
section; interior; elevation; section

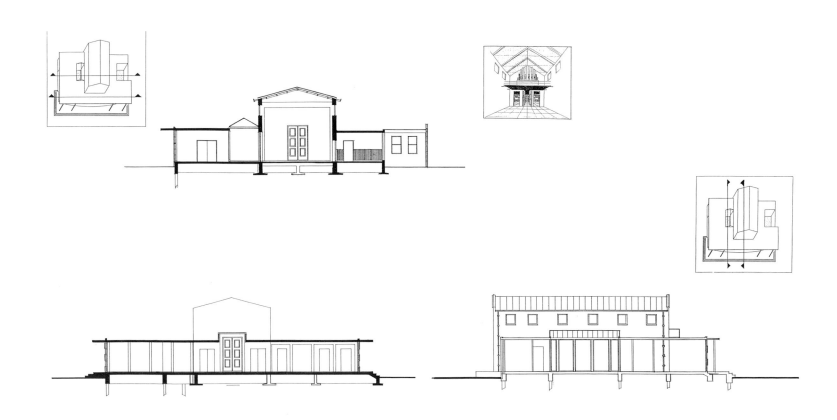

ARNALDO POMODORO

The distinction between architecture and sculpture in funerary art becomes increasingly blurred, and Arnaldo Pomodoro's ambitious and visionary competition-winning scheme of 1974 for an extension to Urbino's necropolis of San Bernardino, Italy, fuses both arts in one of the most imaginative cemetery designs of the twentieth century.

In contrast to the neighbouring cemetery, Pomodoro's designs show a landscape which is carved out of the hillside rather than accrued through a series of buildings or structures. The realm of the dead is both placed and expressed sculpturally below ground. This brings his art closer to the idea of an archaeological site; the notion of the ruins of a town which have been discovered below the ground and partly revealed so that, as at Pompeii, one can wander along the arteries of another world.

Pomodoro saw the design as an attempt to create streets out of the hillside, a landscape of intimate internal corridors and passages to evoke death and prepare the visitors themselves for the experience of entering the other world of death, which Pomodoro sees as the fundamental idea of visiting the cemetery. The idea of carving niches out of the rock contains powerful resonances of the mythological and symbolic ideas of the grotto or the fissure in the mountain as the source of the earth spirit, the primitive shrine for the worship of the mystical power of the Earth Mother.

It was precisely these pagan associations which were to surround Pomodoro's scheme with controversy. The subterranean expression of a literal 'underworld' led to accusations that the design was un-Christian, violated the sacred nature of the burial site and went against all received notions of Christian burial. Furthermore, the abandonment of the traditional hierarchical arrangement (which can be seen at the neighbouring cemetery) whereby sepulchral monuments

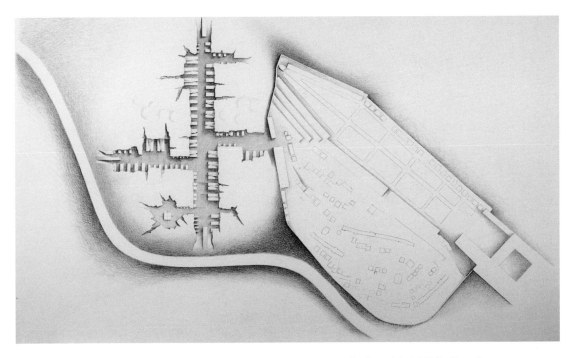

Necropolis Extension, *San Bernardino, Italy, 1974, OPPOSITE: Detail of model; ABOVE: Site plan*

express the wealth and importance of their occupants through opulence, size and decoration, would have been upturned by this proposal. Here there seems to be no class distinction, no difference between the common grave and the bourgeois mausoleum, and no way of maintaining the social distinctions of life from those in death. The furore caused by the design reveals the deeply held conservative ideas about burial and the sensitivity of the subject as an arena for artistic and architectural experimentation, and ultimately explains why the scheme was never realised.

Yet despite its experimental nature and its appearance on the hill as a series of prehistoric remains carved into the hill, Pomodoro's design recalls many profound archetypes drawn from both Christian and pagan sources. Christ himself was, after all, resurrected from within a cave, while the earliest places of worship in Christianity, the catacombs, were similarly subterranean burial places arranged in complicated networks of chambers and corridors. Pomodoro created a series of catacombs which have been revealed, opened out to the sky so that they can be viewed from both above and below, experienced as a network of cracks in the earth or as a series of urban streets, squares and alleys in an exposed city of the dead.

The Urbino Cemetery was to some extent at least an attempt to address what Pomodoro views as the apparent failure of modern architecture to accommodate and embrace public sculpture in all but the most superficial manner as an afterthought or adjunct. The field of monumental and memorial architecture is perhaps the most fruitful in which to engage this debate as it is here that the boundaries and definitions are the most blurred. By sculpting a building, Pomodoro has empowered the landscape with an inherent form, in the way that Michelangelo believed that he was freeing a platonic image from within a block of marble.

OPPOSITE: Perspectives; ABOVE: Site plan and model

To some extent, Pomodoro's highly publicised monument to his great friend Federico Fellini in Rimini (1993) becomes the antithesis of the wholly submerged urban necropolis at Urbino. Here it is the very insignificance of the contact with the ground which gives the monument its essential ethereality. The great baroque acrobatics of the director and his acerbic vision of a superficial Italian society obsessed with celebrity and self-promotion are embodied in the great cantilevered triangle of bronze which teeters on the edge of a sheet of reflecting black marble. The shiny surface of the sheets of bronze are stripped away like the earth in the Urbino Cemetery designs to reveal a complicated network of jagged sculptural forms reminiscent of the dentil-like protrusions revealed at that cemetery. The sculpture is named La Grande Prua (The Great Prow) and Pomodoro explains:

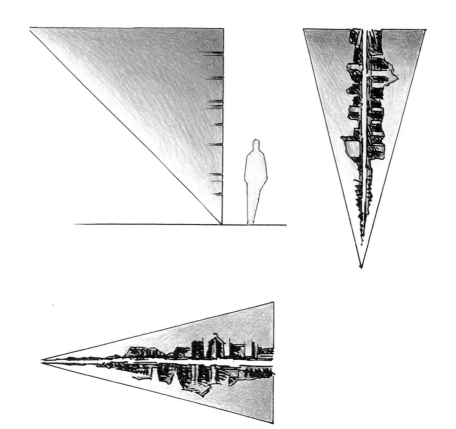

> The prow of this ship seems to cut a path across the land, the water, the air: it represents to me, therefore, the grandeur and the glory of Fellini's works, which now outside of his life, continue to traverse time, history, human experience.[1]

Note

1. Quoted in Sam Hunter, *Arnaldo Pomodoro*, Fabbri (Milan), 1995, p300.

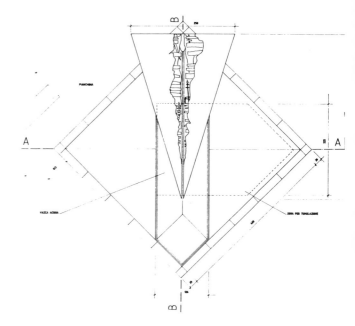

Federico Fellini Memorial, Rimini, Italy, 1993
ABOVE AND BELOW: Sketches; CENTRE: Plan;
OPPOSITE: View of monument; site plan;
section of tomb

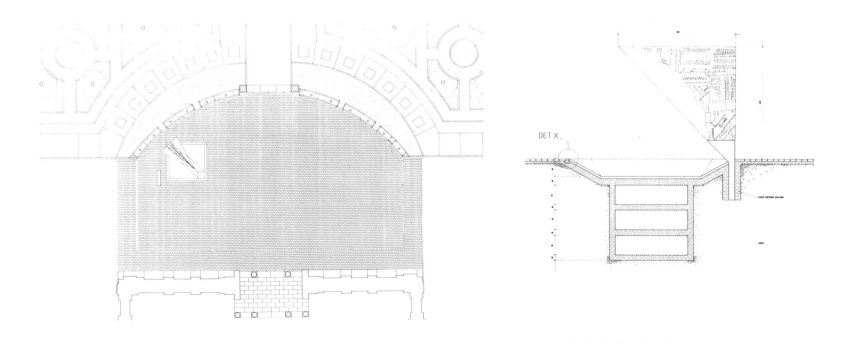

Cemetery of San Cataldo, *Modena, Italy, 1972*
ABOVE: Cemetery in its urban context; OPPOSITE: Compound drawing

ALDO ROSSI

The cemetery, when considered in terms of a building, is the house of the dead. Initially, no distinction was made between the typology of the house and that of the tomb. The typology of the tomb and of the sepulchral structures overlaps the typology of the house: rectilinear corridors, a central space, earth and stone materials . . . Death expressed a state of transition between two conditions, the borders of which were not clearly defined. The urns, shaped like Etruscan houses, and the Roman Baker's tomb express the everlasting relationship between the deserted house and the abandoned work. Consequently, references to the cemetery are applicable to the cemetery itself as well as to the house and to the city. This project for a cemetery complies with the image of a cemetery that everyone has.[1]

Thus Rossi introduced his competition-winning scheme for the Cemetery of San Cataldo in Modena, Italy (1971), designed in conjunction with Gianni Braghieri. In one of the most haunting buildings of the twentieth century, he formalised the theories he had expounded in his book *The Architecture of the City* (1996).[2] The metropolis, seen transformed through the mirror of Rossi's drawings, becomes a necropolis to match Italo Calvino's cities of the dead in his novel *Invisible Cities*, which was published a year after Rossi wrote the opening lines of this chapter.

The most striking aspect of the scheme is its ghostly centrepiece, a massive cubic block, punctured by repetitive rows of one-metre-square openings revealing an emptiness inside. The cube was initially intended to serve as a cenotaph, literally an 'empty tomb' or memorial, but it later became an ossuary. The architect has imbued this structure with many meanings; he describes it as an empty house which is the space of the living's memories. It is the house of the dead and, as such, it remains unfinished; the windows are unarticulated holes, while the roof, the most fundamental form of human shelter, is

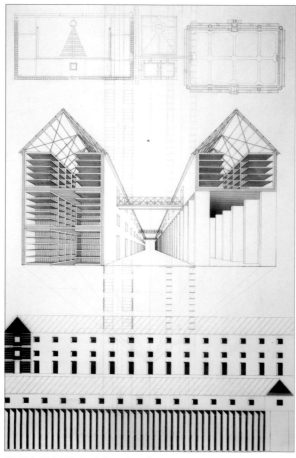

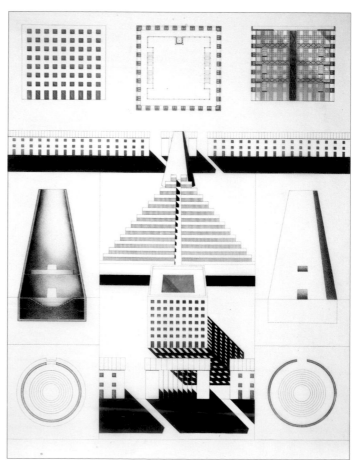

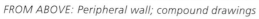

FROM ABOVE: Peripheral wall; compound drawings

conspicuous by its absence. The interior consists of a series of walkways and galleries in steel, allowing access to the remains which are held in concrete cells. Indeed, the effect of the industrial crudity of the interior and the repetition of a series of units allied with the massive solidity the walls is reminiscent of a prison.

On axis with the entrance to the cemetery and this house of memories, a huge, truncated brick cone is seen on the drawings. Its platonic form strongly echoes the *architecture parlante* of Ledoux and Boullée, and the form evokes both the idea of an elemental monument in the tradition of the pyramid or the great round mausolea of the Romans, but also the more recent and more sinister idea of the exhaust flue of a crematorium. This element stands adjacent to a plot set aside for Jewish burials. That Rossi draws this parallel to the single, cataclysmic event which will perhaps define the twentieth century in the texts of future generations – the Holocaust – is a sombre reflection on the existential *angst* of modern humanity.

The cone (which remains only a design element on paper and is not yet built) stands over the communal grave containing the remains of war-dead and those brought from the old cemetery. It is intended as a climax to the main axis beginning at the centrally placed gate. The original design envisaged a progression of gradually tapering ossuaries, arranged like library shelves, which defined a triangle on plan culminating in the circle of the chimney; thus the forms of the Platonic solids all appear along the axis, square to triangle to circle.

Perhaps it is no coincidence that these forms appeared together in Giorgio de Chirico's painting *The Enigma of Fatality* (1914). This ominous composition features the blind arcades so characteristic of the artist and, at the centre, a soaring brick chimney, its height accentuated by the tall triangular form of the canvas. A red 'Hand of Fate' dominates the picture's foreground and further distorts the internal perspective and the claustrophobic sense of space.

Similar brick smoke-stacks appear in other De Chirico paintings of the same period, notably *The Anguish of Departure* (1913–14) and *The*

Philosopher's Conquest (1914). The motif seems to take on the iconic significance of the obelisk of antiquity while reflecting on the industrial nature of the city and perhaps mocking the industrialised Futurists. The chimney becomes abstract memorial and utilitarian object.

Rossi makes it clear that the smoke-stack is the focus of the design. Below it lie the remains of:

> abandoned dead . . . dead whose links with the temporal world have dissipated, generally persons coming out of madhouses, hospitals and jails – desperate or forgotten lives. To these oppressed ones, the city builds a monument higher than any other.[3]

It becomes a symbol of the dispossessed, the victims of the merciless city and of a failing modern society.

Like the neighbouring cemetery dating from 1858, Rossi's scheme is enclosed by walls which reinforce the idea of the scheme as the architect's beloved 'Analogous City'. The depth of the walls contains columbaria which become streets of memories, lined with flowers and memorial lights, and the effect is comparable to a kind of urban arcade; the covered walkway appears again as a transition zone between the old and the new cemeteries where an attenuated colonnade creates a shelter for the flower-sellers and park-keepers – the living who inhabit the city of the dead.

Nearby, the forms that Rossi made so ubiquitous in post-modern design, the curious archetypal houses or beach huts, appear as family mausolea. In an absurd reversal of the lightness embodied by this form of structure (the puppet booth, the stripy beach hut, the temporary theatre) the structures are here formed of grey marble. Gone are the bright colours and the light canvas – in the city of the dead, all is weighed down by its own mass and the burden of grief and memory.

The cemetery's articulation as a conglomeration of individual architectural elements (simplified, dream-like archetypal structures) powerfully evokes a literal necropolis, a functioning as opposed to a metaphorical city of the dead. Rossi, in his explanation, summed up the underlying urban ideas in a fundamentally Jungian manner, building upon the idea of the collective unconscious:

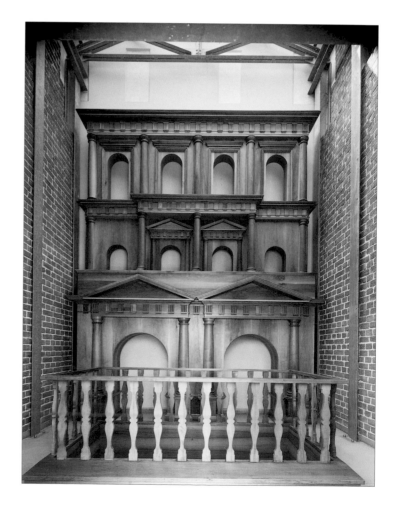

Together, all of the buildings read as a city in which the private relationship with death happens to be the civil relationship with the institution. Thus the cemetery is also a public building with an inherent clarity in its circulation and its land-use . . . The elegiac theme does not separate it much from other public buildings. Its order and its location also contain the bureaucratic aspect of death. The project attempts to solve the most important technical issues in the same manner as they are solved when designing a house, a school or a hotel. As opposed to a house, a school or a hotel where life itself modifies the work and its growth in time, the cemetery foresees all modifications; in the cemetery time possesses a different dimension.

Faced with this relationship, architecture can only use its own given elements, refusing any suggestion not born out of its own making; therefore, the references to the cemetery are also found in the architecture of the cemetery, the house, and the city. Here, the monument is analogous to the relationship between life and buildings in the modern city. The cube is an abandoned or unfinished house; the cone is the chimney of a deserted factory. The analogy with death is possible only when dealing with the finished object, with the end of all things: any relationship other than that of the deserted house and the abandoned work, is consequently untransmittible. Besides the municipal exigencies, bureaucratic practices, the face of the orphan, the remorse of the private relationship, tenderness and indifference, this project for a cemetery complies with the image of cemetery that each one of us possesses.[4]

In his autobiography, Rossi reflects on his being the victim of a serious car accident just before the hand-in of the cemetery scheme.[5] The damage inflicted on his body, he writes, made him aware of the fragility of existence and of the fragmentation of his shattered bones. He began to understand his traumatised body as a series of fractures and breaks, elements which had been dislocated and had to be realigned within the orderly framework of his skeleton.

The rigorously ordered plan of the cemetery must have been drawn, in part, from this traumatic incident and the deep effect it had on the architect while the scheme can be seen as an attempt to reconcile the cities of the dead and the cities of the living from his hospital bed in the city of the transient in-between. The poignancy and power of San Cataldo Cemetery is increased by the tragic nature of Rossi's death, which was the consequence of injuries sustained in another car accident in 1997.

While San Cataldo Cemetery was Rossi's first major work and probably the most enduring of his haunting schemes as an image, his attempts to address remembrance, grief, death and monumentality did not come to an end with what seems to be a project of such brutal finality. Instead he kept experimenting with forms in a field which fascinated him. The funerary chapel which he designed in 1981 in Giussano is expressed through a classical architectural vocabulary which is stripped, fragmented and blended with a stark blockiness which echoes the work of Rossi's beloved Adolf Loos.

Funerary Chapel, *Giussano, Italy, 1981*
OPPOSITE: Exterior and interior views; ABOVE: Drawing of Palladian centrepiece

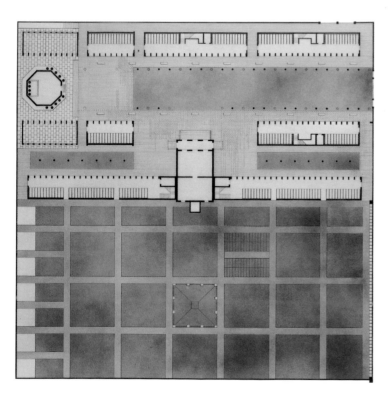
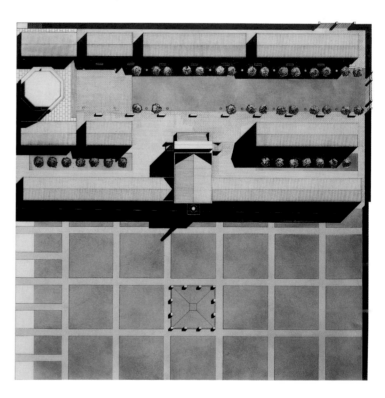

The chapel consists of a tall brick cube raised on a stone plinth. A set of steps is cut into the plinth and rises to a single, gaping door-opening. A pair of square windows, symmetrically placed on either side of the door stares blankly and darkly like the eyes of a dead man. The brick shell is otherwise unadorned except for a cornice which, although complete on the front elevation, only reappears in fragments on the other elevations in an act of wilful Mannerism, rather like the pure classical columns which appeared and disappeared between courses of heavy rustication in much late Renaissance Italian architecture.

On the inside, the Renaissance reference is made more explicit. The visitor to the chapel is confronted with a timber screen based on Palladio's Porta Borsari in Verona, which acts both as the monumental centrepiece to the interior and as a personal memorial to the founder of a company making wooden furniture to whose memory the chapel is dedicated. Above, a fully glazed pitched roof (unseen from the outside due to the high parapets on the elevations) is supported on steel trusses which lend an industrial aesthetic to the upper sections, in the vein of the deserted factory which Rossi talks about in his explanation of San Cataldo Cemetery and which evokes the furniture factory now in mourning for its departed founder.

The section through the building, however, reveals a darker, more sombre space below ground. A well in the middle of the chapel allows light to filter down to a space which is entered separately from a stair which begins outside the chapel. The hole at the heart of the ground floor of the building seems to indicate the absence of a crucial element. It is surrounded by a set of curiously flat, theatrical timber balusters which contrast with the rounded solidity of the wood-work of the classical screen. The atmosphere of the space below is utterly different to the lightness of the ground floor. Simple punched perforations function as high-level windows and complement the light filtering down from the space above. The visitor is confronted with a plain wooden crucifix on the wall opposite. It is framed by two walls clad in marble which seem to accentuate the tunnel-like nature and the inevitability of

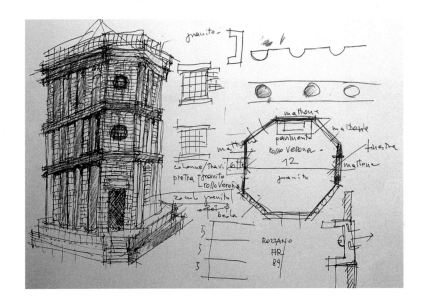

Designs for Cemetery in Rozzano, Italy, 1990

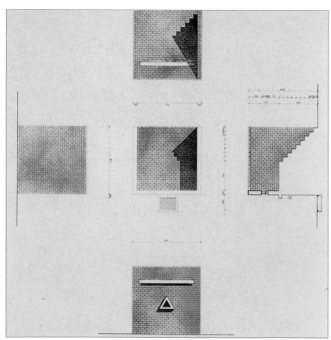

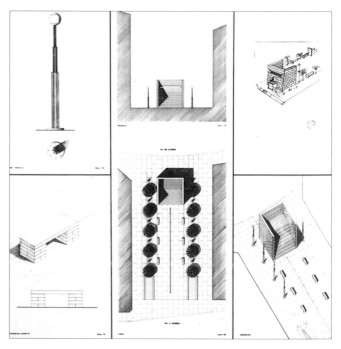

procession or progression towards the cross.

Seen from within, the stair which the visitor has descended seems like a stairway into the blinding light. On the original sectional drawing for the scheme the walls below ground are rendered in rough, coursed stonework which, together with the light from the high-level windows gives the impression of a cell – a dungeon – while the crucifix hangs almost threateningly on the wall. In the built version this vision has been diluted but the powerful division of above and below remains a critical part of the concept.

The building sits in a row of mausolea – a row of houses of the dead. The simplistic, almost child-like composition of base, cornice, door and windows conspires to reinforce the domestic analogy. The chapel evokes Loos' domestic work with its lush materials, in particular the rich marble on the walls, but also manages to echo Rossi's illustrious Italian forebear, Gio Ponti, who managed similarly to combine modern and traditional architectural languages and elements from the architecture of the living and the buildings of the dead to create a number of powerful funerary monuments.

Rossi's other major cemetery scheme was for Rozzano, designed in 1990. Some of the elements which first appeared at San Cataldo reappear in this design, but the conception is different. The plan is based around a 'street' formed on either side by memorial buildings, culminating in a chapel of octagonal plan which seems to evoke a notion of the baptistery, of rebirth through death. Behind the street lies an ordered cemetery, a large garden formally segmented into plots centred around a single, monumental memorial, rather dwarfed by the similar but taller form of the brick chimney, which again makes an appearance and can be seen poking up above the architect's internal urban facades. The garden is bounded to the outside world by a long brick wall which already existed on the site.

Rossi's Pertini monument at the via Croce Rossa (1988–90) in his home city Milan is the exemplary abstract urban monument. Embodying his rationalism, it reworks an earlier design for a monument in Segrate and recalls K M Kerndle's sketch of a sepulchral chapel (see page 34).

Notes

1 Aldo Rossi, 'The Blue of the Sky' (essay: orig 1971), printed in *Oppositions*, Summer 1976 (English translation by Marlene Barsoum and Liviu Dimitriu); reprinted in *Aldo Rossi: Selected Writings and Projects*, edited by John O'Regan, Academy Editions (London), 1983, pp41–47.
2 Aldo Rossi, *The Architecture of the City*, MIT Press (Cambridge, Mass), 1982. First Italian edition 1966.
3 Italo Calvino, *Invisible Cities*, Secker and Warburg (London), 1974. First Italian edition 1972.
4 Aldo Rossi, 'The Blue of the Sky', op cit.
5 Aldo Rossi, *A Scientific Autobiography*, MIT Press (Cambridge, Mass), 1981.

***Via Croce Rossa Monument**, Milan, 1990*
OPPOSITE, FROM ABOVE: Monument in context; studies;
ABOVE: Sketch

MOSHE SAFDIE

Israel itself can be seen as a kind of memorial to the Holocaust. It is true that Zionism as an idea predates the tragedy of the Holocaust, but the genocide of the Jewish people gave a renewed impetus to Zionist ideals and made the international community uneasy about questioning the right of Jews to settle in Palestine. The foundation of the state of Israel was made almost inevitable by the Holocaust – its very existence was seen as fundamental in the light of what had happened, and there was great international sympathy for the Jewish cause. Despite objections, Israel was founded after a civil war and the repercussions on the area are still being felt.

Moshe Safdie has contributed to memorialising the tragedy which gave impetus to the foundation of the new state, and to an individual whose death was a symptom of the continuing unrest and agitation as a consequence of Israel's existence.

With the Yad Vashem memorials and with the tomb of Israeli Prime Minister Yitzhak Rabin (1995), who was murdered by a Jewish fundamentalist fanatic, Safdie has created a series of memorials and institutions which testify to the tragedies which continue to engulf Israel and the Jewish race.

The Yad Vashem Memorial was originally designed by Arieh Elhanani and remains the focus of commemoration, but the site was subsequently developed into a memorial complex and in 1976 Safdie was appointed to design a museum dedicated to the one-and-a-half million children who perished in the Holocaust. The architect's response comprised a significant alteration of the original brief and instead of a museum the building of a memorial was begun, and completed in 1987.

The memorial takes the form of a cave-like structure, a subterranean cavern entered

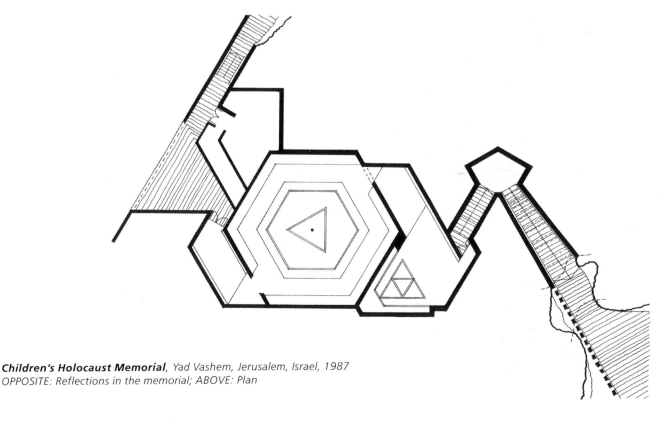

Children's Holocaust Memorial, *Yad Vashem, Jerusalem, Israel, 1987*
OPPOSITE: Reflections in the memorial; ABOVE: Plan

through an archway formed by an outcrop of the rock of the mountain on which the memorial is sited. A ramp has been hewn out of the rock and the visitor descends down this dog-leg path into an octagonal chamber which is illuminated by the flickering flame of a single candle. A plethora of mirrors and glass surfaces reflects the flame and multiplies it, seemingly infinitely, on all sides so that the space is pierced with thousands of tiny points of light. Passing through this memorial chamber the visitor emerges on the far side on to a terrace overlooking the mountains of Judea.

The shape of the octagonal underground chamber is expressed above ground in the form of a similarly shaped amphitheatre located directly over it. Cypress trees surround and define the octagon on seven sides, while the eighth side (to the north of the site) is defined by a series of roughly finished stone pillars, their tops remaining conspicuously unhewn, as if unfinished. The metaphors are powerful and simple and therefore need no further explanation.

OPPOSITE AND LEFT: Interior and exterior details; BELOW: Section

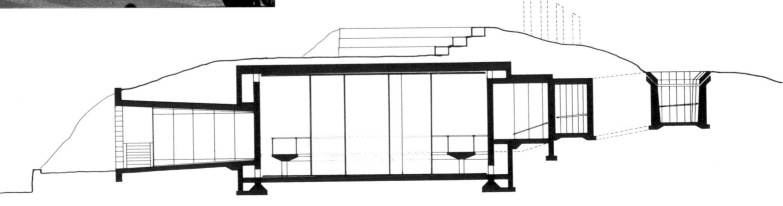

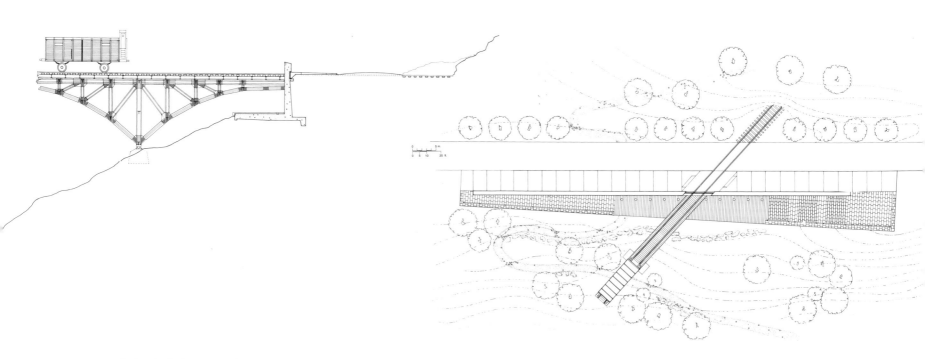

Just as his Children's Memorial takes full advantage of the geography and geology of its impressive and imposing site, so Safdie's subsequent memorial intervention, the Holocaust Transport Memorial (1994), exploits its landscape setting. Two of the original railway wagons used to transport Jews to concentration camps were given away by the Polish state, one to the Washington Holocaust Memorial Museum and the other to Yad Vashem.

Safdie's design incorporates the wagon at the end of a broken section of railway bridge which is cantilevered precariously out from the retaining wall of a road. The timber lattice structure of the bridge is based on a Polish railway bridge; at its broken end the steel and timber elements are twisted and mangled as if the rest had been torn away in a violent explosion. The architect suggests that the wagon, teetering on the brink of the chasm of the valley, could be said to represent a journey into the abyss. The Holocaust represents an irreparable break in the fabric of Western civilisation, symbolised by the fragmented railway bridge, while the wagon on the edge could be seen to stand for the uncertainty and instability into which the Holocaust has plunged modern culture and from which it has never recovered.

Lyotard has compared the Holocaust to an earthquake in Western civilisation and one which has smashed not only the fabric but the instruments of measurement. The break in the bridge is the physical expression of that damage and of the incapability of Western culture to envisage a new start. We are, like the wagon, still teetering on the edge. A wall at the base of the memorial is inscribed with the testimony of a Holocaust survivor relating the conditions on-board the trains. The inscription set in stone represents the hope that by committing these words, the testi-

Holocaust Transport Memorial*, Yad Vashem, 1994*
OPPOSITE, FROM ABOVE L TO R: Wagon and broken section of railway bridge incorporated as part of memorial; elevation; plan; ABOVE: View of wagon representing a journey into the abyss; detail of inscription and cantilevered bridge

Holocaust Museum Extension, *Yad Vashem, 1995*
ABOVE AND OPPOSITE: Model perspectives; BELOW: Site plan;
*OPPOSITE BELOW: **Tomb of Rabin**, Mount Hertzel, Israel, 1995*

mony of the witnesses will be preserved as undeniable proof of the Holocaust; memorials though are poor records of history, and this noble hope may be in vain.

Safdie is also involved in a large-scale rationalisation of the Yad Vashem site, including a substantial reorganisation and extension of the Holocaust Museum. The new design also makes use of the nature of the rocky landscape to emphasise its theatrical forms; the motif of constructed destruction appears in the exploded end of the tunnel (housing galleries) set into the hillside.

The Rabin tomb, which stands in Jerusalem, is composed simply of two blocks of stone, one black, one white, which together form a curved mass focusing on a round vessel at the centre. It is an appropriately simple memorial to a man who was slain for his desire to make peace.

NEW ENGLAND HOLOCAUST MEMORIAL

The construction of the memorial is begun on Remembrance Day.
The horror of the Holocaust is re-enacted in the brutal cutting
of all the trees on half the site. These stumps remain.

Six pits are dug and lined with Black granite.
At the bottom of each pit is a glowing fire.
Six glass towers are raised above.

Once completed many meanings attach to the memorial:

Some think of it as six candles,
others call it a menorah.
Some, a colonnade walling the Civic Plaza.
others, six exhausts of life.
Some call it a city of ice,
others remember a ruin of some civilization.
Some speak of six pillars of death,
others, six chambers of gas.
Some sit on the benches
and are warmed by the fire.
Some think of it as a fragment of Boston City Hall,
others call the buried chambers Hell.
Some think the pits of fire are six death camps,
others feel the warm air rising up from the ground
like human breath as it passes
through the glass chimneys to heaven.

Etched on the glass towers are
SIX MILLION NUMBERS
which flicker with light.

On the black granite ramp is incised:
DEDICATED TO THE REMEMBRANCE
OF THE SHOA
THE HOLOCAUST.
THE ULTIMATE ACT OF PREJUDICE.
THE NAZI THIRD REICH
SYSTEMATIC MURDER
OF SIX MILLION JEWISH
MEN WOMEN AND CHILDREN.
THE ATTEMPT AT THE
TOTAL AND PERMANENT
DESTRUCTION OF JEWISH LIFE.
THE AIM TO REMOVE JEWS
FROM HISTORY AND MEMORY.

Each of the six burning chambers is named after a death camp:

CHELMINO
TREBLINKA
MAJDANEK
SOBIBOR
AUSCHWITZ-BIRKENAU
BELZEC

***New England Holocaust Memorial**, Boston, 1990*
ABOVE: One of the six glass towers; RIGHT: Saitowitz's competi-
tion description of the memorial; OPPOSITE: Site plan

STANLEY SAITOWITZ

In his description of his competition-winning design for the New England Holocaust Memorial in Boston (1990), architect Stanley Saitowitz begins to outline the nature of some of the possible interpretations of the monument. However, even the plethora of associations and memories only constitutes a fraction of the images evoked by the six glass towers on their hollow, fiery foundations.

The prominent siting of this memorial, in the plaza outside Boston's monumental City Hall, makes it one of the boldest and most important of recent public commemorations. It is also one of the most monumental and theatrical of memorials. The glass towers create a specific place within the huge urban plaza and involve the visitor in a number of subtle yet dramatic ways, from the gusts of warm air from the fires burning below to the symbolic tattooing as light shines through the glass, is blocked out by the etched numbers and imprints itself on the bodies of those nearby. Though he originally intended the names of the dead to be etched into the glass of the towers, Saitowitz finally settled for numbers one through to six million to represent the Jewish fatalities of the Holocaust. In doing this, there was a deliberate parallel to the Vietnam Memorial in Washington DC with its wall of some sixty thousand names, as an illustration of the magnitude of the Holocaust.

The six towers are constructed of a frame of stainless steel and a glass skin, and are placed over two-metre-deep pits, at the bottom of which burns a gas fire. Each tower is dedicated to one of the aforementioned death camps. In a deliberate and gruesome way, the burning fires evoke the infamous crematory ovens at the camps. Similarly, their gas-burning source refers to the gas-chambers. more traditionally, they represent the symbol of the eternal flame of memory. The digging of the pits, like that of the inmates digging their own graves, sets the purpose of the construction in motion. At night, they become illuminated beacons lit from the fire within.

The placing of this monument is critical. Its proximity to Boston's City Hall and its location along the city's 'Freedom Trail', along with Paul Revere's house and the Bunker Hill Monument, places it firmly within the history and mythology of the USA. Thus it becomes a highly political monument, stressing American liberty and

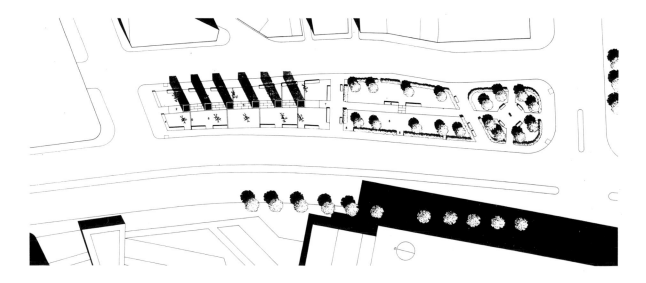

ABOVE: Sequence of glass towers; BELOW: Sections and elevation; OPPOSITE, L TO R: Plans; section; upward view

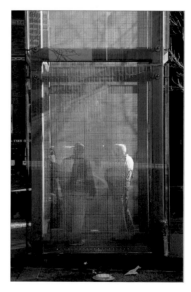

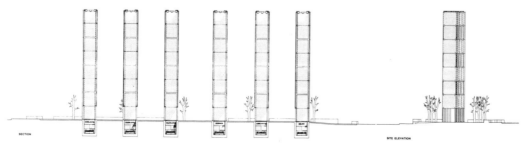

SECTION

SITE ELEVATION

democracy against tyranny and the role of the USA as liberator of the camps. The monuments also become an implicit plea for racial tolerance in the country; a 'what if' warning; also, more controversially, a justification of the Zionism and the idea of Israel. Whether these implications are intended on the part of the architect is irrelevant; like the placing of the Holocaust Memorial Museum in the context of Washington's Mall (constituting a new point in the sequence of that city's memorial trail), the erection of the monument is a political, as well as a purely memorial gesture.

The intense simplicity, almost minimalism of the gesture of the six glass blocks can be seen as part of an emerging tradition of Holocaust memorials: elemental building blocks, towers or slab-like markers of a kind of megalithic simplicity seem increasingly to have become *de rigueur* for Holocaust memorials. Louis Kahn's unrealised proposal for a Memorial to the Six Million Jewish Martyrs in Battery Park, New York City (1966–72), consisted of a series of seven glass slabs on a podium. The pits in which the fires burn can be compared to Horst Hoheisel's Negative Form monument in Kassel (1987) and to Jochen and Esther-Shalev Gerz's anti-Fascist monument (1986–93) in Harburg, Hamburg: both acknowledge the place of the Holocaust in an unimaginable, subterranean nether realm, a realm of darkness and horror.

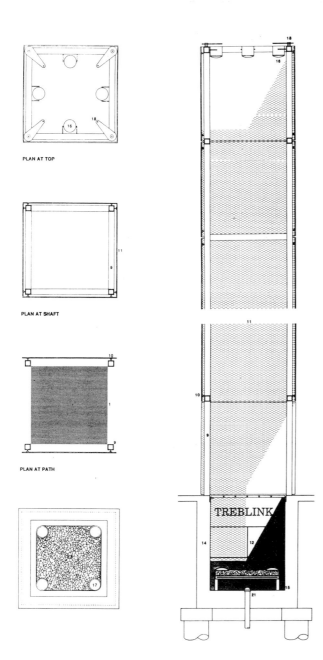

CARLO SCARPA

I have suggested Sir John Soane's house in London as a key starting-point for an exploration of modernism and the architecture of death (see chapter VII). In his house, Soane combined the ideas of a museum as a memorial, of a series of objects and spaces in a set sequence as a theatrical journey through a narrative and of the archaic notion of the dwelling place as the burial place – a house of the dead.

Stefan Buzas (whose photographs can be seen here) has inferred (in conversation with the author) a marked affinity between the work of John Soane and the work of Carlo Scarpa a century and a half later. Both architects thrive on a remarkable attention to detail which infuses their work with meaning and symbolism far beyond what was usual for their historical age and which makes their work personal and poignant in a manner both unusual and striking.

Soane built his house as a kind of memorial to himself; it is less as if he has left his personal signature on the architecture and rather that the building is suffused with his personality, his melancholy, an absurd and maudlin humour and his passion for fragments of the past. C E Vulliamy, in his book *Immortal Man*, writes, 'The worship of the past is the worship of ancestors;

and the archaeologist is really the most religious of men.'[1] In this light, Soane's house becomes a temple as well as a museum, given immortality by Soane's collection of objects, a symbolic narrative architecture informed by a mass of fragments. Scarpa's Brion cemetery is even more literally a memorial to the architect as Scarpa himself is buried there. Whereas Soane was buried in his family vault alongside his beloved wife, Scarpa is interred alongside his patrons.

Carlo Scarpa's great genius was for making museums that were woven into the existing historic fabric of Italy and particularly his native Venice. His approach to the Brion Cemetery follows on logically from his museum building. The museum is a window on another world, a place where we can immerse ourselves in a different time; as in a religious service the visitor to a museum is able to relive moments of a semi-mythical past by communion with the artefacts from that age. This is why relics became such powerful symbols in the medieval church; they create a link with the past which, like the banging of the shaman's drum, facilitates a passage into another state, another time.

Similarly, walking through the cemetery, the fragment, the gravestone or memorial becomes

Brion Cemetery, *San Vito di Altivole, Italy, 1969-78*

OPPOSITE AND ABOVE: Details of entrance to the cemetery

the relic, the last link with the lost, and with the past. Just as Soane's house is both museum and memorial, so Scarpa's cemetery incorporates ideas of the narrative route of the museum, of a journey guided by a series of mystical objects and paths.

The design and construction of the cemetery spanned nearly a decade (1969–78). It is situated in a corner of the small existing cemetery of San Vito di Altivole in the hilly northern Italian landscape. Scarpa created a garden of death, an enigmatic landscape imbued with layer upon layer of meaning and iconography, a single project which is so rich in symbolism that it has almost paradoxically become a palimpsest in itself. Yet the richness of the architecture comes largely from its enigmatic quality, as nothing is obvious – all the symbolism is left open to interpretation or ambivalent.

To each visitor the landscape is one which will evoke different emotions and associations, despite the museum analogy; as a collection of beautiful fragments there is nothing didactic here. Perhaps this is one of the reasons why the cemetery has been so widely written about and analysed. It invites interpretation and speculation in a way that few modern buildings are able and has a depth and enduring enigmatic quality which comes usually only from the layers of a city that has developed organically over centuries.

The cemetery is conceived as a garden of artifice (in a manner closely related to the English landscape garden perceived as a series of events) in contrast to the traditional Italian cemeteries which tended to be densely packed with mausolea and graves, geometrically arranged in blocks. (It is interesting to note at this point that Scarpa turned down the chance to build the cemetery in Modena which Rossi later completed as a vast, rigid symmetrical city of the dead.)

It is a garden of contemplation in the tradition of Islamic courtyards and Venetian walled gardens rather than a necropolis; his own creation at the Querini Stampalia Foundation in Venice (1961–63)

as a refuge from the city, is a helpful precedent in understanding the development of the conception of the Brion Cemetery.

The plan takes the form of an 'L' which wraps itself around a corner of the existing cemetery. It pivots around a concrete bridge-like structure which is rotated at 45 degrees to the cemetery walls, emphasising its importance within the scheme and its role as a hinge. This structure shelters the tomb of Giuseppe Brion and his wife, the client and friend of the architect. It is a curious and enigmatic structure which lies at the heart of the scheme; a bridge which links nothing to nothing.

In the shadows which fall beneath it, lie the two sarcophagi, leaning in towards one another. The soffit of the arch above the tombs is faced with blue-green tiles inlaid with the names of the deceased. This exquisite material is reserved for one of the least visible parts of the scheme; in a detail typical of Scarpa, the blue of the vault of the sky and the green of the water and the grass, flecked with golden mosaic tiles like glints of the sun are reflected back down on to the tomb's occupants.

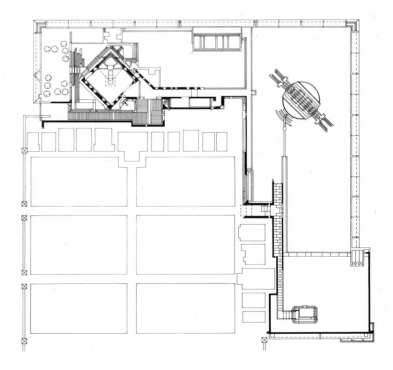

OPPOSITE AND ABOVE: Sarcophagi and watercourse; BELOW, L TO R: Patron's name in gold mosaic; plan

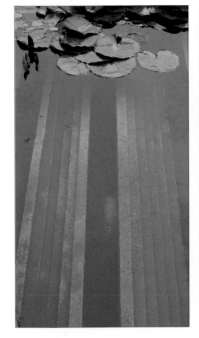

The garden itself is raised above the level of the cemetery around it, and the Brion tombs are immersed in the ground; as if by doing this the architect were revealing the layer below, the underground realm of the dead and the past. The tombs lie in a circular pit, from which a series of partial concentric circular terraces rise back up into the garden, taking with them a sliver of a canal contained in a concrete channel which runs from the entrance and links the tomb to a pool on the other side of the entrance.

Access is gained to the new cemetery through the existing route via a small porch, at the end of which the enclosing wall is visible through a pair of intersecting circles. This favourite device of the architect seems to indicate the view through the stereometric vision of the eyes, as if deliberately emphasising the three-dimensionality of the built scheme. The circles also allude to the cycle of life, to the sacred symbol of the mandala, to the intertwined wedding-rings of the dead couple and to perfection and immortality (like the symbol of the snake coiled around and swallowing its own tail which can be found in Soane's funerary works).

The top of the oddly sloping wall is approximately at eye-level on entry to the garden and bisects the two circles horizontally so that immediately there is an above and below; the visitor is taken up a few steps on to the new level via a stair that is curiously off-centre to the two circles. From this point, the route leads both to the left and right, forcing a choice. To the right, lies a pool. In the water a timber-clad structure is supported on spindly bronze legs to form a pavilion on axis with the Brion tomb. It is reached via passage through a glass barrier which has to be lowered manually into the ground, its mass being countered by an elaborate contraption of pulleys and weights on the wall.

Standing and looking through a lorgnette device built into the underside of the structure, which functions like the eyepieces of binoculars focusing the view on the required framed portion

OPPOSITE AND ABOVE: Details of submerged concrete work

of the landscape, the tomb is seen beyond the water, the tower of the local church and the dramatic hills form the impressive backdrop to this theatrically engineered view and the whole garden is seen in context.

From this pool (on which lilies float and a flat concrete construction of roughly cruciform shape also seems to weightlessly sit on the water) the concrete channel leads away towards the tomb where it re-emerges as a highly symbolic well, indicating regeneration, resurrection and the river of life. The visitor is led alongside the channel of water towards the tomb and becomes aware of the chapel which, like the tomb itself is rotated at an angle of 45 degrees. It is reached by a passage that the architect has designated a 'cloister' and occupies the space between the old cemetery and the street to the other side.

The route takes the visitor past Scarpa's own grave, wedged into the corner, almost on axis with the Brion tomb but just slightly off-centre. The small square building housing the chapel is set in a submerged landscape of terraces, layers and stepping stones like an outcrop sticking up above the water line – all that is left of a greater complex from a past era. In fact, there is a definite Atlantian feel to this aspect of the architecture: the steps, terraces and chamfers seem to derive from some lost Mayan city, and mini-ziggurats crowd the area beneath the water, but apparently Scarpa's inspiration for these motifs was a combination of the architecture of Frank Lloyd Wright and an African cemetery he once saw which was filled with curious stepped sarcophagi.

Scarpa's sketches show the genesis of the chapel's roof form. It is a kind of inverse Temple of Halicarnassus, the original mausoleum, although its complexity is not expressed on the outside, where it appears as a simple barn-like roof. Scarpa once said that his ambition was to find a pharaoh so that he could build a pyramid for him. With this volume above the altar, he seems to have found his pharaoh in Giuseppe Brion. The motif of stepped layers is omnipresent inside the chapel, and each junction and edge reveals sets of layers below, as if the building has been stripped of successive skins like a half-peeled onion.

The chapel is entered through a circular open-ing, the bottom of which is cut-off by the line of the floor, creating a seamless porch. The circular entry motif echoes the twin circles which confront the visitor on arrival and seem to suggest that another twin circle may lurk below the floor, another layer hinted at through the subtle manip-ulation of forms into an internal language. The twin circles are repeated in the holy-water stoup set into the chapel wall (a device which was inspired by a snuff-box given to Scarpa as a present, the hole being the shape of a pair of fingers pinching a dose of snuff).

The focus of the chapel is a brass-fronted altar which suggests a table by the simple device of the now familiar, layered and stepped chamfers at its bottom corners. Viewed from the centre, the little chapel is uncharacteristically symmetrical, as if the restless nature of the fragmented forms around the garden have resolved themselves into a peaceful repose.

Beyond the chapel lies a separate area, accessible by stepping stones. This functions as a priests' cemetery; its sanctity is emphasised by its position at the culmination of the procession – it exists in a realm which is reached through a tortuous route. The sculptural quality of the concrete is stunning in its complexity, and there seems an infinite amount of interpenetration of planes and surfaces so that no part is ever completely separated from another. Space flows across the scheme like the water which surrounds it, while the water seems to be slowly taking control of the site, just as Scarpa's hometown Venice is gradually and hopelessly sinking into the sea.

The complex architecture of the structures, which necessitated the construction of intensely complicated shuttering to form the poured concrete, took what seemed an interminable time to finish, prompting the villagers to ask when the scheme would be completed. To this, Scarpa replied that when the cemetery was finished it would be dead.

Note

1   C E Vulliamy, *Immortal Man*, Methuen and Company Ltd (London), 1926, p176.

OPPOSITE: Chapel interior

HEINZ TESAR

The origins of Heinz Tesar's architecture can be found in his paintings, in which he developed a series of 'Homotypical' forms which lie somewhere between Platonic or Jungian archetypes and primeval shapes that seem to contain the embryos of sculptures, monuments or architectural compositions. At the centre of his Cemetery Chapel in Kleinarl, Salzburg (1977–86) can be found a piece of furniture, the 'Table of Death', which illustrates his way of working through forms redolent with symbolism and archetypal association and transcending many of the debates about architectural style to become readable symbolic centrepieces, appealing to a collective unconscious.

Tesar's work has been compared to that of Plečnik, another architect working within central European traditions, and this comparison is useful not on stylistic grounds, but rather due to the similarity of the architects' search for a language of eternal and timeless appeal through the use and juxtaposition of symbolic and personal sculptural forms.

The skeletal structure of the Table, which acts as the funeral bier, defines the purpose of the chapel and articulates the body, which lies at the centre of its function and ritual. The two metal spikes at either end fix it to the ground at two tiny points in an illustration of the fragility of corporeal life. The coffin is seen against a background of a freestanding screen of richly veined marble, like a headstone which terminates the ritual space of the interior.

The interior of the chapel is pure, simple and bright. The main barrel vault is illuminated by a pair of roundel windows on opposite sides of the building and by a series of twelve smaller roundels, set below the roof in a radiating pattern (vaguely reminiscent of a telephone dial). Two smaller,

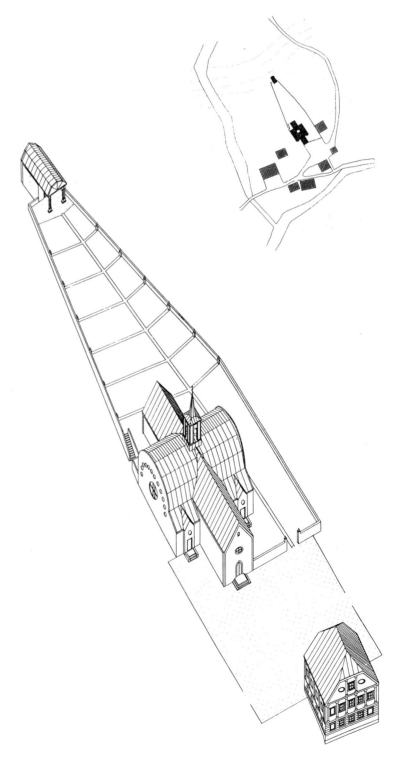

Cemetery Chapel in Kleinarl, *Salzburg, 1977-86*
OPPOSITE: Exterior views; ABOVE: Site plan; isometric

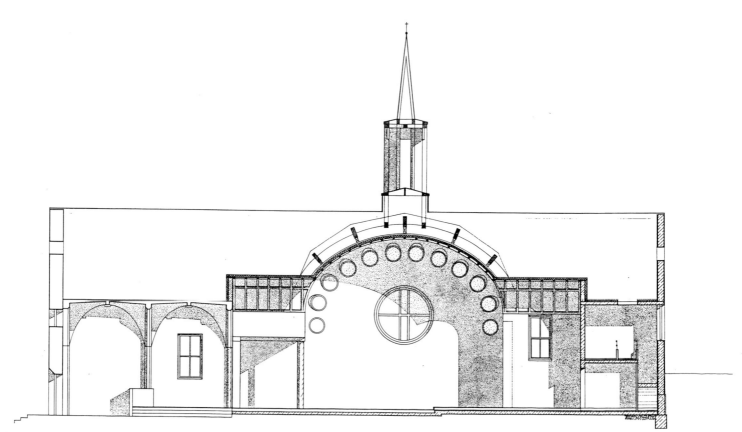

FROM ABOVE: Interior; section; OPPOSITE, FROM ABOVE: Plan; sectional model

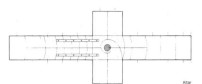

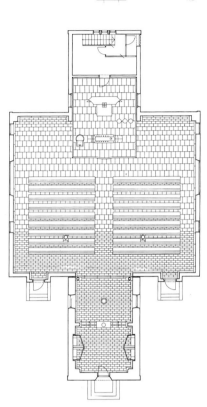

adjacent structures form the lobby and an apsidal chancel but the altar is pushed out into the body of the chapel so that the mourners are brought physically into the service.

The structure is topped by a slender spire which evokes the traditional hillside chapels of the Austrian Alps that form its backdrop. At the other end of the long, thin, wedge-shaped site, the cemetery is terminated by a tiny mortuary building at the culmination of the main path, a steeply ascending route (the nature of the route becomes clear in the sectional model).

The building is an example of the central European type of the *Leichenhalle*, which can be loosely translated as mortuary. The building's function is the laying out of the dead before burial. Its origin lies in the new hygiene dictates set out in the nineteenth century under the Austro–Hungarian Empire, replacing a local tradition of laying out the dead in the family home before burial. The domestic scale of Tesar's building encourages associations of a continuity of this tradition rather than the

bureaucratic impersonality of the mortuary depot.

At Kleinarl, the mortuary building becomes the termination of the site, just as it represents the final resting place for the body. Its gabled roof projects far beyond the building to form a porch (evoking an almost domestic architectural language), the front of which is delineated by two pairs of columns. The right-hand pair consists of a normal, solid column and what Tesar has termed a 'Skeletal Column', a hollow construction of steel bars wrapped around a central core, a device which echoes the skeletal bier in the chapel. The space inside the mortuary is lit by a pair of windows in the shape of a curved gash, as if the flesh of the wall had been slit open.

Tesar's other projects for memorials and monuments spring even more clearly from his ethereal conceptual drawings and watercolours. A design for a wall containing niches for cinerary urns (1984) reveals a dialogue between the pair of walls and the enigmatic space in-between: the walls are terminated by a curving flourish which begins to wrap this space into an interior condition; it becomes at once separate, private, and a part of the broader open space of the cemetery.

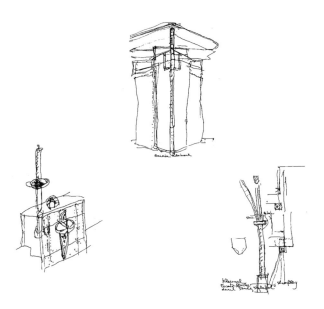

FROM ABOVE: Exterior views; details of skeletal columns and wall for cinerary urns

RACHEL WHITEREAD

The necropolis is often seen as a negative city, a city of empty streets and houses inhabited only by those who live beneath the ground: as a counterpoint to the city of the living. Rachel Whiteread has come to prominence as an artist whose work is based on the notion of the reversal of architectural space; the creation of a negative image of the interior so that what was space becomes solid. In this manner, elusive space can itself be made into a monument by using the room as a mould and this is the basis of Whiteread's successful entry in the Vienna Holocaust Memorial competition (1996).

The monument takes the form of a room, cast as a solid, the dimensions of which are taken from the bourgeois living-rooms of the surrounding dwellings. Its ceiling becomes its roof (with the form of a cast ceiling rose in its middle), its internal walls become external surfaces and its doors lead nowhere - the block is resolutely impenetrable and the true darkness of the Holocaust seems trapped inside this blind block.

The Judenplatz, which forms the setting for the memorial (the first major memorial to the Austrian Jews killed in the Holocaust), is the historical heart of Jewish Vienna. The presence of the inverted room in the centre of the square refers to the displacement of the Jewish bourgeoisie and of the loss of an irreplaceable human element in the cultural firmament.

Closer analysis of the texture of the walls of the monument reinforces this interpretation of its meaning, although Whiteread herself is reluctant to attach meaning to her work. Its surfaces are covered with the impressions of rows of books so that the inverted room becomes a library. The spines – the labels – remain on the inside and so are forever unseen; the knowledge has been lost. Books are analogous to memory; they have particular meaning in relation to the Jews who often refer to themselves in Hebrew as the 'People of the Book'. The Nazi burning of books remains a key image in the history of our century, the destruction of the knowledge contained within books is equated with the genocide, the attempt to obliterate a race. The burning of books (like the burning of the synagogues) is a powerful metaphor for the cremation of the bodies at the death-camps. The finely moulded edges of the cut pages of these thousands of anonymous books seem to have returned to haunt the city

At the same time, the solid concrete block is a permanent reminder of the spaces vacated by the hundreds of thousands of fleeing Jews and the hole that this has left in the city, a gaping emptiness which is as profound and painful as the memorial itself. The inversion of solid and void recalls Italo Calvino's vision, in *Invisible Cities*, of the city of Argia:

> What makes Argia different from other cities is that it has earth instead of air. the streets are completely filled with dirt, clay packs the rooms to the ceiling, on every stair another stairway is set in negative . . . everyone is better off remaining still, prone; anyway, it is dark.

Rachel Whiteread's entry for the Vienna Holocaust Memorial Competition, *1996, Model*

PETER EISENMAN

The drawings on this page depict Peter Eisenman's entry for the Vienna Holocaust Memorial competition. By overlaying images of subsequent ghettoes in the city, and the railway map of the country (Jews were transported by rail to the camps), the architect creates a series of ruptures, a crampling of the earth. The chaotic plan is overlaid with the fanatical order of the grid plan of Auschwitz: a chilling mapping of humanity's most gruesome legacy.

Peter Eisenman's entry for the Vienna Holocaust Memorial Competition, 1996, ABOVE: Bird's eye perspective; CENTRE: Sections; BELOW: Perspective and site plan

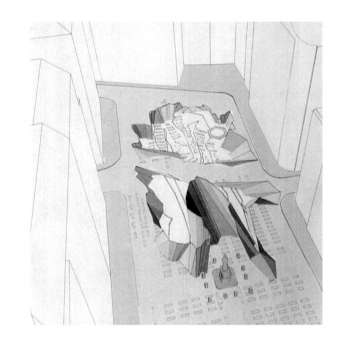

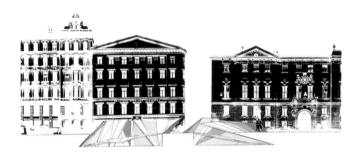

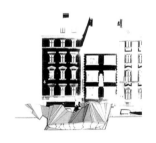

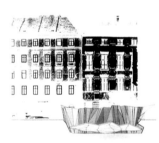

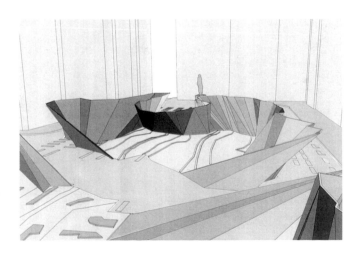

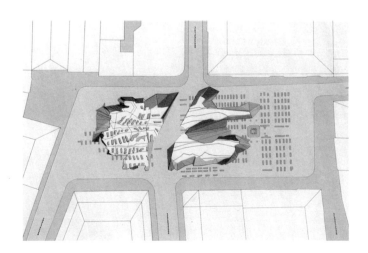

BIBLIOGRAPHY

Ahlin, Janne, *Sigurd Lewerentz - architect*, Byggforlaget, Stockholm 1987 -

Aloi, Roberto, *Architettura Funeraria Moderna*, Editore Ulrico Hoepli, Milan 1953

American Jewish Congress, *In Everlasting Remembrance: Guide to Memorials and Monuments*, American Jewish Congress, New York 1969

Aries, Philippe, *Western attitudes towards death*, Johns Hopkins University Press, Baltimore 1974

Asami, Akihiko, *Rite of Light: Sanbu Crematorium 1990*, Akihiko Asami, Urawa City, Japan 1990

Aulich, James and Wilcox, Tim (editors), *Europe without Walls: Art, Posters and Revolution 1989-93*, Manchester City Art Galleries, Manchester 1993

Bachman, Gabor, *Ravatal-Catafalque*, Meta-R Ltd. NA-NE Gallery, Budapest 1990

Bailey, Adrian, *The Caves of the Sun: The Origin of Mythology*, Pimlico, London 1997

Bonta, Janos, *Ludwig Mies van der Rohe*, Akademia, Budapest 1983

Brion, Marcel, *Pompeii and Herculaneum: The Glory and the Grief*, Elek Books Ltd, Toronto 1960

Borg, Alan, *War memorials from Antiquity to the Present*, Leo Cooper, London 1991

Borsi, Franco, *The Monumental Era, European Architecture and Design 1929-1939*, Lund Humphries, London 1987

Borsi, Franco and Godoli, Ezio, *Vienna 1900, Architecture and Design*, Lund Humphries, London 1986

Boullée, Etienne-Louis, *Architecture, essai sur l'art* (edited by Jean-Marie Perouse de Montclos), Hermann, Paris 1968

Boyd Whyte, Ian, *Emil Hoppe, Marcel Kammerer, Otto Schonthal, Three Architects from the Masterclass of Otto Wagner*, Ernst and Sohn, Berlin 1990

Buchanan, Peter (editor), *Enric Miralles and Carme Pinos: 1985-90*, SITES Lumen Books, New York 1990

Burckhardt, Francois, Eveno, Claude and Podrecca, Boris (editors), *Jože Plečnik, Architect 1872-1957* MIT Press, Massachusetts 1989

Cacciari, Massimo, *Architecture and Nihilism: On the Philosophy of Modern Architecture*, Yale University Press, New Haven 1993

Calvino, Italo, *Invisible Cities*, Secker and Warburg, London 1974

Colvin, Howard, *Architecture and the After-Life*, Yale University Press, 1991

Constant, Caroline, *The Woodland Cemetery: Toward a Spiritual Landscape*, Byggforlaget, Stockholm 1994

Curl, James Stevens, *A Celebration of Death*, B.T. Batsford Ltd, London 1980 (revised 1993)

Curl, James Stevens, *The Art and Architecture of Freemasonry*, BT Batsford Ltd, London 1991

Cuyvers, Wim and Lootsma, Bart, *Wim Cuyvers*, Exhibition Catalogue, Internationaal Kunstcentrum deSingel, Antwerp 1995

Dannat, Adrian, *United States Holocaust Memorial Museum*, Phaidon Press, London 1995

van Doesburg, Theo, *On European Architecture, Complete Essays 1924-31*, Birkhauser, Basel 1990

Dyer, Geoff, *The Missing of the Somme*, Hamish Hamilton, London 1994

Etlin, Richard A, *Modernism in Italian Architecture, 1890-1940*, MIT Press, Cambridge, Mass. 1990

Etlin, Richard A, *Symbolic Space, French Enlightenment Architecture and Its Legacy*, University of Chicago Press, 1994

Etlin, Richard A, *The Architecture of Death: The Transformation of the Cemetery in Eighteenth Century Paris*, MIT Press, Cambridge, Mass. 1984

Fleig, Karl, *Alvar Aalto*, Artemis, Zurich 1974

Friedlander, Saul (editor), *Visions of Apocalypse, End or Rebirth*, Holmes and Meier, London, 1985

Gerle, Janos, *Makovecz Imre Muhelye*, Mundus Kiado, Budapest 1996

Grant, Michael, *Cities of Vesuvius*, Weidenfield and Nicholson, London 1971

Gregotti, Vittorio, *New Directions in Italian Architecture*, Studio Vista, London 1968

Gerosa, Pier Giorgio, *Mario Chiattone*, Electa, Milan 1985

Harbison, Robert, *The Built, the Unbuilt and the Unbuildable*, Thames and Hudson, London 1991

Heathcote, Edwin, *Budapest: A Guide to Twentieth Century Architecture*, Ellipsis, London 1997

Heathcote, Edwin, *Imre Makovecz: The Wings of the Soul*, Academy Editions, London 1997

Hidemark, Ove, *A Conversation with Time*, Anders Nyborg Private Edition

Hultin, Olaf, Johansson, Bengt O H, Martelius, Johann and Waern, Rasmus, *Guide till Stockholms Arkitektur*, Arkitektur Forlag, Stockholm 1998

Huyssens, Andreas, *After the great divide: Modernism, Mass Culture, Postmodernism*, Indiana University Press, Bloomington 1986

Irace, Fulvio, *Gio Ponti*, Electa, Milan 1988

Johansson, Bengt O.H., *Tallum - Gunnar Asplund's and Sigurd Lewerentz's Woodland Cemetery in Stockholm*, Byggforlaget, Stockholm, 1996

Kahn-Magomedov, Selim O, *Pioneers of Soviet Architecture*, Thames and Hudson, London 1983

Kidder-Smith, G E, *The New Architecture of Europe*, Pelican Books, London 1962

Kidder-Smith, G E, *The New Churches of Europe*, Architectural Press, London 1964

Kis, Danilo, *A Tomb for Boris Davidovich*, Penguin, London 1980 (original translation 1978)

Klein, Rudolf, *Jože Plečnik*, Akademia, Budapest 1992

Krecic, Peter, *Plečnik - The Complete Works*, Academy Editions, London 1993

Kundera, Milan, *The Book of Laughter and Forgetting*, Penguin Books, London 1981

Lesnikowski, Wojciech (editor), *East European Modernism*, Thames and Hudson, London 1996

Lethaby, William, *Form in Civilisation, Collected Papers of Art and Labour*, Oxford University Press, London 1922

Marciano, Ada Francesca, *Carlo Scarpa*, Artemis, Zurich 1986 (2nd ed. 1989)

Margolius, Ivan, *Prague: A Guide to Twentieth Century Architecture*, Artemis, London 1994

Minetto, Renato (editor), *Architettura e Spazio Sacro nella Modernità*, Abitare Segesta Cataloghi, Milan 1992

Moravanszky, Akos, *Competing Visions: Aesthetic Invention and Social Imagination in Central Europe 1867-1918*, MIT Press, Cambridge, USA, 1998

Mumford, Lewis, *The City in History*, Secker and Warburg, USA and London, 1961

Nagy, Elemer, *Erik Gunnar Asplund*, Akademia, Budapest 1974

Panofsky, Erwin, *Meaning in the Visual Arts*, Doubleday Anchor Books, New York 1955

Portoghesi, Paolo, *Global Architecture 51 - Carlo Scarpa*, A.D.A. Edita, Tokyo 1979

Prelovsek, Damjan, *Jože Plečnik 1872-1957*, Yale University Press, 1997

Rosenblum, Robert, *Modern Painting and the Northern Romantic Tradition: Friedrich to Rothko*, Thames and Hudson, London 1975

Rossi, Aldo, *The Architecture of the City*, MIT Press, Massachussets, 1982

Rossi, Aldo, *A Scientific Autobiography*, MIT Press, Massachussetts 1981

Rykwert, Joseph, *The Necessity of Artifice*, Rizzoli, New York, 1982

Schumacher, Thomas L, *Giuseppe Terragni: Surface and Symbol*, Ernst and Sohn, Berlin 1991

Scully, Vincent, *Architecture: The Natural and the Man-Made*, St. Martin's Press, New York 1991

Spengler, Oswald, *The Decline of the West*, George Allen and Unwin Ltd, London 1961, reprint

Stamp, Gavin, *Silent Cities*, Exhibition Catalogue, RIBA, London 1977

Starr, S. Frederick, Melnikov, *Solo Architect in a Mass Society*, Princeton University Press, 1978

Summerson, John, *The Unromantic Castle*, Thames and Hudson, London 1990 (contains the essay *Sir John Soane and the Furniture of Death*)

Summerson, John and Watkin, David, *John Soane*, Academy Editions, London 1983

Tagliabue, Benedetta (editor), *Enric Miralles: Mixed Talks*, Academy Editions, London 1995

Udvary, Gyongyver and Vincze, Lajos, *Mestrovic, Szemtol Szemben*, Gondolat, Budapest 1975

Vamos, Ferenc, *Lajta Bela*, Akademia, Budapest, 1970

Vegesack, Alexander von (editor), *Czech Cubism*, Laurence King Publishing/Vitra Design Museum, Montreal 1992

Vidler, Anthony, *The Writing of the Walls*, Princeton Architectural Press, 1987

Vulliamy, C E, *Immortal Man*, Methuen and Company Ltd., London 1926

Waterfield, Giles (editor), *Soane and Death* (exhibition catalogue), Dulwich Picture Gallery, London 1996

Watkin, David and Melinghoff, Tilman, *German Architecture and the Classical Ideal*, MIT Press, Cambridge, Mass. 1987

Wechter-Bohm, Liesbeth (editor), *Heinz Tesar*, Springer, Vienna, New York 1995

Weinberg, J. and Elieli, R. *The Holocaust Museum in Washington*, Rizzoli, New York 1995

Wiesel, Elie (introduction), *Judenplatz, Wien 1996: Competition, Monument and Memorial Site dedicated to the Jewish victims of the Nazi Regime in Austria 1938-1945*, Folo, Vienna 1996

Winter, Jay, *Sites of Memory, Sites of Mourning: The Great War in European Cultural History*, Cambridge University Press 1995

Young, James E (editor), *The Art of Memory, Holocaust Memorials in History*, Prestel Verlag, Munich and New York 1994

Young, James E, *The Texture of Memory. Holocaust Memorials and Meaning*, Yale University Press, 1993

Zabalbeascoa, Anatxu, *Igualada Cemetery, Enric Miralles and Carme Pinos*, Phaidon Press, London 1996

Zabalbeascoa, Anatxu, *The New Spanish Architecture*, Rizzoli, New York 1992

Zevi, Bruno, *Giuseppe Terragni*, Artemis, Zurich 1989

Zukovsky, John and Wardropper, Ian, *Austrian Architecture and Design: Beyond Tradition in the 1990s*, Art Institute of Chicago/Ernst and Sohn 1991